THE MOUNTAIN WITHIN

THE MOUNTAIN WITHIN

The True Story of the World's Most
Extreme Free-Ascent Climber

Alexander Huber

TRANSLATED BY
ANNA BRAILOVSKY

Skyhorse Publishing

Skyhorse Publishing books may be purchased in bulk at special discounts for sales promotion, corporate gifts, fund-raising, or educational purposes. Special editions can also be created to specifications. For details, contact the Special Sales Department, Skyhorse Publishing, 555 Eighth Avenue, Suite 903, New York, NY 10018 or info@skyhorsepublishing.com.

www.skyhorsepublishing.com

10 9 8 7 6 5 4 3 2 1

Library of Congress Cataloging-in-Publication Data

Huber, Alexander.
  The mountain within : the true story of the world's most extreme free-ascent climber / Alexander Huber, translated by Anna Brailovsky.
    p. cm.
  ISBN 978-1-60239-988-4
  1. Huber, Alexander. 2. Mountaineers--Biography. 3. Free climbing I. Title.
  GV199.92.H86A34 2009
  796.522092--dc22
  [B]
                                    2009041598

Printed in the United States of America

CONTENTS

∞

CHAPTER ONE

A BRIEF GLANCE
AT THE END

A huge cracking noise. Beneath my left hand, the sheet of rock that bears my weight suddenly comes loose. It falls on my left foot and knocks me off balance. Instinctively, I try to find something on the rock to hold on to. Nothing. Absolutely nothing. Everything is crumbling. It's all coming down.

At the last moment, I jump, turning 180 degrees, staring into the abyss, and pushing off with both feet. Everything speeds toward me. There's no more time to think. I crash into a steep slab of rock—first with my feet, then with my backside, and then I keep going. I'm catapulted forward in a wide arc, sailing through the air. When I smash into the ground, it's like an explosion.

September 15, 2005, 12:35 PM—I'm still alive after falling a total of 16 meters.

It's been two weeks since Thomas and I arrived in California's Yosemite Valley. We've been here so often in the past ten years that this national park has become our second home. For the millions of tourists who visit Yosemite every year, the roaring waterfalls are the main attraction. But for us climbers, it's the rock formations that call to us, such as the Half Dome and El Capitan, looming majestically over Yosemite Valley. For over a hundred years these rocks have made "the Valley," as it's known for short, into something more than just an incomparable natural spectacle. Thousands of climbers gather here every year to seek adventure on its vertical walls. This unique collection of wild granite escapes is unparalleled in the world—a true mecca for the sport.

The rock that stands out among all others in Yosemite is undoubtedly El Capitan, and the most irresistible route on its wall is the "Nose"—probably the most famous rock-climbing route in the world. It was on this very route that Thomas and I had wanted to set the new record for the fastest ascent. Speed climbing. Normally, time is not the most important aspect of mountain climbing; the point is usually just to make it all the way to the top. But after all the summits have been attained and all the faces conquered, climbers begin to look for new challenges. It is in the nature of the sport that, as time goes by, the achievements become more and more extreme; one is always trying to go faster, higher, farther. On the big walls of Yosemite, too, the race was on. And so the climbing grew increasingly faster: days, hours, and minutes were shaved off the ascent times. One record after another was toppled. By the 1990s, an entire speed-climbing scene had developed, with a horde of young speed demons lining up one after the other to break each other's records.

The previous year, Thomas and I had not only set a new record on the "Zodiac" route, but with a total time of 1 hour, 51 minutes, and 34 seconds, we had also made the fastest ascent ever of El Capitan. Nevertheless, we were not yet 100 percent satisfied. The venerable old Nose is the *ultimate* rock route, and setting a speed record here is the absolute pinnacle—the record that stands above all others. Only when the record on the Nose was ours would we have achieved our aim. Our last great goal in Yosemite would be accomplished.

But it wasn't only our objective that was unusual. We also had with us a fourteen-member film crew that had chosen our project as the subject of a feature-length documentary. Even before we'd left home, we knew that the world of film would be entirely uncharted territory for us. After all, Thomas and I are not actors. And though we were familiar with the presence of a camera from earlier projects, we didn't have the slightest idea of how much work we were taking on. Coordinating fourteen film people is already challenge enough for the production manager, let alone the fact that we would all be climbing a mountain, to say nothing of a vertical wall.

When we arrived in San Francisco, Thomas and I were still alone. We set off by ourselves for the Valley on a mild September evening. It was the calm before the storm—one last peaceful night in a little roadside motel before beginning our climb. Nonetheless, we had a slight premonition that things would soon begin to heat up.

The next morning we were supposed to meet the whole crew at 9:00 AM at a gas station inside the entrance to Yosemite, but no one came. Not at nine. Or ten. And when we were still waiting there at eleven, I tried in vain to reach someone from the production company in Europe on the telephone. Just as I was punching the fifth telephone number into my phone, Pepe Danquart, the director, arrived. Perfect communication: The crew was waiting at a station outside the park, while Thomas and I had sailed right past them, straight into the Valley.

Things went on in this chaotic manner. This was due not so much to a lack of organization, but rather to the complexity of the situation. Filming in the middle of a 1,000-meter-high wall was the ultimate example of how complicated the technical aspects of a production could be: Three cameramen and a sound engineer were supposed to be hanging on the wall. The director, with another camera and assistants, had the choice of setting up either at the summit or at the base. Sufficient quantities of sleeping bags, water, and provisions had to be in the right place at the right time, along with the terribly heavy and expensive film equipment. On top of that, some of the film crew had had very little experience with mountains. It was a monstrous logistical puzzle, as difficult to solve as the undoing of the proverbial Gordian knot.

Despite the perpetually blue California skies, the general mood blackened with each successive day of the shoot. There was hardly a day on which we were able to keep to the production plan, and tensions grew under the pressure. Nerves were raw. Heated discussions became more and more frequent. With an undertaking this complicated, there were hundreds of possible approaches. Although each person had expertise in their own field, we all had to cooperate with everyone else. In addition, the entire crew could rarely be gathered together in one place. While some were on top of the mountain, others were on the way up, still others on the way down, and a bunch more had gone to get camera equipment from San Francisco.

The situation took some getting used to. Of course, an expedition to one of the great mountains of the world is *always* complex. But while climbing the mountain itself is a clearly defined task, a documentary film does not take shape as a tangible product until it is finished. Furthermore, the tools that are used for mountain climbing are relatively manageable and usually fit in a single backpack. And, in a modern expedition, we climbers are the ones doing all the work.

The first day of shooting on the wall turned into an endless wait. Although everything had been well prepared—the cameras and the sound equipment were already in place before Thomas and I showed up at the approach of the Nose—it still took an eternity before a single take could be filmed. Mostly, it was just little details that had to be corrected. But in the vertical, everything takes much longer.

First the rope was in the frame, then it was the soundman, and then the position was too unstable. What took a matter of seconds to film on the ground turned into minutes in the vertical, which ultimately added up to hours. Nonetheless, everyone tried their best. We needed to gain experience as a team, and it took time.

Never before had Thomas and I allowed anything to come between us and our climbing goal. Yet we had agreed to this project, and from that moment on we could no longer make decisions independently. Aside from us, there were the producers, who had taken on significant financial risk; Pepe Danquart, the director; and a large team of filmmaking professionals. All of these people were now just as involved in this project as we were.

Thomas and I began to doubt whether it was possible for us to succeed under these conditions. We were far too constrained when it came to fulfilling our plan. As top athletes, Thomas and I are exceptionally self-centered; we're used to ignoring everything else in pursuit of athletic success. This time we had competition. I suppose we had been somewhat naive, not realizing that, as a director, Pepe would have to pursue his own aims just as selfishly. Inevitably, our two worlds—the world of film and the world of sport—collided. We were made to feel the pressure everyone was under, and the strain became our constant companion.

Each one of us—Pepe, Thomas, and I—protected his own interests. No one wanted to give an inch. There were constant arguments and endless discussions. But in the end, we were always ready to shake hands and find a solution despite our different goals. Our greatest ally was Ivo Ninov, a Bulgarian who had made Yosemite his second home five years before, and who had since become a close friend. He strove to get a halfway decent understanding of everything that was happening on the wall. He was the link between us and the production management, who were clueless about anything concerning climbing.

Indeed, toward the end of the second week, our efforts began to produce results. Thomas and I finally had a chance to get to know the route, and that was important. Only by knowing every last detail of every inch of the Nose would we have a chance of beating the current record held by Hans Florine and Yuji Hirayama. Hans Florine of California is perhaps the most ambitious speed climber of the last fifteen years. But when his countrymen Dean Potter and Timmy O'Neill overtook his previous record on the Nose in November 2001, with a fantastic time of 3 hours and 24 minutes, he knew that he had to come up with something.

In September 2002, Florine recruited the strongest available workhorse—top Japanese climber Yuji Hirayama. The two came up with a significant change to the usual tactic: Hirayama would lead the entire way, from the base to the descent. With nearly a hundred ascents, Florine is indisputably the greatest authority on the Nose, and since the second plays a key role primarily in the organizational and tactical areas, it made sense for this climbing pair to give the lead entirely over to the outstanding free climber. Hirayama and Florine were the first to climb the Nose in under three hours—in a meteoric 2 hours, 48 minutes, and 50 seconds. This record would push us to the limit if we wanted to beat it.

By the end of the second week things had finally progressed to the point where Thomas and I could climb the Nose all the way up. Although we were nowhere near the record time, we were happy just to be able to get through all the pitches. It took us nine hours. There was no getting around the limitations that arose from the film production. Thomas and I felt like we were the victims of circumstance, even though we knew we were the ones who had made the decision. We alone were responsible for the situation in which we now found ourselves.

The main problem was our increasing fatigue. Even on the days we planned to rest, it was necessary to support the production work.

After all, Thomas and I knew the Valley better than anyone else on the team, so we were constantly going off to show the film crew new locations. What we were still missing after two weeks was a vantage point for the camera to get a shot of the wall from exactly opposite El Capitan. That's why, on one of my days off, I was on the way to Middle Cathedral Rock with the two cameramen, Matthias Lackner and Max Reichel. I was convinced that the desired perspective would be possible from there. There was a gully going up, not too steep, but interspersed with some nearly vertical rock steps; although it didn't call for any hard climbing, it was still steep enough that we had to put hand to rock.

I had just climbed over the last step when Max asked for my help. He hadn't chosen the most optimal way up, and had gotten stuck hanging just below the top of the good 15-meter-high cliff.

"Wait a sec," I said. "I'll come and give you a hand." I bent down to reach for his hand, but I suddenly lost my grip. All at once the groundless abyss opened up before me.

The split-second decision I made—not to try and delay my unavoidable fall—was what saved my life. Had I remained in my initial position—where I was still attempting to improve my chances of surviving the fall, with my face to the wall—at some point I would have inevitably dropped into an uncontrollable fall, flipped head over heels, and been unable to protect my head from the deadly impact. By not delaying the inevitable, I was able to maintain an upright position the entire way down through the air, and to make full use of my only effective means of braking—my legs. In this way, the angle at which I smashed into the ground was altered greatly in my favor. Further, I had the opportunity to determine, at least to some extent, where my fall would end. I was undoubtedly very lucky. Still, I'm convinced that my survival was in large part also due to my intuitive reaction.

I hit the ground, did a perfect rollover, and lay there, incredulous, staring up at the top of the cliff where Max was still desperately clinging to the handholds, probably assuming I was dead. I felt at once that I had survived the impact without internal injury, but I also noticed that something wasn't right with my feet. I took off my shoes. Although my feet didn't appear deformed from the outside, I knew that I'd probably broken some bones.

"I'm okay," I called up to Max and Matthias. "But I think I broke my feet."

Despite the injury, I was just happy to be alive.

∞

CHAPTER TWO

THE VILLAGE

I grew up on a farm in the peaceful village of Palling, in Upper Bavaria, together with my brother Thomas, two years older than me, and my sister Karina, five years younger. Back then, Palling had a population of some 1,000 people, since it was located within commuter distance of the industrial town of Traunreut. A few new housing developments had sprung up on the outskirts, but the heart of the village remained as ever its farmsteads. We grew up on the Riedl Farm, one of the smallest in this little circle of farms.

Today, Thomas and I are known as the *Huberbuam* ("the Huber brothers"), but in many areas throughout Bavaria, the name "Huber" is practically a plague. In Palling, too, the list of Hubers is quite long. That's why it was nothing special that our mother, Maria Huber, got to keep her maiden name when she accepted the marriage proposal of our father, Thomas Huber. With so many Hubers in the village, people took their cue from the names of the farmsteads instead. Since we were from the Riedl Farm, we were called *Rialbuam*, according to good Bavarian custom.

When you grow up on a farm like we did, the agricultural routine forms the central foundation of your life. My earliest childhood memories are of experiences on and around the farm. The highlight for me was working in the woods; I loved to be taken along into the forest as a little kid, and enjoyed getting to know its various paths and the different types of trees. Even now, after so many years have gone by, I still know every little corner. I like to see the many changes—seedlings that I planted with my very own hand that have matured into full-grown trees.

It is truly a gift for a child to be able to grow up in such an ideal world. In the woods, out in the fields, in the barn, or anywhere else in the village—for us, it was all one great big adventure playground, large enough to be our entire world.

To all appearances, Palling is the very epitome of the perfect Upper Bavarian village, with a large church at the center, fourteen farms around the periphery, a blacksmith, a baker, two general stores, two taverns, a folk theater, and a *Trachtenverein*.[1] We had everything we needed right there. It's still the custom to gather together in the mornings over a mug of something, and the latest talk in the village is more important than the news in the paper. Life in this Bavarian idyll is so tranquil and unvarying that you could almost call it boring.

We were certainly never bored, however. Our father was not only a farmer; he was also a mountaineer, whose entire heart and soul belonged to the mountains. It was far from easy for him when he discovered this passion at the age of sixteen. Back then, mountain climbing was an entirely novel idea in Palling, and my grandparents

---

1 Literally, a "traditional costume society," these are popular clubs for the preservation of local folk customs, and the source for the stereotypical image of Bavaria as a land of beer gardens filled with men in lederhosen and suspenders (transl. note).

put up great resistance. Whenever my father went off on a climbing trip, his departure would be accompanied by his mother's heart palpitations. Financially speaking, such nonsense was entirely unsupportable. And above all, there was the disgrace of it: Every Sunday, my father ignored the Holy Mass! Nana assured the others in the village that her son was in fact attending mass up in the mountains, which, in a sense, was true. It's just that the cathedrals he worshipped in had names like the Watzmann, the Matterhorn, or Mont Blanc. Many paths lead to God, including the one my father took through the mountains.

Today, it is hard to imagine that in the years following World War II, a bicycle was often the only way for my father to get to the mountains. It was 30 kilometers to the foot of the closest mountain, and no less than 60 kilometers to the Wilder Kaiser and the beloved mountains of Berchtesgaden. He soon began to dream of becoming a mountain guide and making his living in and from the mountains. Still, he could not escape the responsibility of the family farm.

When it came to mountain climbing, our mother was far from the oft-cited "ruin of alpinism."[2] For her, mountaineering was, above all, an opportunity to finally expand her horizons beyond the village limits of Tyrlbrunn, the tiny hamlet of six farms where she spent her childhood. Although she never developed a taste for extreme mountaineering and climbing, on the whole she has spent (and continues to spend) as much time in the mountains as our father.

Often, we went hiking with our mother while our father went up one wall or another with one of his buddies. There was one incident I remember particularly well. Our father had been climbing on the Große Bischofsmütze in the Dachstein region—an outing that

---

2   The legendary Austro-Jewish climber Paul Preuß (1886–1913) wrote an article in the *Deutsche Alpenzeitung* in 1912, in which he ironically claimed that women would be the ruin of alpinism. This phrase is frequently quoted in German (transl. note).

ultimately ended with him in the hospital. He had suffered a major leader fall, and had torn a great big gash in his knee. When we came to visit him in the hospital, I gazed in wonder at his fat bandage, listened to his story, and thought, *Wow, that's so cool! I want to do that someday, too!*

Today, when people describe Thomas and me as extreme climbers, I can only say that the apple doesn't fall far from the tree. Our father left virtually none of the great, classic alpine walls unclimbed, be it the north face of the Tre Cime, the Matterhorn, the Grandes Jorasses, or the Droites. There is only one he missed, and that's the north face of the Eiger. But my father is still quite active as a mountain climber, and I think that one day he will climb that wall yet. At age sixty-eight, he's in excellent shape, and far from too old.

CHAPTER THREE

∞

WE LIVE FOR SPORTS

As in all Upper Bavarian villages, Palling's cultural life revolves primarily around the church and various other clubs and associations. For some, it may be the *Trachtenverein*; for others, the folk theater. For us, it was the ski club. Ski camp, training, the Chiemgau regionals . . . Thomas, Karina, and I were there every time.

When I transferred from the Palling school to the *gymnasium*[3] in Traunreut, an entirely new path opened up for me. The school, the handball team, my circle of friends—for me, it was a brandnew world that led me rapidly and irrevocably away from the old.

---

3 In Germany, public schools are divided into two tracks starting in the fifth grade: the *gymnasium*, which goes through grade thirteen and prepares students for the state university entrance exams with an academically rigorous liberal arts and sciences curriculum; and two types of secondary or middle school, which end in grade ten and prepare students for trade apprenticeships or vocational school. The choice of schools is up to the family, though it's often guided by aptitudes exhibited by the child in elementary school.

Mountain climbing had a similar impact on my life. A village like Palling doesn't have its own local chapter of the German Alpine Club, and mountain climbers are considered utterly exotic birds. Like our parents, we were members of the Trostberg chapter of the Alpine Club, and this activity took us another step away from Palling. The Trostberg Hut on the Sonntagshorn soon became more of a home to us than our village.

Increasingly, even our last strong link to Palling—the ski club—began to lose its hold. For many years, it had been at the center of our lives. I can't begin to count the number of races we entered, or the countless hours we spent training and at ski camp with the club. Konrad Obermaier and the Seehuber boys were a merry crew, and we spent many years together. Our group brought an admirable enthusiasm to the task, even though there was never any chance of an Olympic victory, or even a German master title. Certainly, we were good skiers, and managed to secure a few good rankings at the Chiemgau regionals. But the blood of an Olympic champion was simply not in us. And that, ultimately, was the reason why skiing increasingly lost ground to mountain climbing. Mountaineering offered so much more than just competition. For me, there was something rugged in it; something that promised freedom and adventure. I was now ten years old, fascinated by the world of the mountains. The ski-touring trips we took over the years became more frequent, and also longer. Above all else, I was most impressed with my first 4,000-meter peak.

The year before, my father had already introduced Thomas to the world of the great mountains. Together, they had traversed the Ötztal Alps. Man, was I ever jealous of the experiences Thomas came home with! Not that I would have begrudged him his adventure; that wasn't it. I simply wanted to be there myself. But I was only ten years old, and according to my father, still too young for something like that.

The next trip was already planned for the following year, and it was crystal clear that Thomas wanted to go to the truly big mountains: to the four-thousanders in the Alps. Monte Rosa, Liskamm, Dom, Zermatt, Saas-Fee—these were all names that I would go to bed with at night and wake up to in the morning. Even before I had set eyes on a single one of the great mountains, I already knew all about the Alps. I could quote the exact height of each peak; I knew every route, all the first ascents. *The Alpine 4,000m Peaks* and *Extreme Alpine Rock* were still only dream worlds that I created with the help of books, but I already lived in them as fully as if I were there.

I knew that it wouldn't be long. There was just one small problem: Thomas was not convinced that I was capable of climbing a four-thousander, and so he argued that his little brother ought to be left at home. I was thoroughly miserable and in deep despair. My yearning was overpowering, and my father could see it too. I can still clearly recall the evening when Thomas was out and I got an opportunity to work my father over and break him down. He didn't stand a chance! He would only let me come on one condition: I was not allowed to say a word to my brother to give away the fact that I was coming until the very day of our departure for the Zermatt. My father wanted to spare himself weeks and weeks of arguments with Thomas.

And indeed, my father kept his word. In early April, the day of departure arrived, and I was going. My dream trip to the great mountains of the Alps! Now I would really see the mountains for the first time—and not only see them—I would also get to climb them. Our father had chosen the Allalinhorn for this trip, and I was completely overwhelmed. My brother, in contrast, was already bursting with self-confidence. My father exuded such profound calm that I did not capitulate in the face of the task that at first seemed so beyond my reach.

I still remember with absolute clarity the moment that I followed my father up the last few meters of the ridge at the summit of the Allalinhorn. I set down my crampons more slowly with each step, my legs as heavy as lead. I was utterly exhausted, feeling the effects of the thin air, but my father gave me a sense of security. In front of me, on the summit, I saw Thomas. He had already arrived a few moments before us. He laughed and congratulated me; he was glad that I had gotten my way despite his earlier objections. He was happy that we were together now, and able to discover this splendid world together. I laughed, too, and thanked my father. Then I simply plopped myself down on the summit, completely spent.

To stand on top of one of the great peaks of the Alps as a little boy of eleven—in the cold, completely exposed to the elements in the white desert world of the glacier—made a terrifically strong impression on me. The two weeks we spent in the Valais defini-tively convinced me of the path I wanted to take. I was completely fascinated by these great mountains, their awesome glaciers, and the utterly hostile world in which one could survive, nonetheless. It was clear I wanted more. We were barely on our way home before Thomas and I began to work on our father again. Besides the altitude, we now wanted to experience the other legendary side of mountaineering: the vertical world of rock climbing.

Because of our perpetual badgering, Thomas had just been given the privilege of accompanying our father on one of his climb-ing trips. I myself was not yet in the game, but of course, I had every intention of coming along for the training. Castle Stein was some-thing our father had shown us: a medieval cave castle built into the side of a cliff, with its heavy walls made of Nagelfluh conglomerate, perfectly suited to climbing. Pebbles had fallen out, leaving holes of various sizes. The walls were vertical, full of climbing opportunities ranging in difficulty from easy to challenging, and mostly within jumping distance from the ground. Except when there was work to do in the woods, we were out on our bikes, on our way to the castle in Stein an der Traun. Back then, we still were lucky enough to enjoy complete freedom: No one disturbed us in our undertakings; no one had any intention of spoiling our fun. Of course, these training exercises were not enough to make me a climber, but at least I could show my father and brother that I had the skill to hold on securely. I was biding my time; surely, it wouldn't be long before I'd be allowed to join them.

∞

CHAPTER FOUR

THE SMALL WATZMANN

The wrench in the works was my mother. She was dead-set against my father taking both of us rock climbing at the same time. It was already enough to have the two of us go ski-touring; to go rock climbing together on top of that was just too much for her.

So, I had to go on being patient, content with limiting my climbing activities to the Castle Stein. But to tell the truth, it didn't really take long. No sooner had another winter, and another trip to the Valais, gone by, than Thomas and I ran into two climbers at Castle Stein who quite clearly were there to get an optimal workout before the coming summer season: Gottfried Wallner and Fritz Mussner, the two best climbers out of Trostberg. They could see that the two of us were not too shabby. Of course, they weren't that interested in me, since I was still much too young to consider seriously as a climbing partner, but I didn't care about that. The main thing was to find a partner for Thomas; then I could have my father all to myself!

Just two weeks later, my last obstacle to the vertical world was overcome. Thomas was on a trip to the Wilder Kaiser with the Trostberg crew, so my father had no escape. We started from Berchtesgaden and made our way up to the Kührointalm. I was wound tight as spring. Aside from the joyful anticipation that my dream would now finally come true, I was also a bit apprehensive, uncertain about how I would fare on the rock. At age eleven, was I perhaps too young after all? What would happen if the wall broke off and plummeted down from under my feet—and not just a couple of meters, but a couple of hundred? It was one of those moments when you wish for a way out. But there wasn't one. Tomorrow, we were going to climb the Watzmann.

And anyway, my desire was far too strong. The attraction of the enigmatic world I had yet to discover was overpowering. Though it was only the west face of the Small Watzmann, the aura of the famous name still hangs over it: the Watzmann, hallmark of Berchtesgaden—the most beautiful mountain in the Bavarian Alps. At almost 2,000 meters, its eastern face is the largest wall in the eastern Alps. This would be the first time that I'd actually experience real climbing routes—not just from descriptions. I would touch the rock of this famous mountain with my own two hands!

The next morning, we hiked up to the foot of the west face of the Small Watzmann—a lovely, 300-meter wall of the best-quality limestone that shoots rapidly and impressively up to the sky. The "Alte Westwand" is an expertly chosen route that makes use of the natural weaknesses in the wall to overcome an incline that is astoundingly steep for its difficulty rating of 3. My father gave me the harness and tied me in. I was so agitated that if it had been up to me, I would have bolted. But my father conveyed a sense of calm, and the start of the route was not all that steep. He climbed up and soon reached a good stance. He pulled up the rope, laid it over a rock spur, and belayed me up. Utterly detached from the rest of the world, I took my first steps in this vertical realm. Conscious of every move, I tested every hold

I took in hand, climbing up and searching out the next hold. The climbing turned out to be much less difficult than I had anticipated. I discovered large hand- and footholds all over the place, and often even little ledges that I hadn't seen from below. It took hardly any time at all before I was up by my father's side.

We went on, and with every meter, the wall became steeper. We followed a long ramp that led us up obliquely to the left through the entire lower portion of the wall. At the end of this stretch, the route became truly exposed for the first time. My father took in the rope, which disappeared around the corner directly before me, and I climbed out onto the ledge. Suddenly, the view below me opened up into nothingness; no more rock under my climbing shoes, only air, and a 200-meter chasm. It was a moment that hit me right at my core. I was awash in waves of adrenaline.

I climbed forward, then back again. There, just ahead, was the hold that I needed to reach. I could see it quite clearly! I just couldn't go for it. I had to retreat and compose myself. My father spurred me on, gave me a good pep talk. I knew that I could do it, but I still needed a little time. I took a deep breath, then another, and then I climbed out a second time onto the ledge. There was the hold! I no longer looked down, but rather focused my gaze on the hold, on this small detail in the middle of the vast wall. I moved toward it as if in slow motion, grabbed on, and now there was no going back. My body hung at a slight angle from the ledge, and my feet had to follow. All at once, I was compelled to look down, directly into the abyss. For a moment, everything was completely still. I froze in my position and stared with wide-open eyes into the groundless depths.

"Climb on over here, already!" my father urged, snapping me out of my torpor. Quickly, my feet caught up with the rest of me, and the open stretch was behind me.

I'm sure that I have never again in my life experienced this sense of absolute exposure as intensely as I did then. It was my first encounter with the abyss. Although I would later be confronted with far bigger walls and even more exposed stretches of rock to climb, the intensity of that first encounter would never be surpassed. The experience of my very first time, in complete ignorance and with all my naive dreams, was absolutely one of a kind. That is why, even to this day, my memory of this first encounter is so incomparably vivid, colorful, and clear.

The last pitch was really steep again. Above us was a chimney, and after that, only the blue sky. My father made his way up the chimney spread-eagled, and belayed me up. There were only a few meters left to climb, but I was already completely worn out and exhausted. I struggled on slowly toward the end. Directly above me, the rope disappeared, and I climbed up toward the sun, up into the warm afternoon light. A few meters away stood my father. I was beside myself with joy. I had wanted this so intensely, had hoped and despaired; now, I'd finally done it.

I threw myself into my father's arms, infinitely grateful for the experience he had allowed me to share with him that day.

CHAPTER FIVE

∞

THE SHARP END
OF THE ROPE

Unfortunately, after this first climbing expedition, others did not immediately follow. As always, Thomas exercised the right of the firstborn and monopolized my father most weekends. It wasn't until I was fourteen that Thomas had finally established himself completely in the circle of the Traunstein and Trostberg climbers and began to go off more and more frequently with them—most often with Fritz Mussner. I had to wait a long time for this moment, but now, at last, my turn had arrived.

Naturally, I had already developed a strategic plan—one that would make me a full-fledged climber as quickly as possible. I had climbed a couple of routes by that time, but nonetheless, I was still not a real climber because each time I had only followed my father as second. It's not for nothing that climbing in the lead is called "taking the sharp end of the rope." It's not only that there is no rope above you to show you the way, and you have to find the proper route for yourself; it's also the fact that a lead fall on an alpine climb carries with it a very high degree of risk. Indeed, demanding climbs are often less hazardous than climbs on supposedly easy terrain, since on the most difficult pitches of many traditional alpine climbs, you tend to find sufficient pitons for protection. In contrast, falling on "easier" ground almost certainly leads to serious injuries, as the falling body is not caught in midair by the rope, but instead smashes against the blocks and ledges of the flatter terrain.

Our father had always strived to make us into full-fledged mountain climbers, and lead climbing on rock was central to his training methods. That summer, he had already taken me on more routes than in all the previous years put together, and slowly, I had begun to develop a certain level of self-confidence. My initial apprehension had abated. I was able to move freely and register the full extent of the wall's steepness without becoming nervous. For obvious reasons, we mostly went climbing in the Berchtesgaden Alps and the Wilder Kaiser range. The Northern Limestone Alps are a dream world of high-grade, precipitous rock that is not only easily accessible but also has walls facing every direction of the compass so that climbing is possible at almost any time of the year.

In the fall, we took one of the last opportunities before the winter to visit the Kaiser again, and went up the Christaturmkante, between the Hinterer Karlspitze and the Fleischbank. This is a good old classic in grade 5, not overly long, but a beautiful, elegant bit of climbing—especially if you climb directly up the edge, like we did. Suddenly, and completely unexpectedly, came the challenge: "Now you climb lead on the next pitch!" my father called. I wasn't even particularly nervous. According to the topo map, which marked the route with drawings of the topographical landmarks, there were already some anchors along the length of the pitch. We could even see most of them from where we stood.

I hung the quickdraws and some chocks on my harness and began to climb. At this point I actually did begin to feel the tension rising in me, but it was more the excitement of finally getting to climb for real—to climb on lead, and to experience the freedom of finding my own way, with the prospect of being able to go anywhere I wanted someday. At the time I was still glad to have my father with me. His calm demeanor conveyed his confidence that I was entirely up to the challenge. After just 4 meters, I had already come upon the first fixed pin. I had my hand on a good hold, took the quickdraw from my harness, clipped in to the anchor, and then to the rope. Everything came as naturally to me as if I had done it all before. The rock grew somewhat steeper in the next few meters, but that did not make me any more nervous. Right in the middle was an anchor—the goal upon which I could concentrate my efforts—and the holds, too, were good. I'd climbed much more difficult rock before, training at the castle. Step by step, pull by pull, I climbed over the steepest portion of the ridge, without faltering, without hesitation, without any doubt, and then belayed up my father.

At home, I wrote euphorically in my little climbing journal that I had climbed in the lead for the first time, and was now a "real" climber. And I kept on dreaming bigger dreams. By early spring, it had become standard procedure for my father to send me out in the lead repeatedly on the most difficult pitches, which gave me the chance to develop rapidly into an independent mountain climber.

CHAPTER SIX

THE KAISER CALLS

The Wilder Kaiser is as much my mountain home as the Berchtes-gaden Alps. At the start of the twentieth century, mountaineers from Munich and Vienna were perhaps the most innovative climbers in the Alps; without them, the history of mountain climbing would be quite different today.

For instance, Paul Preuß, the brilliant theorist, was the most talented free climber of the Vienna school. Along with his skill as a climber, his public statements, his influence, his ideas, and the quality of his ascents made him the most significant climber of his time. Preuß was also a vocal proponent of foregoing all technological aids to climbing. He saw climbing as a natural capacity of human beings, noting, "The master's art lies in self-limitation." His guiding principle was that great difficulties demand greater ability. It was out of the question for him to consider that greater levels of difficulty should be attained by the use of artificial aids. According to Preuß, a person ought to live long enough with a problem till he has grown mature enough to handle it. These ideas presaged the attitudes of free climbers today.

The Munich school gave us Hans Dülfer. He was no less talented than Preuß, but thoroughly prepared to neglect the honorable duty of renouncing technology. He is famous for his tension-traverses on the east face of the Fleischbank—master performances of their time and milestones of climbing history.

Early in 1984, we were once again climbing in the constellation that had by now become routine. Thomas and Fritz took on the "Southeast Corner" of the Fleischbank, and my father and I went up the "Wießner/Rossi" over to the left. These climbs were always wonderful experiences. I was extremely content and matured as a climber with each new trip.

If climbing made us this happy, could anyone begrudge us the fact that we no longer thought of anything else? If it had been up to us, we would have gone climbing every free day we had. Unfortunately, we didn't grow up living smack dab in the middle of the mountains, and we felt the effects of this drawback particularly strongly when school was out. We had endless time on our hands; what dumb luck that the adults had to work. There we sat during our summer vacation, in Palling . . . with the mountains far away.

Father completely trusted us to manage in the mountains by ourselves, but it was no easy undertaking to convince our mother. Naturally, since he had been the cause of our mountain fever, Father would be on the receiving end of all the blame if anything should happen to us. Nonetheless, we managed it somehow. During the last week of summer vacation in 1984, under a number of strict conditions, our mother drove us up to the Wilder Kaiser.

It was pretty clear to us that our mother was not overly enthusiastic as she dropped us off in Ellmau. But we had our orders: Every evening, we were supposed to call and make our report. Furthermore, we agreed that I would only climb second, and that we were not allowed to climb any route above grade 5. Of course, we knew that we'd never be able to keep these promises. For us, it would have been a torture akin to the misery suffered by Tantalus in the Greek myth. To be in the middle of the Wilder Kaiser and not be allowed to climb the great classic grade-6 routes would have been no easier than standing, like Tantalus, parched with thirst and waist-deep in water that receded whenever he bent down to drink from it. I believe that our father must have known, deep down, that we would never keep to this agreement.

I was already familiar with the Kaiser, of course, but on previous trips, Father had always been with me, a powerful source of confidence. This time, everything was different. As Thomas and I hiked up to the Gaudeamus Hut from the Wochenbrunner Alm, the Kaiser seemed much steeper, sleeker, more remote. I was utterly in awe of the high walls. Although I knew that Thomas already had many difficult routes under his belt by now, still, like me, he too had always climbed with a partner who was significantly more experienced than himself. Nonetheless, my brother was full of confidence, while I felt rather overwhelmed.

In the end, we were good boys; at least, we limited ourselves to the classics. On the first day we climbed up the "Göttner" on the Karlspitze, and when we found ourselves back down in the talus by noon, we naturally couldn't refrain from going over to the Bauernpredigtstuhl and climbing up the "Alte Westwand." On the first route, we had kept our word that I would follow. But on the approach to the Alte Westwand, I began to insist on having my way after all. It's not that I particularly wanted to be first on the rope, nor did I think I could equal Thomas's skill as lead climber. It was just that, unlike the experience of climbing with my father, above all else I wished that someday Thomas and I would become equal partners on the rope. If that were to happen, I had to start somewhere.

It was obvious that Thomas was pretty uneasy as I climbed up the first pitch; however, he understood that my taking the lead someday was unavoidable. And so we made our way up this wonderful, very steep wall. With each new pitch, I began to be confronted with something that I had never experienced to such a degree before: I had cramps in my hands and forearms. For one thing, the number of pitches we had put behind us was rapidly growing, and for another, the wall was dead vertical, and therefore quite exhausting. In the last difficult pitch, things got really tricky. Repeatedly, at just the moment I needed to reach up, my hands would cramp, so that I couldn't grab the holds at all. In despair, I tried to find a resting point so that my hands could recover. I had lost my holding power completely. It was clear that Thomas would have to take over the lead. I had to admit to myself that I was utterly spent. Although I was upset about this, I was also glad that Thomas was able to masterfully complete the route. I had given it all I had, and was overjoyed at what we had accomplished.

In the evening, back at the Gaudeamus Hut, we were once again busy making plans. We had called Father and told him about our ascent of the "Göttner" on the Karlspitze. This was the most difficult of the routes that we had discussed with him, and we had already completed it on the first day—whereby he gave us a talking-to and admonished us to "Take it easy!" Moreover, Father advised us that the next few days were likely to bring some rain. Sure, we would take it easy!

The next morning we were off to the "Neue Südwand" of the Hochgrubachspitze. The peaks were lost in the clouds, which only motivated us all the more. We thought it was exciting to climb up a wall we couldn't even see. But after we had covered the first half, things really did get exciting. Because of the deplorable condition of my arms, Thomas had obviously taken over the lead again. Suddenly, it began to rain above a steep layback flake that led up to the right. *Shit!* We argued back and forth. Finally, Thomas started to descend and climbed back down the entire length of the pitch. No sooner had he arrived back at the belay then, naturally, it stopped raining, and we began the whole discussion all over again. Surely the route would still be there tomorrow, as they always say. But if we completed the route today, then tomorrow we could be climbing another one! *We're here, and the route is here, so let's go!* And that's what we did.

It turned out that we were very happy about our decision, as we ended up with terrible weather for the following two days. Everything had gone perfectly; we had finished our route, and we were now so exhausted from all the climbing that we would have needed a day off anyway. During our time at the hut, we had won the goodwill of caretaker Hansjörg Hochfilzer, and enjoyed special treatment, particularly at dinnertime (we were as hungry as we were young). Hansjörg had closely observed the routes we had completed over the past few days. On the one hand, he took his guardian's responsibilities seriously; on the other, he liked the way my brother and I went off to explore the steepest walls of the Wilder Kaiser.

On the evening before our last day, Hansjörg even offered us a little prize. Thomas and I were going to attempt the "Lucke/Strobl Crack" on the Bauernpredigtstuhl—a classical route rated VI-/A0, and an upper-6 free climb. Free climbing was just coming into its own in the Alps.

"If you two can get yourselves through the Lucke/Strobl without hanging on to the bolts," the caretaker said, "drinks are on the house!"

And that's exactly what we did. Spurred on by Hansjörg's promise, we put everything we had into it. We struggled, and more than once found ourselves at the end of our abilities, but in the evening we were able to claim our prize. For me, there was only soda pop, but Thomas got the privilege of a beer shandy—a perfect ending to a wonderful trip.

∞

CHAPTER SEVEN

THE *HUBERBUAM*

At the time that Thomas was going around with the Trostberg and Traunstein crew and I was climbing with Father, we were much more fanatical about climbing than we are today. There was only one thing in our heads from morning till night, and that was our next climb. But as much as our passion for climbing united us in the mountains, Thomas and I were still far from a real climbing team. Both of us were still dependent on other people to *take* us to the mountains with them. We didn't mind this very much, however; the main thing was to be up on one wall or another every weekend.

With our father's help, we had set up a little climbing training area in the hayloft of the stable, and we would practice here during the week. There were climbing routes spread throughout the whole hayloft, for both free and aid climbing. We had pounded long nails into the heavy timber beams, grinding off their heads and bending them into large U shapes for perfect protection points. We either went hand over hand along the beams until our strength gave out, or we dangled from the etriers (webbing ladders for aid climbing) until we were dizzy. Hanging belays, pendulum traverses, rappelling down from the roof, 15-meter-long hand traverses—it was all possible in our little climbing playground.

After we first came across the fascinating pictures of the American cult route, "Separate Reality" in Yosemite, we even built the Bavarian version of this famous, 7-meter overhanging roof crack. Our roof was in fact more difficult than the original, and far too hard for us. But we had created a project that would serve as a long-term goal— albeit, one that was still very far away, and continually demonstrating to us how much more we still had to do.

There was also a Boskop apple tree on our farm with branches growing in all directions and at all angles, onto which we projected our fantasies of the wildest routes. *Extreme Alpine Rock,* written by Walter Pause and Jürgen Winkler, was our guide, and cult reading material at the time. It listed the 100 most-significant extreme-climbing routes in the Alps. According to the rating system, the hardest route in this climbing bible was the south face of the Torre Trieste in the Dolomites. Thus, the hardest route in our apple tree was meant to represent this climb. Naturally, we weren't allowed to wrap our hands around the branches, but instead limited ourselves to the holds offered by the bulbous bark on the sides and undersides of the thick branches. We finished up with an extremely long aid-climbing haul, for which we had to step up on the last rung of the etrier, and so our route earned its VI+/A3 rating, just like the original in Torre Trieste.

Even our little village of Palling had something to offer: a large neo-Gothic church built of solid Nagelfluh conglomerate. Thomas and I had often climbed its walls and had earned nasty looks for such misuse of sacred property. Eventually, after we had gotten the inevitable slap on the wrist, we made our way to the quarry, from which the Nagelfluh had been dug 150 years before. The abandoned quarry lay not far from the village, but over the years it had become extremely overgrown, and our father didn't allow us to climb on the broken-down heap by ourselves. Indeed, the 30-meter-high wall had an extreme alpine character, and a telephone booth stood nearby in the likely event of an emergency. Father couldn't stand watching our doings on this wall of horrors, which became our best bargaining chip. Naturally, we preferred a real training area to this crumbling wall, but the nearest climbing crag was 30 kilometers away. Thus, Father was forced to drive us to the crag to prevent us from returning to the quarry.

As the opportunities to visit the crag increased, our previously wide horizon of activities began to narrow accordingly. Climbing became the central aspect of our lives. The handball team had to do without my participation as a pivot player. I didn't mind the training sessions, but whenever there were games on the weekends, or the weather was good, I was noticeably absent. Obviously, this didn't encourage team spirit, and after we had gone on like this for two seasons, I had to give it up. It was no different with gymnastics, which I attended more and more sporadically. My skill level dropped accordingly, and eventually, I lost any connection to the sport.

Another important facet of climbing was that it opened up a brand-new social sphere for me. I was at school during the week, but from Friday afternoon till Monday morning, I belonged to the world of the mountains: on the rock during the day, and at night, in the Festung (the Fortress), the climbers' bar in Traunstein (I was by now fifteen). At the Festung, Thomas and I were suddenly no longer the *Rialbuam*, but the *Huberbuam*—the Huber brothers.

We were not yet allowed to hang out at the bar very late, but still, the few hours until 10:00 PM were important for me. After all, climbing isn't just about climbing; it's also about community—meeting up with people who share your passion and exchanging ideas. Though the "big" climbers still considered me a child, with time, I was becoming a familiar member of the clique: the *Weiningerbuam* and Peter from Färbing; Weizi and Winni; Godl and Dave; Woidl and Schübl Sepp; Sundance; and the leader of the gang, Karl Schrag. It wasn't that Karl had climbed harder stuff than the others; he simply radiated a special aura from having toured the world's most legendary mountains. There was a kind of magic about him.

For me, Karl represented a living connection to the great mountains of the world: Annapurna, Cerro Torre, El Capitan. He had all those grand names written in his tour book. In my mind I could see him struggling up the last few meters of an eight-thousander in the brutal cold. I could see the way he battled his way up the ice mushroom on Cerro Torre, and how he climbed the vertical granite wall of El Capitan.

Of course, there were many books about climbing; I had read them all a long time ago. Books by Hermann Buhl, Kurt Diemberger, Reinhold Messner, and above all, Reinhard Karl. Himalaya, Patagonia, Yosemite, the great north faces of the Alps—for us, these books contained not just descriptions of great climbs, but concrete goals to accomplish. The special thing for me about this clique was that I was by far the youngest, making the completely natural relationships I had with the older climbers all the more wonderful. I had no problem distancing myself from my parents to become more independent, and for their part, they had similarly few problems letting us kids go out into the world.

Growing up truly begins when you have found your own circle.

CHAPTER EIGHT

HUNTING FOR
NEW GROUND

Throughout the history of mountaineering, nothing has inspired a climber more than virgin territory—to go forth on paths that no human foot has touched before, as though the eternal rock had waited there for thousands of years especially for you to climb. Many of the grand narratives that have been written about mountaineering are stories of significant first ascents.

The reports of explorers and discoverers like Sir Ernest Shackleton or the famous Robert Falcon Scott also fall into that category. I can't remember where I got Scott's journals of his adventures, but I still recall how deeply they moved me: how Scott and his four friends made their way to the South Pole, putting their requisite quota of miles behind them each day while pulling the heavy sleds laden with supplies. It was a slow, laborious march, spurred on only by the ambition to be the first human beings to reach the Pole, this point on our globe that, more than any other, stands for the inaccessible, the inhospitable, and the untamable. The explorer is a man who works against his own primal instinct—the instinct to keep far away from such hostile and life-threatening conditions.

How much harder, then, must it have been for Scott to get to the South Pole only to find Roald Amundsen's tent already there. He had lost the race. Amundsen's tactic—to rely on sled dogs—had paid off, and Scott had lost, just barely, to his competitor. How difficult it must have been to have to admit defeat after expending such a huge amount of energy! The return march was a harrowing journey, its sufferings exacerbated by the fact that any remaining motivation must have plummeted in the wake of their failure. Scott and his friends never made it back alive. They died one after the other, and the journals that were later found with their bodies are staggering accounts of the difficulties faced by the early explorers of our planet.

As distressing as this story was for me, I was also fascinated. In fact, back then, I actually dreamed I could work in the Antarctic one day as an explorer. Later, when I was studying physics in Munich, one of the forces that motivated my studies was the desire to set off for the most inaccessible regions of the earth.

The fascination of mountain climbing also consists of a search for new ground. As a climber, you're often in situations where you have to venture out beyond the limits of what you've previously known, to leave the realm of security behind and step across the imaginary border into the unfamiliar. You are confronted with a new horizon.

Thomas and I were in search of this new territory—our very own vertical horizon. At first, we looked for it on the south face of the Wagendrischlhorn, one of the three high peaks of the Reiteralm, which is one of the seven great massifs of the Berchtesgaden Alps. The Reiteralm has a certain fame among climbers due to the Mühl-sturzhorn, or, more precisely, the south arête of the Mühlsturzhorn. This classic route in the Northern Limestone Alps was first ascended by Andreas Hinterstoißer and Toni Kurz in 1936. Shortly after, they attained tragic fame when they lost their lives attempting the first ascent of the north face of the Eiger.

The south face of the Wagendrischlhorn is made of the same fantastic limestone. It is not particularly high and stands somewhat out of the way, behind the large wall of the Häuslhorn. Its size and remoteness, combined with its smooth, compact structure, are probably the reasons why climbers did not begin to show any interest in this 300-meter rock until our generation. Just one year earlier, the Berchtesgadeners had inaugurated the first route, and given it the fitting name of Zauberplatte ("Magical Slab"). Thomas had bagged the first repeat of the route with Fritz Mussner and was full of enthusiasm for this discovery of the Berchtesgadeners. Moreover, he was convinced that still more precious virgin terrain was there, just waiting to be explored.

Thomas had brought pictures of his route home with him—including one on which every detail of the wall was evident. We projected this slide up on a wall in his room and eagerly discussed the path "our" route should take. To the right of the Zauberplatte, the image showed wonderful erosion grooves—thin little runnels cut into the rock by flowing water—that ran throughout the wall like a spiderweb. The trick was to find the most useful combination within the bewildering network. We drew up a little sketch of the best possibilities. This sketch was meant to help us later, in case we got stuck up on the wall and couldn't go on.

The plan was made. Now, we just had to convince our parents— since, after all, someone was going to have to drive us there. At the time, Thomas was seventeen and I was fifteen. It was clear that we could not tell them the entire truth, or our mother would never allow it. It was early September. Another week and summer vacation would be over. We argued that we would be much more motivated for the start of the school year if we were allowed to take one more trip. And anyway, it was only a pleasure trip—the south face of the Großer

Häuslhorn, a grade-5 classic, beautiful and not particularly difficult. Disarmed by our extremely logical and convincing arguments, our mother did actually take us to the mountains at the crack of dawn the very next day. With the most solemn promise to be careful and to take no risks, we said our good-byes and set off from Mayrberg on our way to the south wall of the Wagendrischlhorn.

For a good hour, a small path led us toward a rock gully, which in turn took us in a steep and direct line to the foot of the wall. We stopped beneath it, sat down in the grass, and analyzed our projected goal in the warm morning sun. While Thomas already knew the wall from his ascent of the Zauberplatte, for me, it was the first time that I'd seen the 250-meter-high rock directly before me. It was a compact wall, not particularly steep, but very hermetic in structure. There was only the rather delicate net of water runnels spread like filigree over the slab, which was otherwise seemingly devoid of any features. It looked truly extreme! I was thrilled. Thomas had really found something quite extraordinary for us. I couldn't believe that such a wonderful piece of rock had never been climbed before.

We didn't stay at the bottom for long. A great wave of solid limestone rose above us into the blue sky, and we felt the agitation of standing on the brink of the unknown. The first few meters were moderate, structured in clear sections, and not yet very steep. Still, it was intimidating. I climbed up the first 40 meters and stood directly at the point where it was obviously going to become very difficult. This time, there was wordless agreement between us that Thomas would lead the difficult pitches. I was just glad to be allowed to come along.

Expertly—at least to my eye—Thomas went through the routine of hanging the gear on his belt. Besides the usual chocks and friends, we had also packed a whole assortment of pitons. At the end of a narrow crack that climbed upward until disappearing, Thomas had managed to drive in a pin. What followed looked very difficult. With rapt attention, I observed Thomas's progress as he climbed diagonally up to the left.

"Don't look so scared!" he yelled. From my end below, the terrain looked far from easy. He was attempting to reach the beginning of the first water runnel. It was a good 15 meters, and I couldn't even hazard a guess as to how he meant to protect them. But after some 6 meters, he found a hole in the middle of the slab and placed another stopper in it. "That's a bomber!" he assured me. After a good hour on the pitch, he arrived at a tiny ledge right at the start of the water runnel.

I went up after him, enjoying the role of novice. As second, completely free of anxiety, I could fully experience every meter that Thomas had just robbed of its virgin state. It had taken millions of years for billions of organisms to build up the limestone upon which we climbed. Surely, what we were doing just then was utterly insignificant in the context of the Earth's history. We were nothing but a flash in the grand scheme of things, two little people on this rugged wall. A wall that, in comparison to the dimension of the Alps, was absolutely tiny. Just as the Alps themselves were in turn only a tiny mountain range among the other great ranges of the Earth—a planet that was practically lost in the infinite expanse of the universe.

It was as if the wall had been waiting millions of years just to be touched by us.

Directly above us began a 25-meter-long, deeply cut erosion groove—an absolute dream. It was, however, also very difficult, protection-wise, and so I readily let Thomas take the lead again.

The great overhang above our heads was impossible to climb, but a nice hand traverse to the right would clearly avoid that problem without much difficulty. There were good holds all over the place as I continued my ascent up around the overhang—but the wall broke off directly under me, so my feet had no grip. It's hard to say whether or not I was enjoying the situation. A flood of adrenaline coursed through my body.

Fortunately, the pitch really did go pretty easily from there, and after a short time I had the 30 meters in grade 4 behind me. Above us, we could see a sheer wall shot through with two shallow water channels. In comparison to the stretch I had just climbed over, it looked intense. This was clearly a task for Thomas.

The passage demanded all the skill he had. In the middle of the pitch, there was a break where the wall became absolutely vertical for 2 or 3 meters, and so the water channels were lost. The last protection point was already a few meters under Thomas, and it was clear what a fall here would mean—a stay in the hospital at the very least. I suddenly thought of the promise we had made to Mother. It didn't help to worry about it now.

"Be careful!" Thomas called down to me. He climbed cleanly, searched for holds, tried things out, came back, analyzed the situation again, until, finally, he had found a solution. It went quickly, then. Three, four climbing moves, and he was up. He stuck a friend into the water runnel and the major difficulties were now behind us. The rest of the wall was less steep and shot through everywhere with a dense network of climbable water channels. We made quick work of it, and another adventure had been completed.

Full of energy, we descended, marched up the length of Almstraße from Mayrberg to the highway, and hitched a ride home. But not straight home, of course; first, we made a stop at the Festung.

We called our very first ascent "Raunachtstanz." It had been at least a hard grade 6, without protection.

∞

CHAPTER NINE

KARLSTEIN

I can still remember clearly when the first articles about sport climbing began to appear in the magazines. There was an issue of *Bergsteiger (Mountain Climber)* that showed all of the grade-10 routes in Germany. These were all names that, for me, inspired down-right reverence. "The Face," by Jerry Moffat, the first European route in grade 10; "Zombie," by the old master, Sepp Gschwendtner, who had given the route to himself as a present for his fortieth birthday; "The Problem," by newcomer and rising star Stefan Glowacz. And last but not least, all the early masterworks by Wolfgang Güllich, such as "Kaum Zeit zum Atmen" (Barely Time to Breathe)—a nod to Reinhard Karl's cult book, *Zeit zum Atmen (Time to Breathe)*—and above all, "Kanal im Rücken," the most difficult route in the world back in 1984.

I was fifteen, and Thomas and I were about as fanatical as you could possibly be. But while we devoted all our energies to mountain climbing, sport climbing didn't really spark our interest. What kind of experience could you possibly have on such a small rock? It was all just nonsense made up by climbers who had come off badly in the rock department and didn't have an endless supply of alpine walls in their backyards. Why should we be satisfied with a 10-meter route when the mountain cliffs were so close at hand?

But the article by Wolfgang Güllich suggested that climbing is a high-performance sport regardless of how high the wall is—whether it's 1,000, 200, or 10 meters. If we're talking about a short route, then the holds are that much smaller, the movements more complicated, and the reaches much farther. The photos of the various routes showed us a whole new dimension of difficulty. Here, the heroes of the new sport were getting by with holds so tiny I would not even have considered them holds. And Wolfgang Güllich actually managed to convince me that an eight-thousander was not necessarily harder to conquer than a 6-meter sport climb.

We heard that the Traunstein climbers met on Friday afternoons to climb the crag over in Karlstein in preparation for the coming alpine season: sport climbing as training for the really big goals. And so, every Friday after school, Thomas and I hitched a ride to Traunstein. We wanted to start the alpine season in perfect condition too. Karlstein is an idyllic little climbing crag, and close by in an untouched wood is a large rock outcropping up to 40 meters high. The climbing routes are all on the south side, facing away from the town. This creates such a sense of seclusion it's hard to imagine you're only a few steps away from civilization.

The climbing in Karlstein is challenging. The limestone is unusually compact and demands advanced skills to find holds. Our first climb was therefore a bit on the frustrating side. At the time, Thomas and I thought we could hold our own with most people on alpine terrain, but we'd never been confronted with such intricate climbing moves before. All the other climbers had memorized every single sequence necessary for the climb, which came as a surprise to me; until then, it never would have occurred to me to memorize the technique I used on every single meter of the rock. Why would I? Our goal had always been to climb as many different routes as possible in a season. It had never occurred to us to climb the same route a second time.

We watched with astonishment as Dave (whose real name was actually Erwin Praxenthaler) climbed a route. Although it was a mere 8 meters long—hardly worth mentioning—the line (a lower VII) even had its own name: "Ikarus." Dave made the climb look easy. But then again, he was wearing Fires, the best climbing shoes you could get at the time. This was the ultimate secret weapon, whose existence was more rumor than reality for Thomas and me. But Dave had just come home from Arco, one of the climbing hot spots of the time, where the secret weapon could actually be found on store shelves. Fires be damned, I thought; it had to be doable in any case!

Soon I was on the route, although not climbing lead. The others advised me to try it on a rope secured from above—called "top roping" in the new climbing jargon. I barely made it up 3 meters with my stiff, knobby climbing shoes, which nowadays would more likely be described as mountain boots for use with crampons. I'd been convinced that the holds couldn't possibly be as bad as they looked—but they were. Moreover, they were extremely far away from one another, and at the time, I was still a late-blooming little shrimp. I let go after my arms truly had absolutely nothing left to give; trying to go up again after a short break was not an option. It was unbelievable. The shortest route I'd ever climbed had me utterly beat before I'd even finished half of it. At least Thomas fared a little better; in the end he was able to climb what for me had been completely impossible.

Even today, at five-foot-six, I'm no giant. And since back then I was always going climbing with people much older than me, I was the smallest by far. The more intensely I pursued sport climbing, the more frequently I found myself constantly struggling to reach the holds. I often felt it was terribly unfair that the holds were always just a tiny bit too far away for me, while the others simply had to stretch a bit to reach them. Somehow, my ambition never allowed me to be left behind.

The "Fata Morgana" is one of the absolute classics in Karlstein. At the time, it was legendary. A completely compact, nearly vertical slab that rises 20 meters high. Ranked a solid 7, it was a proving ground on which the Traunsteiners tested their mettle. There were rumors that only three people had ever been able to climb it: Sepp Gschwendtner, Rudi Klausner from Berchtesgaden, and Axel Eidam (aka Fax) from Ruhpolding. I already knew from the magazines that Sepp was one of the best. Of Rudi and Fax, it was often said that they were hulks. Fax could supposedly do ten one-arm pull-ups in a row. That's exactly how I imagined the masters of our sport should be, too; you could tell just by looking at them that they were ultimate athletes, able to climb a grade 8.

Though I was still considered "the little Huber kid" more than a real athlete, I didn't let that stop me from trying the Fata Morgana myself. Obviously, the "impossible" stretches were far too difficult, and, in the beginning, it wasn't even so much a question of climbing as hanging on the rope. But it didn't really matter; we were keen to improve at sport climbing and to appropriate its technical and tactical habits. The same thing went for our climbing gear. Just a week later some friends sent us a couple pairs of Fires from Arco, and we got ourselves the same super-cool white painter's pants, just like the others wore. We were, in short, total sport climbers.

What soon differentiated us from our friends was our attitude. For everyone else, Karlstein was just a training camp for the really big rock faces. But for Thomas and me, it was a world of its own. Maybe there were no big cliffs, but here it was the grade that mattered. Pretty soon we had our hard-won redpoint for Fata Morgana and were dreaming of grades 7 and 8 just as much as of the big mountain walls.

It was not just the new sport itself that had captured our enthusiasm. It was also a new lifestyle that had developed in and around

Karlstein, a community of climbers that not only loved their sport, but also just liked to hang out together, to spend their free time in the little crag, preferably from morning till night. Just sitting around, taking turns belaying each other, talking people through the difficult moves, shouting out encouragement, trying it out themselves, maybe climbing all the way through a route, taking a rest in the sun. It was a lifestyle that we never grew tired of.

The Kugelbachbauer pub also played a major part in this social life. Not an evening went by that we didn't make the five-minute pilgrimage to the Kugelbachbauer to give the day an appropriate send-off. Heidi, the pub's cook, became a den mother to our climbing fraternity, and she was always there waiting for us. Over time, our visits became so frequent that Heidi became practically the center of the climbing community. She knew the scene better than anyone, and was always guaranteed to have the latest news. She also knew that after a full day of climbing, we would show up with an appetite and a thirst to match. Heidi is an excellent cook, and there was often something to celebrate—whether a new route or someone's birthday. Then we would celebrate the day not just with one beer, but often two or three.

Out of this tradition evolved the idea of an annual celebration. The first Karlstein Festival was such a great success that Thomas and I organized another one the following year. Often, there were over 200 climbers from the entire area converging on the Kugelbachbauer to celebrate together with the extended climbing family, with the best food, lots of beer, and live music from various bands. Celebration is an integral part of life, just as essential as sleeping, eating, drinking, working, and climbing! There were often a few too many beers in the mix. (When I look back at the many parties we had over the years, it was probably much more than just a few too many.) But as climbers, we never let it get out of hand. After all, what we wanted was to be able to climb our hardest, and if we were to party every day, that goal would certainly have suffered for it. It really all came down to the right measure, to finding a healthy balance—the proverbial golden mean. If you don't know how to party, you haven't really lived! The Karlstein Festival is alive and well to this day, over twenty years later, and it continues to be a central part of our little world.

"He's crazy, but not insane."
Andreas Kubin, chief editor of the alpine magazine Bergsteiger, *on Alexander's climbing career*

THE FOLLOWING IS AN INTERVIEW KARIN STEINBACH CONDUCTED WITH ANDREAS A FEW YEARS AGO

Karin Steinbach: *You have been following Alexander's career for more than twenty years, not least in your professional capacity.*
Andreas Kubin: Yes. And I have the deepest respect for the path he's taken. Alexander has managed to go down in climbing history with his achievements, and his name will always be written in the alpine history books.

When did you meet?
I think I had seen the two Huber brothers for the first time at some point in the mid-'80s, at their local crag, Karlstein. There, we were the "good" climbers, and the kids had looked up to us. But that all changed pretty fast.

Did you ever go climbing together?
I never climbed together with Alexander in that sense [on one rope]. He was much too good, and I wasn't nearly good enough for that. It was more like we drove together to go climbing. In the late '80s, I had a car and lots of free time. Mostly, we went to the Schleier Waterfall climbing

area in the Wilder Kaiser. The boys had their big projects there, and I had my small ones. At some point, everyone made it up their routes. We all spurred each other on. It was just a super time, free of envy or resentment. We were a whole clique, and no one begrudged anyone anything. On the contrary, there was a great spirit among all the climbers back then.

How long did that last, and why did it end?
I think this "golden age" lasted two or three years. We were out climbing together two, three times a week. Why it ended? Well, all good things must come to an end sometime! I don't know—probably because our interests developed in different directions.

What did each of you get out of the relationship?
I always enjoyed being out with him. Somehow, we were emotionally on the same wavelength. Maybe I was in a position to be a bit of a friend to him? And if I thought the *Buam* were being bloody idiots, I never kept it to myself.

Which of Alex's qualities—as a climber and in general, too—really stand out for you?
In the first place, his incredible determination! Alexander is not a naturally gifted climber. All his achievements are due to hard work and deliberation: 10 percent inspiration and 90 percent perspiration, as Einstein supposedly said.[4] Above all, he has analytical abilities that allow him to solve problems that others would dismiss as impossible. In many respects, he is like a good chess player—which he

---

4   Actually, it was Thomas Edison (transl. note).

is at the chessboard, too, by the way. Of course, as a sport climber, he does have a couple of physiological advantages that are genetic. For instance, there's his enormous powers of recuperation: He could hang on a big hold in the middle of an overhang and just shake it out as long as he needs to until he's completely rested.

What would you criticize him for?
Since we've only been in contact sporadically for a long while now, I can only speak about the early years. Back then, he could sometimes be damned selfish. But you have to be, when you're uncompromising about working toward your goals.

Now that he's in his late thirties, are his "glory years" over?
No, I don't believe that. On the contrary, climbing has made him so strong physically and emotionally that he could still have many glory years to come.

Where do you see him in the future?
Definitely on the big walls in the major mountain ranges!

You were not as deeply involved with Thomas. How do the brothers differ?
There's already been so much said about that by other people! Alexander is the rational one, Thomas is the emotional one. Alexander has both feet on the factual ground, Thomas sometimes drifts off a bit in his dream world . . .

What makes the two such a good team?
Well, what I just said—that two brothers of the same blood but with such different characters are united in their

unbelievably high motivation to achieve the same goal as a climbing team through their different abilities.

In the last ten, fifteen years, Alexander and Thomas have made regular "guest" appearances in the Bergsteiger. *What do you see as the role of the media in the "alpine circus"? Is it the public that creates the stars?*

Alexander and Thomas are featured in the *Bergsteiger* not because they're popular, but because the two have always drawn attention to themselves through their sensational athletic achievements, and it's the task of an alpine magazine to report about it. And there's no such thing as an "alpine circus," thank goodness! I can only speak for the alpine journals, not for the Yellow Press or television. Specialty alpine magazines don't make stars. The top mountain climbers do that themselves through their achievements. And by the way, the word "star" doesn't really apply that well to the top alpinists.

Alexander is one of the few professional mountain climbers in Germany. Making a living from climbing—doesn't that mean having to make many concessions to the wishes of the sponsors and the media, since you're always having to market yourself?

At one point, when all was still well with the world, I myself had earned a few bucks with climbing. What kind of pressures the sponsors put on the top alpinists nowadays is not something I'm in a position to judge. But I don't believe that Alexander bows down to business interests! And if I ever thought he did, I would feel free to call him up and give him a piece of my mind.

Can you tell how much of what Alex does comes from his own motivation and how much is in response to the needs of his sponsors?

I am convinced that Alexander did not do a single one of his important climbs in order to attract or satisfy a sponsor. If this ever becomes the motivation for climbing one day, then we might as well close up shop and wash our hands of extreme rock climbing. If you want to see what happens to people who try to exploit alpinism for fame and fortune, look at Bubendorfer and his cohort; no one even talks about them anymore. Alexander is a climber with passion. He would never let a sponsor force him into something he wouldn't have fun with—I'm convinced of that.

What do you think of the film, Am Limit?

I think it's a great documentary—but it's not a film about climbing. Rather, it's a sincere film about two crazy guys that just happen to be climbers. With his vivid images, Danquart manages quite impressively to convey all of the "ex-centricity" of this world, which is so remote from normality—just as he had done earlier for biking with his brilliant film, *Höllentour*. The dynamic nature of climbing—in this case, speed climbing—is of course a further advantage for the dramatic potential of such a film. And the fact that the two failed in their pursuit of the speed record makes the film even stronger and adds a romantic dimension—in the original meaning of the term.

In the film, speed climbing almost appears as a somewhat questionable, relatively risky variant of climbing. The rope may provide the illusion of security, but in fact the protection is so poor in the event of an actual fall that you can no more afford to stumble here than if you were climbing solo.

This kind of sport climbing is not more questionable than any other kind—just more difficult to understand, because the logistical and technical aspects are so complicated. Speed isn't any more dangerous than other forms of climbing—if you leave out the wimpy version of plaisir climbing, and well-protected climbing in the highest-difficulty grades. You just have to be crazy enough to get involved with it properly, and you won't die.

It's even more difficult for outsiders to comprehend Alexander's solo ascents, which have ultimately made him so exceptional—on the one hand, fascinating, and on the other, "insane" for taking on such a risk.

That depends on what you mean by "insane." If that's meant in the literal sense of the word, I have to object. Alex is by no means irrational, and none of his solo climbs have been uncalculated in any respect. Alex is an ice-cold deliberator who analyzes his extreme solos precisely and prepares himself for them systematically down to the last detail. He optimizes each individual move to such a point that the remaining risk appears small enough for him to handle. The fact that even at this point he is taking on risks that appear much too high from the perspective of us "normal" people is what makes him stand out so far from the rest. He is simply an extraordinarily strong climber, both physically and mentally; he knows his fears and his weaknesses, and he has them perfectly well in hand.

Have you ever done any solo climbs yourself?

Yes, a whole bunch, but it was ages ago, and it was completely different! You need to define the concept of "solo." What Alexander is doing, and what Wolfgang Güllich has done, is "free solo." That means nothing but your climbing shoes and chalk bag allowed, and that's it—no carabiners, no slings, much less a rope. What we used to do is make an ascent on your own, but using all the usual climbing paraphernalia available in the '70s, including grabbing at bolts and swinging from the etriers. That sort of thing was more dangerous than difficult, because it wasn't calculated, and therefore dumb! Pulling yourself up on wobbly pins without the protection of a rope is simply idiotic. For a time, I was really into stuff like that because you could feel a little like Reinhold Messner doing it. But then, thank goodness, sport climbing came along! Later, I always experienced free soloing as a fantastic pleasure—but it was always at least two grades below my personal ability, only in the 6th- and 7th-difficulty grade. I was simply too afraid for more, and I only did it in the mountains.

How does it feel to climb with absolutely no protection at such a difficulty rating, with so much empty space beneath you?
I can only tell you that the feeling you get in the seconds, the minutes immediately after a successful solo is absolutely incredible, and you've got to be damn careful to dole out these huge doses of adrenaline in moderation—otherwise, at some point, you're going to come off the high with a horrible crash, and before you know it, you'll be in a box underground. For me, solo is the absolute essence of climbing. Because with solo, there's no excuse. Because it's pure climbing. Because the payback is as high as what you put in. Because there's no possibility of screwing around. Because it's just totally awesome to be hanging on to a tiny

hold and playing around with the thought, what if I let go—just absolutely nuts!

Where does Alexander get the incredible mental strength that enables him to make such climbs?
No idea. Perhaps the good Lord had a soft spot for him? Or maybe he's a psychological mutant whose brain cells were pathologically altered by the rarefied air in Berchtesgaden? But seriously: I have no idea. Let's just leave it at that. He has this mental strength, and it has made him who he is. By the way, there have been others before him throughout climbing history who have shown the same kind of strength. Recall Reinhold Messner's solo ascents of the eight-thousanders, which were just amazingly strong; or Wolfgang Güllich's solos of "Sautanz" and "Separate Reality" in 1986.

Is climbing an addiction?
If by addiction you mean a psychic deformation, then climbing is one of the many forms of the addiction to adrenaline. You can get the exact same thing with extreme mountain biking, hang gliding, or parachuting as with climbing—it really just comes down to what makes you tick. For us, climbing just happens to be the way to happiness, since climbers are only happy when they're pumped full of adrenaline. So we climb.

What does climbing have to offer to the average climber who's very far from Huber's level of difficulty?
No idea. That's something everyone's got to find out for himself! I only know that what climbing gives you is entirely independent of numbers, names, and grades of

difficulty. Let me quote an American climbing pioneer of my generation, Leonard Coyne, who opened up the Black Canyon in Gunnison: "It's not the question of fuckin' numbers or egos. It's just the question if you got this fuckin' spirit of the rock—and if you don't, you're a sport climber!" No one's ever gotten to the heart of it better.

∞

CHAPTER TEN

FIRST FORAY INTO THE GREAT WORLD OF SPORT CLIMBING

Joining the Traunstein climbing group opened up the possibility for Thomas and me to start taking big trips without our parents. As in many other chapters of the Alpine Club, the youth group often got together to go climbing somewhere. Over Christmas 1983, a trip to Buoux, France, was planned—an absolute dream for Thomas and me. Buoux had recently become world-renowned as a sort of epicenter of the sport-climbing scene in France, where this kind of climbing was particularly popular. Everybody who was anybody met up in this canyon near the little town of Apt in the south of France.

When Hannes Weininger asked us whether we wanted to come, I could hardly believe it. What a question! By now, we were already climbing a pretty solid 7 at Karlstein, and were even starting to inch our way toward grade 8. There couldn't have been anything more fabulous than being able to experience all the famous routes and stars of Buoux up close and personal. My whole entire life had begun to revolve around nothing but hard climbing—and now I stood there with an invitation to paradise.

It was also the first time I'd gone so far from home without my parents. Hannes and his brother, Sepp, simply packed us in their cars and took us along, through Switzerland to Grenoble and further south. At some point during the night, in the middle of Provence, we just stopped and threw our sleeping bags down in the middle of a field. Why has this made such an indelible mark on my memory? Perhaps because it was all so different: There was no looking around for a hotel, to say nothing of booking in advance; there was no turning off the road to find a campground. Instead, we simply lay down in our sleeping bags in some field, and the next morning, we got up, shook the hoarfrost off our sleeping bags, and without further ado climbed in the car and made our way to the closest bakery.

When we arrived in Buoux, I approached this new world wide-eyed with anticipation. The great world of sport climbing—this is where the most difficult routes of the world are put up, such as the "Rêve de Papillon." I immediately learned that Sepp Gschwendtner was there too. At the time, he was one of the best sport climbers in the world, and there we were, a few days later, sitting just like that at Sepp's table in some bar in Apt. I think I must have peppered him with questions: Had he done the "Rêve de Papillon" yet? How big are the holds in grade 10? What did you have to do to be able to climb at that level? Sepp was quite relaxed, and seemed happy just to sit around and answer my questions, drinking wine at a table full of Bavarians.

I excitedly told him about our new projects in Karlstein, and how he just had to come by one day and look at them—see if maybe there was a grade 10 in there somewhere. Poor Sepp had to sit there and let it all wash over him. That's just the way it is when a young climber, completely obsessed with the sport, meets his idol. Nowa-days, I smile when up-and-coming climbers pester me with such questions, because I recognize that earlier version of myself, and it makes me nostalgic for a time that is long past for me.

Of course, judging purely by results, it wasn't a particularly exceptional trip. We didn't care. We had tried just about everything that was at all within our reach, even routes in grade 7b and 7c, which were much too hard for us. For me and Thomas, the trip was above all an inspiration—a lesson in what one is capable of and how to achieve it.

When we got home, we immediately built a climbing wall for ourselves in the basement: a bouldering wall with a 30- and a 60-degree incline, and even a complete roof. To this, we attached strips of wood in all shapes and sizes, drilled holes for one or two fingers in the wooden wall, and thus made a highly efficient piece of training equipment with the cheapest possible means. From this moment on, it was nothing but training, training, training. When spring finally arrived, we were accordingly well prepared to assault the routes of Karlstein again. Not a weekend went by without some new project. The grade-8 routes fell one after the other. Thomas climbed the first 9 in Karlstein, and I eagerly tried to keep up.

And then there was Arco; today, this little town in the Sarca Valley has been a climbing hot spot for some twenty years. It really is absolutely perfect in every respect: Lake Garda, the weather, the countless crags, the little town, and with the 300-meter-high Colo-dri—even the opportunity for alpine climbing in a Mediterranean climate. To this day, I recall with great pleasure the wonderful time we had in that community of climbers, which was still quite small in the mid- to late '80s. Every spring and every fall, they would come together down south, when the weather at home was not very coop-erative. After all, why should one grapple with the endless rain on the north side of the Alps when the best cliffs were waiting under the clear blue skies on the south side?

Arco was a sensation—the ambience, the rocks, the weather, and, not least of all, the people. Arco was a sport-climbing mecca like no other. That year, we went to Arco so often that all the trips have combined in my memory to create an overall impression. The tents at the Zoo Campground, where peacocks wandered around freely; the evening outings to the town; and the utterly disorienting walk back, which, now and again, someone would invariably fail to manage, and wind up lying down for the night under an olive tree. And then the difficulty of deciding which café had the best cappuccino . . .

The contact with all the other climbers was really important for us. It was in Arco that Thomas and I finally realized that these other climbers put their pants on one leg at a time, just as we did.

∽

CHAPTER ELEVEN

CLEANING UP IN THE DOLOMITES

A very special day for the *Huberbuam* was the day that Thomas finally had his driver's license in hand. Of course, there was still the small problem of having to ask our parents for the car. This milestone was really important to us because of our big plans. By now, we had pretty thoroughly gone over all the ground in the Berchtesgaden Alps and the Wilder Kaiser, and were dreaming of our next goal: the Dolomites in Italy. What *didn't* we want to climb there!

The Tre Cime, Torre Trieste, Tofana, and the queen of the Dolomites, the Marmolada—now that Thomas was eighteen, these were finally no longer just dreams but actual, concrete goals. At the start of the summer vacation, we began to work on our parents to let us have the car for ten days. They couldn't resist us for long, since there's nothing more unpleasant than having to endure life with two sullen boys who have absolutely no interest in anything—except climbing in the Dolomites. We must have been quite impossible to live with, and very soon we got what we wanted—no doubt with the hope that we would return from the Dolomites as much happier and more even-tempered young people.

We plundered the pantry, and our mother slipped us a little money besides, so we could afford a hut for a few nights as well as our tent. And then we were off. Thomas was eighteen and I was sixteen, and it would be just the two of us, alone in the Dolomites. Of course, we weren't entirely unfamiliar with the range. We had already been hiking and climbing there with our parents. But it's a completely different feeling when, suddenly, you're alone in the car, going on a great big trip—especially since neither one of us yet spoke Italian.

Our first goal was going to be the Tre Cime. As the symbol of the Dolomites, and as one of the most famous massifs in the world, the "Three Peaks" were at the top of our list. We'd already hiked all around them and had gazed in awe at this sheer rocky world, but we hadn't yet been allowed to enter it. It was high time!

Following our father's advice, we drove up in the middle of the night to avoid the shamelessly expensive toll. In absolute darkness, we pitched our tent somewhere near the Auronzo Hut. The sky was black. Not a single star, not a bit of light—nothing but dense, dark clouds. We had barely climbed into the tent when a heavy storm front dumped everything it had over us: It rained, and hailed, and blew, and thundered, and flashed with lightning for all it was worth. We threw our weight against the walls of the tent to keep it from being blown down. We were terrified. It was the first time we'd experienced the full force of nature so close at hand. For hours, we sat up inside the tent, our backs pressed against the violence of the storm. We suddenly had an inkling of what it would mean to be unprotected somewhere up on the mountain at this moment.

In the morning, as dawn was breaking, our tent finally gave up the ghost. One of the seams burst and it quickly got really cold and wet. It was not long before we gave up, too. The storm raged on without a break; a few centimeters of snow had already begun to accumulate on the ground in the meantime, and we had had enough. We threw all our stuff in the car, broke the tent down, stuffed it in the trunk, and ran over to the Auronzo Hut. We spent the entire day getting warm again, drying all our things, and waiting for night to come so we could avoid the toll when we left. At 10:00 PM, we made our way back down. We left the snow behind us and drove down through rain. It rained and rained and rained. It was fucking cold. The tent was trashed. What could we do? Where could we spend the night? A hotel or a pension was definitely too expensive for us.

Slowly, we wound our way toward Cortina d'Ampezzo. And then Thomas had a brilliant idea—a cableway station! It was perfect. The cable cars weren't in use during the summer. We'd have a roof over our heads and we wouldn't have to pay anything. Soon, we found a lift station right next to the road and inspected our possibilities. There was even an open attic in which a great deal of equipment was stored. We just had to get up there without a ladder. But weren't we climbers, after all? A few minutes later, we were up, and clearing away the things to make room for ourselves. We holed up there for two days, cooking, studying the climbing guides, and dreaming all sorts of dreams. We sheltered undisturbed until the cold front had finally moved through.

Once again, we waited for nighttime to go up the toll road back to the Tre Cime. But this time, we set out near dawn and reached the Auronzo Hut at five in the morning. Man, was it cold! There was still snow all over the ground. We'd get nothing out of the north faces on this day, so we decided to warm up on the famous "Yellow Arête" on the Cima Piccola. Finally, sun! And how warm it became all at once—so brilliant that our long, cold wait was forgotten. The two of us alone in the Dolomites, on the Tre Cime. It was amazing!

The next day followed with the north face of the Cima Grande. But the "Comici" turned out to be much more severe, and the going was not easy. Although the temperature had gone back to normal and it was truly a beautiful summer day, we hadn't considered that the sudden cold spell would leave some ice in the large chimney at the exit of the Comici. And of course, with the temperatures climbing, the ice didn't stay put. We had hardly put the most difficult and steepest portion of the route behind us when we found ourselves right in the unimpeded path of the icefall. For us, the experience offered something similar to the north face of the Eiger—by which I mean that although what we felt at that moment was not exactly pleasant, it was definitely a rush. Following in the footsteps of the brilliant climber Emilio Comici, under these conditions, was truly a dream come true.

And it was a dream that we continued to live for another eight days. Catinaccio, Pilastro di Rozes, Sella Towers, Piz Ciavazes, the "Via Niagara" on the Sass Pordoi, the "Vinatzer," the "Messner," and "Moderne Zeiten" and "Via Fortuna" on the Marmolada. With one day left, we headed back to the valley quite late after climbing "Moderne Zeiten," cooked some food real quick, and went to sleep with the plan of getting an early start at five the next morning. For the last day, we planned to undertake "Ezio Polo" on Piz Serauta. Since the tent was still in a pretty abysmal state, we had simply resorted to sleeping in the car with the seats put down. We didn't have an alarm clock, so we agreed that the first one up would wake the other.

I awoke at five o'clock the next day and snuck a quick peek at my watch. Thomas was still sleeping deeply. Good—I really didn't feel like getting up yet. I dozed off again, and when I checked my watch an hour later, same thing: Thomas was still sleeping. By seven o'clock, it was too late. We'd both overslept and it was too late to begin our climb. There was nothing for it but to head home. The car had to be back the next morning without fail. For our parents, it had surely been more than worth it to loan it to us, as all of the unbearable qualities we'd made a point to exhibit before we left had completely disappeared upon our return.

Many years later, Thomas and I discovered that both of us had in fact been awake in the car, just pretending to be asleep, each hoping the other one would oversleep. After the incessant pursuit of so many routes, that one last climb would have simply been too much. Our exhausted bodies had finally gotten the upper hand over our determination and our insatiable ambition.

∞

CHAPTER TWELVE

THE "WEG DURCH DEN FISCH"

After the experiences Thomas and I had had in the Dolomites, we were in a much better position to assess our next goals. We weren't arrogant. It's not like we thought we could climb anything in the Alps—but at least we thought we should try. And so, as soon as we returned from our trip to the Dolomites, we immediately began to plan our second trip to the queen of the Dolomites, the Marmolada.

When Thomas and I were going up the "Via Fortuna" during our first trip, we had run into Igor Koller, who was there with a Slovakian climbing party. Koller had opened the "Weg durch den Fisch" route, considered one of the most demanding in the Dolomites. Heinz Mariacher had repeated the "Fisch" (as we called it for short), and Thomas and I had read his article about it. Everything about the route sounded extremely difficult. With great respect, we read about Heinz Mariacher's progress as he fought his way up with the help of skyhooks. According to the article, the communication on the rope was quite monotonous: "How's it going?"—"Hook!"—"What's it look like?"—"Hook!" More than any other route in the Dolomites, the "Fisch" was synonymous with adventure. Thomas and I had no idea if we were really ready for it, and that was why we hadn't attempted it on our first trip to the Dolomites.

When we'd met on the route, Igor Koller had wanted to prod us along a bit. He was bivouacking with his two friends, and Thomas and I sat up in the warm sleeping bags the Slovakians had brought with them, listening spellbound as Igor told us all about his route. He was sure we could manage the "Fisch" too. The conversation went on late into the night, and we were in no hurry to end it; as long as we were talking, we could partake of the warmth of the Slovakian sleeping bags. Eventually, we could not escape our fate; the Slovakians lay down to sleep on the comfortable bivouac ledge, and we rolled ourselves up in the space blanket that we had brought for sleeping. It was cold as hell, and we were freezing, but the thought of the "Fisch" helped us bear the discomforts of the bivouac, even as the Slovakians snored, and the Mylar began to tear, and the cold crept deeper and deeper into our bones. At the first sign of light, we left this wonderful place and our Slovakian friends. Keller had planted the seed, and the idea of attempting the "Fisch" did not take long to mature. Soon, Thomas and I would be in the Dolomites again.

The "Weg durch den Fisch" was listed in the climbing guide published by Heinz Mariacher as grade VII/A1, 850 meters high, and 37 pitches long. Even at the time, this was not extraordinary. "Moderne Zeiten" had been rated VII+, and we had climbed that without any problems. The greatest difficulties apparently stemmed from the fact that hardly any pitons had been left behind, and the structure on this portion of the wall is extremely compact. For the most part, the available protection points are few and far between, and the protection is very difficult to place. It is above all a mentally demanding route, not dependent solely on being able to climb a grade 9 or hang on to tiny holds; to succeed here, you need to be able to climb in grade 6 or 7, even without bolts, and far above the last protection. You need to know what you're capable of and possess the necessary self-confidence.

With some reverence, Thomas and I climbed up to the Falier Hut at the foot of the enormous south face of the Marmolada. This time, we even allowed ourselves the luxury of staying there. We didn't want to leave anything to chance, and planned to get an early start the next morning, as well rested as possible. Moreover, we had been advised by Igor Koller to try out a tactic that was new to us. On this climb, we would use a full rope for protection as well as a half-rope, which we'd use to haul up the backpacks. That way, the second could also climb unencumbered by the weight of our gear. It worked splendidly, although the climbing was extremely demanding. Most of our time was taken up with placing protection. There were hardly any cracks, and on Igor's advice, we mainly protected with tricams, which we inserted in the holes that were a common characteristic of the rock on the face of the Marmolada. In the afternoon, we finally reached the actual "Fisch" itself—a cave, 4 meters high and 8 meters wide, in the middle of the vertical wall. The perfect place for a bivouac!

Before us lay the hardest pitches—precisely the pitches that Heinz Mariacher had so vividly described. Now things were really going to heat up. The wall was a notch steeper. The utterly blank rock shot upward in an impressive overhanging curve. We deposited the backpack with the bivouac gear in the cave and Thomas got busy with the first pitch. According to the topo, the route led up around the left edge of the cave by means of pitons and skyhooks. Thomas analyzed the situation; after thinking it over briefly, he decided not to follow the directions and left the cave on his right side. Here, he could free-climb. There were more holes, and it was much easier to place protection. Then, he executed an impressive, airy traverse directly over the Fisch. The whole thing turned out to be far less difficult than it had first appeared. Good holds on steep terrain brought Thomas back to the original route. He had found a brilliant solution: Instead of struggling with pitons and skyhooks, he had taken the sting out of the crux of the route by free-climbing.

I led through to tackle the next pitch, and it, too, went quicker than we'd expected. Though it was the first time in my life that I had climbed with the help of skyhooks, the holes in which I set them were deep and solid. And so, by five o'clock, we had already accomplished our mission of climbing the two crux pitches before bivouacking. If we hadn't left our bivy gear in the "Fisch," we could have managed the remaining two pitches up to the big ledge terrace, and perhaps even all the way to the summit. Instead, we went back down to the cave on the fixed rope.

It didn't matter. We knew that nothing could hold us back now. One more bivouac, two more hard pitches the next morning, then 400 moderate meters, and the "Fisch" was ours.

CHAPTER THIRTEEN

THE REITERALM

The Reiteralm is something of a second home for me, much like Karlstein. The Berchtesgaden Alps were our primal rock, made of the best limestone. Of all the massifs in the Berchtesgaden Alps, the Reiteralm was our favorite. Its walls were not only the best limestone the Northern Limestone Alps had to offer, but there were still untouched walls that provided plenty of undiscovered territory. In the midst of the most interesting walls stood the Old Traunstein Hut—back then, the heart of our Alpine Club chapter, and our home away from home. The hut, and the parties held there, were legendary.

Every year, in November, the youth group of the Traunstein chapter organized a big party to mark the end of the climbing season. Of course, climbing continued to go on year-round, and it would soon be time for ice climbing. But the end-of-season party had another function: It also served to commemorate the comrades we had lost to fatal accidents.

The very first time I was on the Reiteralm, there had been a memorial gathering to honor the memory of a friend, and also to remind us that what happened to him could have happened to any one of us. Scharrer Beze, Schrag Koni, Sundance, Dave—it was stunning to see the list of the Traunstein chapter casualties get longer every year. Dave lost his life in a particularly tragic manner. While leading an expedition in New Zealand, he had his clients cross a stream using a little rope bridge. He himself crossed the water by jumping from stone to stone, during which he slipped and hit his head on a rock. Because he immediately lost consciousness, he was washed away by the current and drowned.

At the end of our minute of silence during that first memorial gathering, we partied—and we partied unimaginably hard. The beer flowed in massive quantities. There was no consideration for one's physical well-being that night. On this one day of celebration it didn't matter how much we had trained or whether excessive partying would disrupt our conditioning. Everyone, man and woman alike, drank, staggered, and fell in memory of those who were no longer among us.

I was allowed to experience my first end-of-season party on the Reiteralm after my brother had attended the previous year and returned unscathed. I went eagerly after many promises to my parents. The evening got pretty wild! As a novice, I was clearly the victim of many attempts to dispatch me. I managed to stand my ground for a while—after all, I'd practiced at many a party with my school friends—but at some point, my body failed me and I had to puke my guts out outside. Partying with friends is as much an integral part of our lives as family and work. And, ultimately, it's also one of the reasons why the chapters of the Alpine Club have built all those huts in the mountains—not just for shelter, so we could climb the mountains with more comfort and ease, but also to allow climbers to congregate and have a social life.

Today, the legendary end-of-season parties on the Reiteralm are a thing of the past. The reason is that the chapter leadership saw the wild partying in its sacred hut as bad publicity. The membership of the Traunstein chapter of the German Alpine Club is now over 4,000, and it maintains four huts, but there is no longer an active youth group. The most important thing for this chapter is servicing its 4,000 members, and maintaining its huts in perfect condition and the growth of the chapter's membership seems to justify the leadership's actions. But what matters to me is quality, not quantity. Although on paper the club has more young people in its membership lists than ever before, their main goal is simply to have a cheap place to spend the night. Getting together to socialize is not in the plan; instead, the chapter leadership would rather sit all alone and keep watch over its Old Traunstein Hut—which is in top condition but has degenerated into a museum piece. Poor Alpine Club . . .

The morning after my first end-of-season party was extremely hard, but after some palliative measures, things began to look up again. The remains of the party were cleared away, and in the early afternoon, we set off into the valley. The mountains had remained hidden the previous evening, as we had driven up in the dark. I had never seen the northern precipices before. I was fascinated. In the afternoon light stood walls that continue to inspire me to this day, even after I've seen so many of the world's mountains.

The next summer, Thomas, together with Fritz Mussner, put down his first new line on the north walls. "Sundance Kid" was born—at VII/A2, a demanding route that, to this day, has not yet been freed. Shortly afterward, the two of us together managed another first ascent just to the left of that, "Dave Lost." Though we did put in a bolt, the tour is very demanding. At grade 7, "Dave Lost" is not just hard; above all, we tried to be as frugal as possible with the protection devices. We followed through with what we began on "Raunachtstanz," and to this day, when I make a first ascent in the Alps, I only use as many bolts as are absolutely necessary.

By 1986, Thomas and I had developed as climbers, training not just in alpine terrain, but also in climbing crags. The good protection there allows you to experiment with everything. Falls are par for the course at the crag. It's not unusual for an enthusiastic sport climber to come home at the end of the day having taken no less than fifty minor falls. But climbing at the crag also enables you to try out new techniques, new and unfamiliar kinesthetic patterns. All of this plus the routine of climbing more-difficult grades increased our skills, which, as always, we practiced on the north side of the Reiteralm. "Utopia" was our first ascent in grade 8; the name alone shows what the route meant to us. Although it was compact, without structure, sheer, and unclimbable in the classical sense, nonetheless, we climbed it. And we kept going. Every year, something more, and something more difficult.

In the fall of 1987, Thomas and I cracked our first 10 in sport climbing. Our next goal was to translate this grade as quickly as possible to alpine terrain. In fact, at this time, there was as yet no route of this difficulty in the mountains. The Reiteralm, the grand realm of rock in our own backyard, had opportunities in great abundance. At the start of the year, we chose a wall directly to the left of the Schrecksattelsteig trail, the path to the Old Traunstein Hut. There was not yet a single route on this 300-meter-high, super-sheer wall of the Scharnstein. Compact structure and superb rock—it was exactly what we were looking for.

We had a difficult struggle on our hands. Over the course of two months, we spent days and days on this wall. On August 18, 1988, we had finally done it: the first ascent of what we named "Vom Winde Verweht" ("Gone with the Wind"). The technical difficulties were exactly what we hoped they would be. It was the *first* alpine route in the lower 10th grade—and not only in the Berchtesgaden range, but in the entire Alps. Just like with our other first ascents, it wasn't just the grade that made it a 10; it was also the placement of protection points that made this climb more difficult than all the pseudo-alpine routes that are open in grade 10 today. Nowadays, such qualitative differences between routes are generally ignored, a mistake perpetuated above all by the numerous specialist climbing magazines. Aside from the height of the wall, the technical grade is the only measure provided—although it wouldn't be hard for any competent, interested editor to find out how demanding the route really is. The fact is, however, that the media is almost exclusively interested in nothing but the grade. Today, if it doesn't say "grade 10" on it somewhere, it's just not getting published.

Anyone who undertakes one of our first ascents in the Berchtesgaden Alps should know what they're in for; you'll find nothing given away for free here. You'll have to really earn your stripes, and struggle hard to repeat the route. But in the end, you get something very special in return—an unforgettable day. Our routes are not light consumer fare, the details of which you can hardly recall a year later.

This whole consumer attitude toward the mountains—the preparation of pitches on which climbers can perform thoughtless gymnastics in the air—signifies the loss of our passion. It was precisely because of its adventurous aspect that climbing inspired me more than any other sport. But increasingly, commercial interests are trying to standardize everything. The activities people pursue in their free time are reduced to a consumer good so as to encourage mass consumption and thus maximize profits. This locust mentality is not just a phenomenon unique to the world of big industry; it has also gripped our society when it comes to leisure activities, whether on television, at the movies, in books, or whatever else. Success is not measured in terms of quality, but of quantity: Turning a quick profit is preferable to producing something lasting; doing five grade-8 plaisir routes (a "pleasure" route is usually one that has bolts or pitons in place for an easier climb, often placed there by the government to encourage climbing tourism) in one day is preferable to the quality of a single demanding route in grade 7 where you have to place your own protection.

I feel very sorry for the new generation of mountain climbers. When I see the many classic routes that have been bolted in recent years under the guise of "renovation," I wonder where they're supposed learn what Thomas and I can do today, if not here at home in the Alps? Many of the routes don't even exist anymore as classics, but have simply been retrobolted and turned into plaisir routes. In the meantime, more than half of the worthwhile classics in our Alps have not been "renovated," but rather turned into bland, boring plaisir routes. They have been robbed of their original character, and thereby destroyed. There's much talk about safety, but I feel that they're missing the point. Poor climbing world! Not even in the mountains do we have the freedom to decide where we wish to go. Today, we have the best equipment imaginable, and yet there are those who would convince us that anything other than a bolt is irresponsible. This is just as frustrating as what the clever insurance companies write in their policies: Above grade 5, climbing is a high-risk sport, and accidents are therefore not covered.

And in the middle of it all sits the Alpine Club. There has been a great deal of discussion on this topic. I lobbied for the values of classical mountain climbing at countless club meetings and was invariably met with great hostility toward my "elitist" point of view. My argument was that less-experienced climbers also want to enjoy the pleasures of quality rock, and therefore some of the classic routes should have appropriate protection from being standardized. The state of things today is that here at home, there are hardly any classic routes left that have not been entirely retrobolted. The routes *are* standardized: a bolt every 3 to 4 meters. Today, with fifteen quickdraws and a double rope, you can climb just about anything, whether in the south of France, in Switzerland, in Allgäu, in the Kaiser, or in the Berchtesgaden Alps. The variation among the routes that once gave them character is fading away; the maximum degree of difference between them is reduced to the kind of difference one finds in the range of products offered by competing supermarket chains. In the end, everyone offers pretty much the same stuff, the only difference being the price.

The future of alpine climbing doesn't look very different. The boundless, almost sacred reverence for the fixed bolt as a means of protection destroys variety. No matter where I climb, I know exactly what awaits me: a fixed bolt every 3 to 4 meters, and fifteen quickdraws per pitch. Some routes are in the 6th or 7th grade, some even in the 8th and 9th. But even that is being standardized in modern plaisir routes, since above grade 7, the bolts are drilled only a meter apart, so that everything is flattened out to a 7, or even VII/A0. It just wouldn't be reasonable to expect a weekend climber out on the rock after a hard week's work to have to break off his tour because it was too hard.

Nowadays the fixed bolt is practically the sole means of protection used in our Alps. In contrast, regular pitons are all too readily dismissed by the plaisir faction as irresponsibly dangerous. In light of this development, I fear that eventually the insurance companies and the legal establishment will follow suit and take action to classify natural protection as criminally negligent. I've had the pleasure of taking part in many discussions on the redevelopment of classic routes. Quite often, we traditionalists have been characterized as radicals—an elitist, narcissistic, and egotistical bunch that won't let the others have a share in the vertical pleasures. Frankly, there should be enough room in the Alps for all kinds of interests. Plaisir routes, classical routes, and adventure routes could all exist side by side without hampering one another.

But the discussions led nowhere, and talk is cheap; the plaisir faction proceeded—and continues to proceed—unchecked. Today, it's normal for classical routes to be bolted and afterwards presented to the public as "renovated." The consequence is that no one asks whether such action is right or wrong, which comes down to a complete loss of ethics—precisely what mountain climbing cannot do without.

It was for that very purpose we individuals originally organized ourselves into a club—to pursue a common goal. For me, personally, the Alpine Club was initially a point of social contact, but to my mind, what has now come to be the primary and most important task of the club is the care of our common heritage. And now, my club is allowing this heritage to be raped and pillaged on our watch! In the entire history of climbing, no one has ever managed to destroy the alpine legacy, and my generation will have done it in just a few years. I will feel quite ashamed of myself twenty years from now if I have to confess that I did nothing to preserve it.

That's why, as long as I live, I will at least make sure that my own routes are not brought into line with these forces of conformity. Some-day, I will pass on, like most of the first ascensionists of the routes that are considered classic today. And that is why I would at least like to make it unmistakably clear here, in this book, that the placement of additional bolts on any of my first ascents would be expressly against my will, and I would strongly condemn such action.

CHAPTER FOURTEEN

∾

FIRST ASCENTS OUR WAY—PURE AND HARD-CORE

At the end of the 1980s, alpine first ascents were still the measure of all things for Thomas and me. We were also heavily involved in sport climbing, and invested a lot of energy in the pursuit of our sport-climbing projects. Early in 1989, I accomplished something that was very important: my first climb at grade 10, at a time when there were no more than three routes in the lower 11th. Slowly, I was reaching the very limits of what I'd been capable of doing up to that point.

My unconditional love, however, belonged to first ascents on alpine walls, and not a year went by that Thomas and I did not work on one project or another in the Berchtesgaden Alps. These Alps are made up of seven massifs in total. Besides the Reiteralm and the

Untersberg, the Hohe Göll is a real showpiece for climbers. The west face is a classic destination, characterized by its two hallmark formations, the Großer and Kleiner Trichter. Cut into the middle of a vertical wall are two enormous gullies that narrow, funnel-like, toward the bottom and then break off with compact, overhanging walls. Between these giant funnels is the slender Trichterpfeiler, and to the right of the Kleiner Trichter is the more massive Westwandpfeiler—names that signify the very essence of extreme climbing in the Berchtesgaden Alps.

Thomas and I were particularly interested in the Westwandpfeiler. There was as yet no direct line through this impressive section of the wall. Sheer, structureless, and forbidding, it shoots straight up into the sky. But it was not just difficulty that we were after; rather, it was the elegance of the line, the particular beauty of the west face of the Hohe Göll.

September 12, 1989, was perhaps for most people a Tuesday like any other. The usual routine: get out of bed, down a cup of coffee, and get to work on time. How lucky are the few who can go climbing instead! Our "job" site that day was once again the west face of the Göll. We had been working on the Hohen Göll for a total of four days over the past two weeks, to put up the first ascent of the direct line on the Westwandpfeiler. Now it was nearly finished, and we had given it the name "Scaramouche." It still waited for a complete ascent, the redpoint—a clean free climb in one day from the base to the summit without any falls.

Thomas completed his ascent the previous day, while I had spent the day with community service duties, riding on the ambulance and manning the first-response station.[5] But on this day, I would have my chance. At 7:00 AM, I left my government-issued apartment to

---

5 Germany mandates a year of compulsory military service immediately after high school, but conscientious objectors may perform community service instead (trans. note).

go pick up my partner, Steff Alder. As we got out of the car at the Scharitzkehlalm, the parking lot was still deserted. One and a half hours later, we were standing before the stone wall. Over the weekend, Thomas and I had practiced the route together, finding the simplest and most economical solutions for the crux sections of the climb so that we could have everything perfectly under control later on, for the redpoint attempt. Once again, I tried to mentally review the most difficult moves of the first pitch. The crux: first, the undercling with the left hand, switch to the right, left up to the tiny one-finger pocket, right to the pinch grip. Step up high, push down, and move dynamically into the undercling. Clip the next piece of pro.

Steff set up the belay while I put on my climbing shoes, chalked up my hands, and tried to concentrate on the task. A little nervously, I came to the crux, clipped the first bolt—and pulled through. Everything went perfectly, and, in a short while, Steff began to follow. Steff had come along on this trip because he's a strong climber himself; he wanted to experience the "masterwork" Thomas and I had created. He was not disappointed. Of course, lacking practice, he couldn't make it all the way through the first pitch on the first try, but he was happy to see the individual sequences of the climb and excited by the quality of the climbing. I was glad he felt the spark, too, so that his coming along was not just doing me a service, but giving him as much pleasure as it did me.

On the second pitch, there was another memorable moment. A difficult spot awaited me along the last few meters before the belay. It's not steep, but difficult technically. Somehow, I had managed to confuse the sequence I'd worked out perfectly in training, and soon, I was on the verge of falling off.

I started to see images of the fall I had taken during my first ascent of this climb. This was the very spot on which I'd fallen, at least 12 meters. I hadn't given up, though, and after ten minutes I was ready for another go. But just a short time afterward, when the shock of the fall had receded, I realized that I could no longer put any weight on my foot. During the fall, I had massively bruised my ankle joint. We then rappelled to the base of the wall, where I was taken away by soldiers who were serendipitously there doing a mountain-rescue training exercise.

These images were now swirling around in my mind and refused to be dispelled. I felt the shaking slowly setting in. There wasn't much time left. I had to pull myself together! I had to at least try. And somehow, I managed to switch gears, shut it all out of my mind, and do what I came here to do: I pulled through and stayed on the rock.

Further up, on the penultimate pitch, everything went wrong again. Once more, I'd failed to correctly commit the sequence to memory. A small error, a bit of bad luck, and suddenly I was hanging from the rope. Steff stared at me in bewilderment. He hadn't been expecting this any more than I had; only a little while earlier I had told him that we had put the roughest part behind us with the previous pitch. Now, all at once, things were getting tight. My strength had been gradually ebbing, in any case, and now I had to do almost the entire pitch one more time. So, it was back to the belay, starting all over again. As I came to the problem spot, it was pretty clear to me that there was nothing left in me. Too short of a rest, no recovery; all of my strength was gone. Oh, man, and so close to the goal! Now there was only one thing left to do: wait. Time was running out. At 6:00 PM, I had to check in for night duty. No matter. I had to take fifteen minutes. I simply couldn't throw away the entire day just because I was short on time.

The next attempt. Although I didn't actually have the strength for the pitch anymore, this time I executed the technical sequence perfectly. I had the feeling that I'd long since gone beyond my physical limit, and wondered over and over again how it was that I kept making it to the next hold. How was I able to summon up enough spirit not to let go? I gave it everything I had left and somehow managed it. Steff followed, and an hour later we topped out.

There was no time to rest, to relish the joy. I was already late. In a great hurry, we rapped off, ran down into the valley, and drove back at breakneck speed. I started my shift at six o'clock on the dot.

At the time, Thomas and I were not sure how we should grade the "Scaramouche." The difficulties were comparable to sport-climbing routes in the lower 10. At the same time, we knew that the subjective experience of the conditions in alpine terrain could easily inflate the technical grade. We erred on the side of caution by rating the first pitch in the higher 9th. But we rated the entire route a IX+/X-, whereby we wanted to indicate that the difficulties of "Scaramouche" cannot be reduced to the first pitch. Although, nominally, the first pitch represents the crux, during a redpoint attempt, it is the last pitches that tend to be more decisive. At IX, IX-, and another IX-, these pitches may be easier in themselves, but when you have been climbing at the extreme of your personal limit, the completion of the route will be determined by your ability to climb these last pitches under conditions of increasing exhaustion.

Many years later—in fact, it was no less than seventeen years—I had the pleasure of returning to this place. For a long time, I had thought of this sheer, upper pillar on the west face of the Göll and the routes that remained to be conquered. I wanted to go up to the spot where the "Scaramouche" led away to the left, joining the classic West Pillar Route for its last pitch. This time I wanted to climb straight up—and not just because of the line, but above all because of the fantastic quality of the rock. Slightly overhanging, the column soars upward with a sweep. Smooth, compact rock, peppered with round holes.

Over the years, nothing had changed in the style of our first ascents. Thomas and I had always put up our first ascents using as few bolts as possible. What *had* changed, of course, was our overall level, which we were continually working to improve. Consequently, the "Kleine Feigling," the direct exit out of "Scaramouche," contains no more than one bolt per pitch; 30-meter-long pitches in grade 9, and not more than one or two points of protection per pitch. Here, it's no longer a question of whether or not you've mastered grade 11. It's your nerves you need to master! Only someone who can keep a cool head 15 meters above the last piece of pro will succeed here.

And indeed, though I would still rate the first pitch of the "Scaramouche" in the lower 10th, whereby it would remain nominally the crux of the whole route, it really isn't. Although the isolated difficulties of the "Kleine Feigling" lie almost an entire grade lower, these pitches still constitute the crux of the route as a whole. I am speaking here of difficulties that can no longer be expressed in a numerical grade, but rather those that lie far above the purely technical aspects of climbing.

In the seventeen years between "Scaramouche" and "Kleine Feigling," Thomas and I put up a good assortment of routes in this style. The only one that actually became famous was "End of Silence," which Thomas was the first to redpoint in 1994, and which was, at the time, one of the most difficult alpine climbing routes in the world. Thomas and I made our first ascent of this route on the Feuerhorn in 1990, at a time when we were not yet entirely up to the task of putting up such a difficult line in "our" style. That's why, by our standards, it has a relatively high number of bolts—though that doesn't mean it comes even remotely close to being a plaisir route. On the contrary, on the "End of Silence," you often have to climb far from protection. But ultimately, the purely technical grade-10 difficulties of the route dominate in comparison to its psychological demands.

It's a whole other story with the later routes on the Feuerhorn, which Thomas and I redpointed in 2003. The "Firewall" at grade 10 and, above all, the "Monster Magnet" at grade 9 are routes in which the psychological aspect is predominant. Here, you've got to find your own way far above the last piece of protection because there aren't any bolts to guide you. The few protection points are placed so far apart that you can seldom see the next one. You stand a chance here only if you're prepared to venture into unknown territory, placing yourself in a certain amount of danger. Even though the walls are not particularly high in the Berchtesgaden Alps, it is here in these "small" mountains that you can still find, in the midst of our civilization, that oft-cited sense of adventure—more so than on any well-trodden path in the eight-thousanders, or on the super-hard alpine sport-climbing routes of our day. It is here that you can still expose yourself willingly to danger and test yourself against it.

∞

CHAPTER FIFTEEN

MOUNTAIN GUIDE CERTIFICATION

My parents grew up on a farm during World War II. Farmers suffered the least during wartime; as the supply chain collapsed everywhere else, farmers still had their own reserves. The way our parents and grandparents told it, while provisions were not exactly plentiful, there was always enough to eat. My father was expected to take over my grandparents' farm when he grew up; however, he wanted to go to high school. He wanted a way out of these obligations. In the end, he didn't stand a chance. His duties and responsibilities were too apparent, and the path before him too clearly marked to simply turn away.

During the economic miracle of the postwar era, the farmers' advantage, which manifests in times of crisis such as war, began to disappear in just a few years. While the German economy skyrocketed, farmers fell further and further behind. With the increasing industrialization of agriculture, only those with a great deal of land could survive. As my mother tells me, she often urged my father to train as a mountain guide and move to Berchtesgaden. But it's not that easy just to up and leave a farm. There was the farmstead to think about, the grandparents, the family, and us kids. There was one ambition in which my parents would not be deterred: They wanted to provide us kids with the education they had been denied. Thomas and I, as well as our sister Karina, were encouraged to pursue as much schooling as we wanted.

All three of us went to the *gymnasium* and then to college in Munich. I'm often asked what my physics degree has contributed to my present life. I believe that one can learn much by way of a detour. I can say that as a child, I first got a practical education on the farm. Later, as a physicist, I got a theoretical education—something that perhaps seems to have no immediate benefit in my life, but was extremely important to my way of thinking and my mental development. I apply my education to every aspect of my life, even if unconsciously. And I cannot thank my parents enough for giving us such a broad practical and theoretical education.

Their desire to provide us with a well-rounded education was the reason our parents urged Thomas and me to train as mountain guides in addition to our academic studies. Our father thought that the mountain guide training course would benefit us as climbers. I can certainly confirm that this was the case. Although Thomas and I were autodidacts, and had developed our extensive skills and knowledge on our own after receiving our father's basic training, we profited tremendously from guide training.

I believe I can say with confidence that there is nothing in my life I have been able to do better than mountain climbing. Nonetheless, during the three-year mountain guide training course, I struggled far more than I had with any other kind of schooling. Until that point, I'd never had much trouble with my studies—not at the *gymnasium*, nor in my community service job, training as an emergency medical technician, nor at the university. But when it came to the mountain guide certification, things were different.

It was my own fault. I had always been something of a trouble-maker, and wouldn't hold my tongue if I felt something was improper or unjust. Back in school, I'd already had some difficulties with a certain teacher. It would have been simpler to keep my mouth shut, but the more my German teacher (for example) tried to correct me, the more stubbornly I cleaved to my own opinion. Unfortunately, I had the terrible luck of having just this very teacher—the one I hated the most—follow me through all nine years at the *gymnasium*. What began as a vague dislike grew to be full-blown hatred over the years. I couldn't accept that even if something was unjust, I was still just the student—and that the teacher had the last word.

There were two reasons why I decided to register as a conscientious objector to military service after graduating from high school. It was, of course, a matter of conscience above all. In my written application, I explained that I could not reconcile it with my conscience that someday I might have to stand in a field across from someone with whom I had once climbed a mountain and be told that he was the enemy and I had to shoot him dead. But there was, in fact, another reason: It was clear to me that I would have a lot of problems dealing with the military system. Unconditional obedience is not a concept that exists in my world. I knew there was no way I would ever fit into that order, and also knew how I'd likely end up. My brother's friend had to spend most of his military service in the stockade, and even after his discharge, the conviction remained on his civilian record.

I knew myself pretty well by then, and suspected that I wouldn't have fared much better. That's why I chose the path of least resistance, despite the fact that twenty months of community service was a far longer commitment. This isn't to say that even in the civil corps, I didn't get rubbed the wrong way from time to time. For one of the senior EMT supervisors, community service conscripts were nothing more than dirt, and he treated us accordingly. A shift on his watch was pure torture, and at the first opportunity I sent a written complaint to my community service representative. And there it was, the small advantage of community service: I did not have to obey unconditionally. The head of the first-response station actually granted my request, and in the future, scheduled my shifts so that I never had to encounter that supervisor again.

But when it came to the mountain guide training, it was an entirely different situation. I was the one who wanted something from the trainers—namely, the mountain guide certification—and therefore, I would have done well to give a little less vent to my protest against all forms of injustice. There were certainly many moments in which I was quite unnecessarily pigheaded with my instructors.

As a candidate for the certificate, you are frequently asked to lead a demonstration lesson, a kind of mutual exchange of instruction. At the end, the instructor discusses your performance with the group, evaluates it, and suggests improvements. During one of my demonstrations, the instructor had zoned out, lost in his own thoughts (instructors are people, too). I simply stopped in the middle of my demonstration and we waited patiently a good couple of minutes until the instructor noticed. Later on, when the head instructor called on the trainees to pay more attention, I couldn't help but recall that episode. Unnecessary and inappropriate, perhaps; once again, I just couldn't manage to bite my tongue.

When the weather in the Dolomites turned too nasty for training, the course was moved for a few days to Arco. This, of course, was just the thing for the sport climbers. No sooner had we arrived than we were hanging on the rocks. We were scheduled to have rescue training at nine in Massone, one of the climbing areas in Arco. The sport climbers among us were naturally there by seven, so we could have a chance to wear ourselves out before the long training day began. By half past nine, no instructors had yet appeared, so we went on climbing. Finally, the entire cadre of instructors showed up a little before ten. I was just at the fourth bolt of a 7c+ when the order came to begin the training.

"Don't rush me, now," I shot back. I wasn't even thinking of breaking off. We had waited a whole hour for them, so, to my mind, they could wait five more minutes until I was done with my climb. I believe this line of thought was justified, but it wasn't exactly a good way to avoid conflict.

One of the training highlights was a presentation I gave at the Grödner Joch House in the Dolomites. For obvious reasons, I chose the theme of first aid. After my presentation had been picked apart and I was told I should take another first-aid course to keep abreast of the current methods, I saw red. I made it clear with a few well-chosen expressions that I felt I was the one who possessed the real foundation of technical know-how. The heated review of my presentation came to an abrupt end when I asked my interlocutor whether he was "particularly experienced in mountain rescue." This comment pretty much sealed my fate for the mountain guide course.

And I went merrily along in this vein.

Two weeks later the whole retinue went off to Chamonix for the ice-climbing unit. We trainees could barely contain ourselves as, during the "model guided tour" on the Midi-Plan ridge, our instructors argued openly about how it should be led. While the training leader explained how we should lead a certain passage on a short, tied-off rope, the other instructors remarked that the demonstration we were witnessing was nothing short of a straight F. After such a "model" tour, the atmosphere during the subsequent two weeks of training was predictably poisonous.

Of course, these were the same instructors who were supposed to evaluate me for my examinations. But why should that be a problem? In my entire life I had never failed an exam. The rock-climbing exam was a breeze, of course—although I did wonder how anyone could possibly consider giving me a B for personal ability.

The other shoe dropped a week later, at the exam for the ice-climbing course. As dumb luck would have it, one of my examiners was the very one with whom I got along the least. It was time to pay the piper for my unpleasant dealings with the instructors.

We started the exam route on the Zinalrothorn at 5:00 AM. As I had done throughout the course, I demonstrated my leg power, and accordingly, we made our approach at a good clip. My "client" followed behind me. I began to uncoil the rope, and as the devil would have it, it chose this very moment to get all tangled up. The examiner observed me in silence while I damned the accursed thing to hell. Nervous as I was, it was a good five minutes before we could continue. The whole thing made me sick. During our descent he was hardly paying attention to my instructions, and I could pretty much guess how he would rate my performance on the exam.

The final test was a teaching demonstration that really appealed to me. I was happy with my performance. According to the examination criteria, I should have been in the clear.

The evaluation came a day later in Zermatt. Guiding technique, "D." Teaching demonstration, "F." Personal ability, "D." I suspected that I'd failed the guiding technique after my less-than-brilliant "model tour" on the Midi-Plan Grat. But why had I failed the teaching demonstration? Apparently, I'd failed to address the theme! The assignment (I was now told) had not been to "teach" my group how to move over the firn as I had done, but rather to "improve" their technique. I felt an overwhelming sense of powerlessness. Tears of rage welled up in my eyes, and I had great difficulty restraining myself from screaming my head off at the lot of them on the spot.

The final result of the examination, an "F," was disputable. To be reevaluated I would have to take a makeup examination with the same team of examiners, whose grading policies I wanted to dispute. I had to concede.

A year later, I decided to try again. Of all the instructors, I had once again drawn my nemesis in the exam lottery. Naturally, I had no right to arbitrarily refuse an examiner that had been chosen at random. Everything had been done by the book, and I was simply the victim of bad luck. Nevertheless, I knew I couldn't possibly spend another minute on the mountain with this examiner; I would rather have thrown everything, my entire training, to the dogs. I appealed to the leadership for another examiner.

I had to wait an hour until Sepp Gloggner, the head examiner, informed me that I could do the test with him and Christoph Schellhammer. I thanked him, and happily accepted the offer. The following year, I was a certified mountain guide.

CHAPTER SIXTEEN

GRADE 11 IS ATTAINED

Our father is an alpinist. What he imparted to us was classical mountain climbing, and for a long time, our dreams were ruled by high mountains and big walls. And yet by the early 1990s, I was actually doing sport climbing almost exclusively. I climbed absolutely everything there was to climb in Karlstein. Although the area is not particularly extensive, it is divided up into countless small walls, and the structure of the rock allows for climbing almost everywhere, and above all, in every possible grade.

If you look at this climbing crag today, with 120 individual routes and the popularity the little cliffs enjoyed among the local climbers, it is difficult to imagine that Karlstein was practically unknown when we first began climbing. With every day that we spent there, our enthusiasm grew, and we were not alone. Pretty soon, Karlstein became the meeting ground for a great many climbers who were also showing symptoms of the same disease. As a sport, climbing did not have anywhere near the kind of recognition it has today, and in the eyes of the mountain climbers, we were seen as bloody idiots, messing about on mossy boulders in the best of weather instead of doing *real* mountain climbing.

So when Thomas and I first showed up in Karlstein in 1982, there were only about fifteen routes, and they were obvious—along the weak points that constitute the path of least resistance up the walls (some, up to 30 meters high). After we had knocked off just about all the existing routes that Karlstein had to offer, we now had to turn to the new, less-obvious, and above all, more-difficult lines. And what *wasn't* there to do! Overhangs, arêtes, dihedrals with tiny holds that were just begging to be climbed—when you looked carefully, there was an almost infinite variety of possibilities. The energy was quite infectious when, early in the spring, all the climbers in the area would come together again in Karlstein with a common goal: to climb more and harder lines than the previous year.

It was a simple life, reduced to a very few things. Give us Karlstein and the Kugelbachbauer pub, and it was a perfect day or weekend. The spontaneous gatherings on the rocks gave rise to many lifelong friendships. We were all highly motivated to give it everything we had, and we were slowly but surely developing into top athletes who train as hard as the best athletes in any other sport. Our training center was still at the time located at home in our basement, but also at Felix Sitton's place on the Traunsteiner Stadtplatz. He was one of our best friends, and had a large apartment in which he was able to keep a room free for our training purposes. We built a wall—a real torture chamber—and met there during the winter, usually five times a week, so that we could climb another grade higher next season. We wanted to fulfill our goal of being able to climb the hardest routes in the world.

In 1991, with the ascent of "Action Directe" in the Frankenjura, Wolfgang Güllich introduced a full grade 11 into the world of climbing. This route was undoubtedly the most difficult route in the world at the time, and it set a provisional limit to the rapid development of increasingly more difficult grades in sport climbing. The first route in the lower 10th grade had been opened in 1983 by English climber Jerry Moffatt. From that point on, Wolfgang Güllich turned out to be single-handedly responsible for pushing the limits of maximum difficulty further and further. "Kanal im Rücken" in the full 10th grade, "Punks in the Gym" in the upper 10th, "Wallstreet" in the lower 11th, and last but not least, the now-infamous "Action Directe" in the full 11th, were each respectively the first routes in their standard of difficulty.

There was a reason why Wolfgang Güllich emerged as the chief protagonist of sport climbing in the extremely difficult grades. He was one of the first to transfer to the systematic training methods developed by other high-performance competitive sports disciplines. Wolfgang Güllich was our guru, and he made it clear to the rest of the world that you couldn't attain grade 11 without professional training.

In 1989, I achieved a personal goal when I was first able to climb in the upper 10th. This opened the door to grade 11, and I knew I'd manage that someday. Luckily, Karlstein continued to be an excellent place to find new territory. I found a line on the Schlangenfels that, in its difficulty, far surpassed any upper-10 route I had climbed up to that point. "Shogun" is a good 20 meters high and typical for this kind of climbing in Karlstein. Strength alone won't get you very far in the hermetic structure of these rocks. All the routes are highly complex. They demand extraordinary kinesthetic sensibility, and the optimal solutions to the individual sections of the climb are difficult to find.

The crux of "Shogun" may seem at first glance to have a simple construction—a concave, completely blank wall, which becomes increasingly more overhanging as it rises, like a cresting wave. A thin geological fault shoots up through it diagonally toward the right, but as obvious as this line may be, it turns out to be quite complicated to keep a hold on this structure. The only way to succeed is to keep your whole torso in constant tension while taking advantage of the tiny few available features—if you have the fine motor skills and creativity for it.

The goal seemed to be within reach, and in fact, I ought to have been able to make this move into the 11th grade. But, for the first time in my life, there were certain responsibilities in my way: I was serving my twenty-month-long community service commitment, while also working sixty hours a week as an assistant paramedic on a first-response team. My schedule was anything but ideal, and I simply couldn't put as much sweat into climbing as the leap into the 11th would have required. I had to be patient and bide my time until the situation improved. For someone like me, to whom the 11th grade meant everything at the time, waiting was no easy task.

I was also a student in Munich, and university life was exactly what I needed to fulfill my dreams. Studying was something I could take care of practically on the side. I was never on campus more than twice a week, and still managed to pass every exam. Above all, there were a whole bunch of highly motivated climbers in Munich who trained with me in my modest student lodgings in Sendling.

Without a doubt, grade 11 would soon be mine.

In 1991, it was finally time. After many attempts, I was able to climb "Shogun," and knew that this route could be placed solidly in the lower 11th grade. Even though Wolfgang Güllich had raised the bar to a full grade 11 with "Action Directe," I was as happy with my lower 11th as if I'd won an Olympic medal.

CHAPTER SEVENTEEN

THE SCHLEIER WATERFALL—MY PERSONAL PARADISE

"**S**hogun" had been long overdue, and it was the pressure I put on myself to meet my own extremely high expectations that had made me work so hard to succeed at it. When I was finally able to climb it, I was liberated. I was ready and willing to devote myself to scholarly life. I worked particularly hard at my studies in the winter so I could free up as much time as possible in the summer for my climbing projects.

Indeed, the feeling of being right at the forefront of things had given me a special sort of motivational kick, and the three years that followed "Shogun" very likely represent the most disciplined era of my life. I was, first and foremost, a high-performance athlete. Everything else was secondary to my athletic goals. With the goal of climbing a full grade 11, I began my systematic training.

Only a few years before, Thomas and I had had no substantial knowledge about training, just like everyone else in our little climbing world. In the early days of sport climbing, training was thought to be "uncool" among the climbers in our circle. "A good climber doesn't need any training," was the expert opinion. And in truth, up until that time, all you needed was good technique and the right attitude. Even the hardest alpine routes were generally not inclined beyond the vertical. But times had changed. The difficult routes were increasingly overhanging, so climbers were forced to think much more about their sport and the training that was necessary for it.

In the early years of sport climbing, the best training was just bouldering itself—whether you climbed on rock walls or on indoor artificial bouldering walls. This is still one of the most effective ways of building up strength in the muscle groups specific to climbing. Another method of training to maximize strength, which has by now become a world standard, was the Campus Board, the brainchild of legendary training master Wolfgang Güllich. But there were naturally others who also gave the matter considerable thought. One of them was Rudi Klausner, the longtime trainer of the German sport-climbing team.

In the early '90s, following Klausner's idea of a systematic training program for climbing, Thomas and I designed a bouldering wall with systematically ordered holds, which we accordingly called the System Board. It is, in principle, similar to the Campus Board in its organization of holds, but the big difference is that, unlike the Campus Board, we not only could hang by our arms and hands, but also involve the whole body in training. This took into account the fact that the maximum transfer of energy in climbing—the ultimate key to achievement on the rock—is only made possible through a perfect interplay of all the muscles in the chain between the fingertips and the toes. We put our first System Board into practice in our student digs in Sendling.

We trained three times a week on the System Board, two times a week on regular bouldering, and once a week, we did upper-body strength training. Thomas and I had never had a strict training plan set down in writing, much less a trainer. But over the years, we had acquired such a great deal of knowledge about training method-ology that we never suffered from our lack of a trainer. The most important thing in any training is actually motivation. If the moti-vation is lacking, not even the best trainer will be able to help. This was a wonderful period in our lives, and we were full of energy and enthusiasm.

The university and my various student jobs kept me bound to Munich, so that, with the exception of semester breaks, it was my center of operations. Just around that time, Tyrolean climbers had discovered one of the greatest sport-climbing areas in the world at the foot of the Wilder Kaiser: the Schleier Waterfall. It was here that, in 1991, as part of my preparation for the first ascent of "Shogun" (XI-/8c), I was able to do the first repeat of Gerhard Hörhager's masterpiece, "Mercy Street" (X+/8c). This is one of the best routes in the world, a dynamic, powerful climb that rises up along the left edge of a wild, far-overhanging arch. Since Munich had now become my base, I started looking around the Schleier Waterfall and its practi-cally virgin overhangs for some good projects.

The crag consists of one huge overhanging rock dome, a good 80 meters high, with a 20-meter overhang. In the middle of the dome, a lively mountain stream cascades into a plunge pool some distance away from the base of the wall. On the lower portion of this tremendous rock dome, some routes had already been put up, which all ended after 15 or 20 meters at a natural fracture line—just at the point where it got really steep. Some roofs jutted out a good 15 meters at an angle that was practically horizontal. All these overhangs were still untouched. What a time! It was heaven for me: a land full of surrealistic lines, with overhangs that I had never seen before in such dimensions. Project upon project just waiting to be climbed.

But first, I had set my sights on a line just to the right of Hörhager's "Mercy Street," a fantastic line that follows the course of the far-overhanging arch exactly. "Résistance" (XI-/8c), set in 1992, was just the prelude for what was to follow in subsequent years. The big prizes at the Schleier Waterfall are to be had only on the central overhangs of the great rock dome, and nowhere else.

Two years later, I was finally ready. At the top of my game, having concentrated on nothing but sport climbing for several years, I was prepared to give the best that was in me. I had set up two lines right through the middle of the huge overhang of the waterfall and worked on these continually. My studies were sufficiently under control so that I could pursue climbing virtually nonstop for the entire summer. The two days a week of rest my body needed to recuperate were enough to take care of whatever was required for the university. For anything else, I had neither time nor interest to spare. I was making my way through a narrow tunnel, and there would be no exit until I had achieved the objectives I had set for myself that year.

The "Weiße Rose" (XI/9a) is one of those dream lines that runs through the entire central overhang of the rock dome. For 35 meters, the route grows steeper and steeper, ultimately becoming nearly roof-like, before leading to a gradual transition back into the vertical. While the extremely steep portion of the overhang has a relatively good structure, the transition is the crux. The holds, to the extent they're there at all, are so far apart from one another that it is not immediately apparent which holds should be used in what manner. The correct solution must first be found. In the end, you have to link the individual moves together in such a way that you somehow remain on the rock while simultaneously gaining enough momentum to get over the 1.5 meters to the next hold.

For two weeks, I perfected this sequence of highly difficult moves until it was automatic, and then I had my first breakthrough: For the first time, I was able to climb through the crux of the "Weiße Rose" taken in isolation. It is probably the most complex climbing problem I have ever solved. Over many attempts, my body understood the movements more and more, and with each repetition, I was standing a little better on the rock. I didn't really know what it was I was doing better; I only knew that my body was in a position to learn, and to internalize these complex sequences of moves. Still, I needed a good four weeks more before I was ultimately able to climb all the way through, and thus open my first route in a full 11.

The "Weiße Rose" is one of my loveliest routes, not only because of its difficulty, but also because it has a very special name. The path I took in Munich to the university often led me over the Geschwister-Scholl-Platz (Scholl Sibling Square). This square is dedicated to Hans and Sophie Scholl, members of the anti-Nazi resistance group "Weiße Rose" ("the White Rose") who were executed on February 22, 1943. Often, between classes, I would stand on the mezzanine of the main university building and look down into the atrium of the entrance hall—the very same spot where Hans and Sophie had stood on February 18, 1943. This is where they had thrown their protest leaflets down into the hall, calling for resistance to the Nazis and their senseless war. Hundreds of pages fluttered in the air while Hans and Sophie fled down the staircase toward the exit. But they were observed by the porter, who recognized them and had them arrested. Four days later they were dead. I tried to imagine Sophie as she took up the leaflets and cast them into the air.

Today, the university looks just about the same as it did back then, and every time I saw the place where it happened, it would touch me all over again. I have a very deep respect for the courage of the members of the "Weiße Rose," and I wanted to express that respect in the name I gave to my route on the Schleier Waterfall.

A good month after the first ascent of the "Weiße Rose," I was able to open another big route, "Black Power" (XI/8c), which goes up through the rock dome like a twin sister just a few meters to the right.

Thus, by September of 1994, I had reached a level of sport climbing that forced me to ask myself where I wanted to go next. I didn't want to just climb another dozen routes in this grade. My personality demanded such tremendous discipline that I had to find new motivation—and quickly. That's why my path turned away from grade 11, and took me back to my beginnings, back to the mountains.

In 1995, I allowed myself to skip an entire summer semester and travel to the great mountains of the world. As I was no longer motivated by the local sport-climbing crags, I knocked about in Yosemite and Karakoram. It was exactly what I needed—fresh air, a change of scene, and new walls. It rekindled my motivation just as sport climbing had lit the fire within me five years earlier.

In 1996, I had completed all my qualifying examinations and would be working for the next twelve months on my master's thesis in the department of theoretical meteorology. I had chosen an interesting subject—namely, the connection between LIDAR technology and photometry. LIDAR (Light Detection and Ranging) is a measurement system that uses laser pulses to measure atmospheric backscatter in order to determine the composition of the upper atmosphere, among other things. This may sound complicated, and it is. Since I occasionally had to go up to the more-rarefied atmosphere of the mountain summit to calibrate the photometer, my thesis even had a small connection to the mountains.

On the one hand, the work was interesting. But on the other, it tied me to Munich and left me very little opportunity to travel. Professor Quenzel and my adviser Jörg Ackermann were very understanding of my goals. They gave me a great deal of leeway, so that while great mountain ranges or other projects abroad were beyond my limits, I still had ample time to visit the Schleier Waterfall.

The central rock dome provided one final opportunity for a really difficult project. After 35 meters of extremely demanding climbing in grade 10, I found a good resting point. Just like in the neighboring routes, "Weiße Rose" and "Black Power," I had to work on the complex crux of my new project for a very long time. From the transition, you had to go for an extremely small sidepull and then make an incredibly long, dynamic move up to the left into a two-finger pocket. After two weeks, I had figured out the sequence and could gradually begin to think about making an attempt on the route. But when it comes to long routes with such difficult cruxes this far above the starting point, success can be a long time coming.

Over and over, I would climb the long, demanding stretch until the resting point. And over and over, I would founder on the crux. The climb became a psychological torment. Again and again, I was thwarted by my performance anxiety—the fear of standing just on the verge of success, of having it practically within my reach, only to fail once again a mere meter before the finish line. The full dynamo to the next hold really was extremely far, while the finger hole was very small and a difficult mark to hit. Over and over, I could only reach the edge of the hole, and gradually, I began to doubt that there would ever be a different outcome. The finger hole was so small that I could barely see it. Yet I knew that if I let my thoughts spiral any further, I would fail. There was only one way to succeed: I had to trust myself, and have confidence.

On my next attempt, I was set up in the right position. First, I needed to lower my body so I could get enough momentum to propel myself over a longer stretch. Now I didn't have to think anymore—couldn't have even if I'd wanted to. The muscles in my body engaged 100 percent. The movement was perfectly rehearsed. Against the force of gravity, my body flew up in a wavelike motion. My left hand rocketed toward the hold on which I'd set my sights. Spot-on, I jammed my fingers into the hole, which had just enough room for two fingertips. My fingers were squeezed tight inside the rock. For a brief moment, my body froze; I pressed for all I was worth, and everything went black. I waited to see what would happen.

I didn't fall.

I opened my eyes, placed my left foot, and pulled through to the first good hold.

I worked on the first ascent of "Open Air" (XI+/9a+) for over six weeks. It was truly a difficult birth, at the very edge of my abilities, but that was also why it was so brilliant. It demanded not only all my strength, but also all the creativity and kinesthetic sensibility I had developed over years of high-end sport climbing. For me, it had been a journey to my absolute limit in the psychological sense. From that perspective, the two routes at the Schleier Waterfall, "Weiße Rose" and "Open Air," represent my masterwork—the legacy I have been able to bequeath to the climbing world.

Open air. The phrase is synonymous with crowds of people, alcohol, loud music, excess—things that actually have nothing to do with my route. But anyone who climbs the crux will experience this tremendous exposure, astonishing for a sport-climbing route: 40 meters above the ground, and a 25-meter overhang. It is the dimensions of the rock dome together with the waterfall that create this extraordinary exposure.

"Open Air" makes you think of an open-air concert. Outdoor events have something unique about them. More than the program, it's the setting that can make an open-air event an unforgettable experience. Similarly, the experience of climbing in the "open air" is also more than just the climbing itself, but is rather composed of many factors. Nature is probably the most obvious building block: On a beautiful winter day, who wouldn't rather leave the fog of the valley to stand at the Schleier Waterfall and look up, squinting in the sunlight, at the play of colors in the cascading stream? And the social environment, too, determines whether or not you feel good on the rock. False ambition and resentment often create a negative atmosphere, which is not conducive to a satisfying performance. But a day on the Schleier Waterfall with my friends—what more could I ask for?

CHAPTER EIGHTEEN

"SALATHÉ"—1,000 METERS OF VERTICAL GRANITE

With my achievement of a full grade 11, the ultimate grade 9a, I had not only put up what was likely the most difficult sport-climbing route in the world at the time, but I had also attained something that I had always dreamed of as a climber: reaching the absolute pinnacle of my own potential. It is an unbelievably wonderful moment of realization—to understand that you need not go any further. Especially after all those years in which I had subordinated everything else in my life to the dictates of attaining the most extreme level of technical difficulty. Where should I go from here? I could have fallen into a deep hole, like many others. But for me, attaining this personal high point was simply a new beginning. Finally, I was free to set my sights on other things.

Of course, I could have continued with sport climbing, but I felt I had reached the limit of my abilities. I'd made great sacrifices to bring my body into a condition that would allow me to climb in grade 11. My body is, by nature, rather solidly built, and apparently I have an excellent mechanism for metabolizing fat. I can go for days without eating and experience no loss of energy; I simply live on my fat reserves. This is ideal for long, alpine expeditions. But for sport climbing, the fact that everything I eat is immediately stored as fat tends to be a disadvantage. In order to climb in grade 11, I had to maintain a fighting weight of 62 kilograms (137 pounds). When you look at me today, with my 72 kilos (159 pounds), it's hard to imagine where I could have found any place to take that weight off. I'm not naturally one of those skinny modern climbers whose body type enables them to hang on to the teeniest hold.

And that's why it was a constant battle—just to get thin and nimble enough to conquer the 11th grade. I also had to avoid anything that would contribute to the development of more muscles—since, no matter what I do, I tend to develop a great deal of bulk. That's why, during those years of intensive sport climbing, carrying any kind of backpack was absolutely taboo. Leg muscles are also totally useless for sport climbing, and mine were massive. I also kept away from strength training, since I already had trouble enough keeping my arm muscles in check. It was important to tease out the coordination with the muscles I already had, while at the same time starving myself like an anorexic. In those days, I looked like one of those lean and hungry supermodels in the fashion magazines.

I had attained my sport-climbing goal, and was certain that I would go no further than what I had already achieved. If I kept going down this path, every new grade-11 climb I accomplished would not take me beyond what I had already experienced up to this point, and this knowledge set me free.

Despite the fact that, to all appearances, I had become purely a sport climber, in my heart I had always remained a mountain climber.

My activities may have been temporarily limited to the short sport-climbing routes, but not my horizons. The dream of going up the big walls and climbing the world's great mountains was as alive in me as ever.

In 1995, I had finished all my preparatory coursework and completed the two most important requirements in theoretical physics. I was therefore in a strong position at the university. I had made good progress and could afford to slum it from March until the start of the fall semester.

I wanted to climb the big walls, and my biggest dream was the wall of El Capitan—the incredible granite monolith in Yosemite Valley. Impressive walls have made Yosemite a climbing mecca for over a century. But it was the big successes of the 1960s—the ascents of the great granite walls of El Capitan and the Half Dome—that first thrust the Valley into the limelight of the climbing world. In 1958, Warren Harding opened up the very first big-wall route on El Capitan with the "Nose." Three years later, Royal Robbins followed with the first ascent of "Salathé." Robbins laid the foundations of big-wall climbing through the mid-'60s, and put up the most difficult routes in the world at that time. With his first ascents in Yosemite, the uncompromising style of his repeats, and his development of new techniques of big-wall climbing, he set the tenor of the times—and fought to maintain it. Royal Robbins was the undisputed leader of American climbing for over twenty years. He was not just an exceptionally talented athlete; with his charisma and his farsightedness, he also shaped the style of extreme climbing in our time with big-wall climbing.

The 1970s once again brought a revolution in climbing. Big walls were no longer the measure of all things. Instead, routes like "Midnight Lightning" and "Separate Reality" were the symbols for a new generation, and climbers such as Ron Kauk and John Bachar were the idols. Free climbing was the message preached by the constantly growing community of the Yosemite climbers: They used their technical equipment only for protection, not to help them make upward progress. Climbers from every continent met here year-round, at Camp 4, in order to pursue the "most important pastime in the world."

Long before I was actually able to experience Camp 4 for myself, I had already climbed many of Yosemite's big routes in my mind, leaving the horizontal world of ordinary mortals behind me to follow a single aim: to reach the end of the route. With Reinhard Karl's books as my guide, I dreamt of 50-meter-long traverses on nothing but bad pitons and skyhooks. I imagined how—parched with thirst, my fingers bloodied, my clothes sweaty and torn—I would arrive at the top.

And so I made my way to the climbers' Promised Land with a pretty good idea of how I wanted to realize my dreams. It was no longer enough for me to climb up any old route on El Capitan in any old way. I had some very concrete ideas in that department, for I was already too much of a free climber to be satisfied with anything less than a free ascent. Just a short time earlier, Lynn Hill had completed the first redpoint on the "Nose." Why, then, shouldn't I invest everything and attempt to free-climb the famous "Salathé"?

Mid-April 1995. With great reverence, I stood in the dust of legendary Camp 4. English was only one of the many languages spoken on the venerable campground. Climbers from all over the world had come to Yosemite to climb. I was not disappointed. On every route, you could relive something of Yosemite's storied climbing history.

High up on El Cap: "Sous le toit"—a tiny terrace 40 meters under the great roof at the beginning of the famous headwall of "Salathé." Gottfried Wallner and I had set up our bivouac on less than a single square meter. There wasn't even enough space for one of us to lie down. Still, it promised to be a comfortable bivy. We huddled up next to one another in our sleeping bags. The night was warm, the sky, clear. Suddenly, just as I'd shifted into the best possible sleeping position, it began to rain in buckets. Before Gottfried could even disentangle himself from his sleeping bag, the freak episode was over—and we were all wet. We sat in silence next to one another and stared miserably up into the darkness. I was in the process of trying to find a flashlight in my backpack when we were hit by a second flash torrent. Damn it. By the light of the flashlight, we saw the problem: 100 meters above and 50 meters to the right, a meltwater stream ended at a huge roof to the right of the "Salathé" headwall. During the day, this waterfall had remained hidden from us. The strong tailwind in the valley had sent the cool spray in the opposite direction. But as the sun set, the direction of the wind had changed, and the mountain wind was now ensuring that we were getting increasingly soaked with showers at irregular intervals.

In fact, I had had quite enough water already. The weather since my arrival in the Valley had been marked by rain, snow, and floods. "Below-normal temperatures and above-normal chance of rain," ran the weather report in the papers for the last six weeks, and for once, it was right on target. Accordingly, El Capitan looked more like a vertical waterworks than the brilliant hunk of climbing rock I'd expected.

That day, I had already climbed through water—first on the "Ear" (an ear-shaped loose flake), and then again in the late afternoon, in the waterfall pitch underneath the "Block," a bivouac spot 700 meters above the valley floor. When the "Block" didn't seem to offer secure-enough protection from the various waterfalls, we thought we'd be more assured of shelter on the tiny ledge we were now stuck on.

The next morning, there was not a dry centimeter left anywhere, and I hadn't slept at all. Everything was soaked: the sleeping bags, our clothes, the climbing gear, the rope, our shoes . . . At first light, we willed our stiff, hypothermic bodies through the exposure of the headwall, the last pitches of "Salathé." Completely drained, we climbed out onto the top plateau around midday. Finally, sunshine! An end to the drudgery! But nonetheless, this first trip through "Salathé" was a valuable experience: I now knew that my dream of free-climbing one of the great big routes of the world was doable.

In 1988, Todd Skinner and Paul Piana had caused a real sensation on the climbing scene when they claimed the first free ascent of "Salathé." Over a period of several weeks, they supposedly free-climbed every single pitch; but some in the community had doubts. Skinner and Piana had given a 5.13a rating to the long and narrow dihedral before the El Cap Spire, a pillar standing some distance away from the wall, two-thirds its height. But this pitch is pretty tough, and many a prominent climber has been thwarted on it. Clearly, the dihedral is much more difficult than Skinner's proposed rating would suggest. This flagrant factual misjudgment had strengthened doubts about the claim that the 1988 ascent of "Salathé" had been free all the way through.

But even from El Cap Meadow, at the foot of El Capitan, I had already noticed the wide crack running upward about 6 meters to the left of the original dihedral. A fine undercling flake leading down to the left would enable the airy traverse in an easy grade 9 away from the original line into a 50-meter-long brutally demanding off-width crack. With that, I had solved the crux. Only the headwall remained. After our waterlogged bivouac, I hadn't been in any shape to attempt even a single meter free up there because of the hypothermia, but I could see that my project was possible. There wasn't any doubt. The headwall—and with it, "Salathé" itself—was definitely possible as a free climb.

Sunny California . . . right! It rained, it snowed. I waited down on the floor of Yosemite Valley an entire week before the weather finally decided to cooperate. The meteorologists had forecast decent weather for the coming days. I was ready: Laden with climbing equipment, bivouac gear, and five days' worth of provisions—more than 30 kilos on my back—I set off alone over the East Ledges toward the summit of El Capitan. No sooner had I set up my bivy under a little rock roof on the top plateau than—of course—I found myself standing in the middle of a sudden storm. Unfortunately, I hadn't learned my lesson. I had neither a tent nor waterproof clothing. In the middle of the night the wind rose up, and not much later the first snow-flakes were swirling about my head. A sudden cold front with massive snowfall; if I wanted to avoid impending hypothermia, I would have to come up with something. And so, in the middle of the blizzard, I went off in search of a drier bivouac spot.

Luckily, after a short while, I discovered a little cave—an ideal place. I would, in any case, find no better shelter out here on the otherwise-naked plateau of El Capitan. My dungeon was, however, already occupied by a large, mummified body of a bird, which lent the place a truly macabre character. I pierced its parchment-like skin with a stick and transported it outside the cave entrance. As I was about to lay him down on his final resting place, he collapsed into a little cloud of dust.

For two days, I holed up in my meager "hotel room," brooding, wracked with doubt, and stamping my feet constantly against the cold, before the fine weather promised by the forecast finally arrived. For the next few days I threw myself into rehearsing the climbing moves on the headwall. According to what Todd Skinner reported, the headwall could be freed in three pitches—two at 5.13a and one at 5.13b. The belay between the first two pitches, however, was about the exact opposite of a no-hand-rest; it was most definitely a hang-ing belay, which I would have to avoid at all costs on a redpoint. For that reason, I decided to string together the first two headwall pitch-es into just one. Furthermore, my plan was to redpoint "Salathé" as a whole, in one go—to lead every single pitch without falling in as few days as possible, including setting the protection required in crack climbing.

The headwall. A wall within the wall—the crux of "Salathé." It starts with a V-shaped crack. There are tiny flakes on the rounded edges, making it possible to free-climb. The beginning of the main crack is reached, ultimately, with a dynamic move 900 meters above the valley floor. Luckily, I was long accustomed to the disorienting view of the unbelievable, vertiginous depths. The crack runs up the headwall for 70 meters without a break. That means that up until the first no-hand-rest, which ends the first free-climbing pitch after 55 meters, the difficulties are dominated by open-hand jams. The second, considerably shorter pitch begins with an exquisite finger crack, and after a second no-hand-rest, narrows into a hairline crack, which can only be overcome by face climbing. Hard work, then. By the end of my day on the wall, the snow flurries were swirling around me again, so I beat a hasty retreat from El Capitan before the cold front could descend on me.

Waiting for good weather, one day, two days, a whole week long. At last, I went up again, this time with the comforts of a tent. Like a gymnast rehearsing his routine, I practiced every single move again until, two days later, veteran Yosemite climber Mark Chapman showed up to meet me, as we had arranged. He had agreed to belay me as I led the most difficult pitches. We rappelled down the top five pitches to the start of the headwall. I was nervous—damned nervous. Still, I went into the first pitch with full concentration. Quickly, everything around me faded away; with my thoughts focused on the next move, my field of vision narrowed to a point. I saw before me only the next jam, the next hold.

Finally, 3 meters before the belay, I placed my last chock. With my final bit of strength, I tugged at the rope and tried to clip it, but I had no more power left. The last protection lay some meters below me, and the next few meters were the hardest! No matter. I wanted to try it, and there was only one thing to do: Go for it, despite the fact that a big, huge fall was a very real possibility. Forget everything and keep going; get through it.

After we'd completed the climb, Mark congratulated me, shaking his head and saying, "Hey, this run-out was fuckin' crazy, man!" With our chips and Budweiser, we celebrated the first redpoint ascent of probably the best pitch in the whole world.

I was now ready for the ultimate ascent of the entire route, this time with photographer Heinz Zak. Naturally, first it had to snow and rain some more. The weather gods showed us no mercy and flushed us down into the valley with another downpour. And so we waited until the meteorologists finally announced the end of the "rain season."

For the umpteenth time, I climbed up the flat first third of the "Salathé" wall. On the legendary "Hollow Flake"—a 30-meter-long off-width chimney with no possibility for protection—we caught up to a slower climbing party, which had been stuck there for quite some time. So, blinkers on and into the passing lane!

We finally reached the infamous wide crack before the El Cap Spire, known today as the "Monster Off-Width." It's a crack of the worst possible sort: just a smidge too narrow to wedge your entire body into the mountain, and far too wide to be able to effectively jam any portion of your body between the parallel walls of the crack. Protection? Forget about it! For this crack width, all protection gear is way too small. With 40 unprotected meters, the rope provides nothing more than moral support; the potential fall factor is striking. Making progress here is abnormally strenuous, nerve-wracking, and slow. Inch by inch, you scrape your way toward release. It is pure struggle.

At 6:00 PM, I finally reached El Cap Spire, drained and exhausted, but happy to have put this pitch behind me. Five pitches above us lay the "Block," our goal for the day as the planned bivouac site. At the last great hurdle, the 5.12d pitch shortly before the "Block," it happened. I hung for two minutes on a tiny hold edge, unable to recall the right solution for the spot, a crossover move. As my nervousness increased, the image of the correct sequence faded from my mind. I fought desperately to hang on, my muscles burning. Then it was all over. I tumbled backward out of the wall. The rope pulled at my harness, and I was safe but frustrated.

I had to set it up three more times before I found the correct solution. Back to the beginning once more for another attempt at climbing the entire pitch without a fall before it got dark. I returned to the belay, but there was no time to recuperate. Dusk was fast approaching and wouldn't let me rest. My arms were tired, but I simply had to do it. I pulled off the crossover. Now, I just needed to make it up the overhanging dihedral. My arms had almost nothing left to give, and my fingers kept cramping up. The only thing that was still halfway functional was my leg work, which saved me over the remaining meters. We had to set up for our bivouac on the "Block" in the dark.

The next day, there were only ten more pitches above us, so we had a lot of time. I took it easy and didn't really get going until around midday. Still a bit stiff, I climbed up the first pitch toward "Sous le toit." Although it wasn't all that difficult, it's a while before I'm relieved to feel the fresh blood washing away all of yesterday's gunk from my forearms. At the start of the headwall, I was extremely nervous again, and so the predictable happened. After just a few meters, I fell off the wall during the dynamo in the main crack. I fumed at myself. Slowly, I came back down, the tension dissipated, and I started the pitch anew.

After my experience during the practice run with Mark Chapman, I planned to do without the placement of the penultimate piece of pro in order to save my energy for the placement of the last. This time, I didn't want to have a "fuckin' crazy" run-out at the crux. Everything went smoothly, but just as I was placing this last protection, the hand that was jammed in the crack suddenly slipped. I didn't need to look down to know that there was a 20-meter fall waiting for me. With full force, I drilled my fingertips into the narrow crack, with no regard for pain. The 1,000 meters of El Capitan are reduced only to this. The crack became a microcosm in the infinite expanse of its granite walls. This was pure masochism. Put this much pressure on your fingertips a few times, and pretty soon you won't feel much of anything anymore—until the pain dissolves into ecstasy. Adrenaline can make you drunk, and I'm sure I must have been plastered.

Up on top, at the exit of "Salathé," on El Capitan's plateau, I took time to look back down into Yosemite Valley. In my mind, a film plays out; a film about a dance on 1,000 meters of granite.

CHAPTER NINETEEN

LATOK II—BIG-WALL CLIMBING AT 7,000 METERS

The fact that I—a country yokel from the Bavarian hinterland—could pull off a redpoint ascent of "Salathé" was a sensational personal achievement. I had dreamed about it, and I'd had high hopes—but just as many doubts. Now I could move on granite as though I had never done anything but. That, of course, was the reason I had gone to California that year. I had wanted to undergo the strenuous schooling of Yosemite. I had put up some of the most difficult routes in the world on limestone, which is replete with holes and edges. But crack climbing on granite has truly little in common with the natural gripping and mounting movement known to limestone climbers. It had made sense to learn granite climbing more systematically, and I couldn't imagine a better school than Yosemite.

I therefore was well prepared in the fall of 1995, which is when I had planned to undertake the west face of Latok II with some friends. Located in the Pakistani portion of the Karakoram Range, this 7,108-meter summit is an impressive mountain, and its 2,200-meter west face a fantastic challenge. The symmetrical pyramid of rock rises majestically up from the end of a long glacial valley and is split right down its middle by a huge ice couloir. Above the middle of the face, the couloir ascends up to the left in the direction of the ridge, while above it, a single, sheer ocean of granite leads up to the summit. This was one of the greatest challenges that mountain climbing still had to offer. Never before had a big wall been climbed above an altitude of 6,200 meters. With an ascent of Latok II, we would be the first to bring big-wall climbing to a height of over 7,000 meters. This was what really attracted me to the enterprise: No one had ever tried it before.

We wanted to climb in the Karakorams at the end of the season when, as we figured it, the steep west face of Latok II would be free of ice and easier to climb. I was still far too inexperienced in such big mountains, or I would have known that the huge couloir leading up to the start of the big wall would become more dangerous with each summer day. When we finally stood under the wall and realized how brutal and unpredictable the rockfall in the couloir actually was, we had no other option but to abandon our plans. But success frequently comes by way of a detour, and big projects in the Himalayas and Karakorams provided an excellent opportunity to reconnoiter. I knew how important it was to gain experience, and that's just what I wanted to do in 1995.

After saying good-bye to the west face of Latok II, we turned our attention to an alternative: the Northwest Ridge, which borders the west face on the left. We broke off the assault just before a storm hit. This decision showed me how important it is to pay heed to your sixth sense in the mountains. Upon returning to civilization, we found out that just 30 kilometers away, seven mountain climbers—

including Englishwoman Alison Hargreaves, world-renowned for her achievement on Everest—had died in the storm.

Back at school, I discovered my semester's sabbatical was not without far-reaching consequences. The trips that I took during that time brought about a real change in my life.

Up to that point, climbing had been nothing but a hobby for me. Although I certainly trained for it like a professional, the only compensation I ever got was personal satisfaction. Indeed, in order to fulfill my dreams, I first had to rustle up the money to pay for the trips. That all changed after my redpoint of "Salathé." It was my first successful climb that found widespread recognition beyond the specialized world of sport climbing.

Heinz Zak and I had wanted something more than just quick snapshots for a scrapbook. We spared no effort, put three days of work into getting really good photos, and only stopped when Heinz felt he had the perfect pictures in the can. When you look at alpine magazines today, pictures of this quality have become the standard. But back then, the fact that we brought home such photographs from a wall like El Capitan was a real novelty. The photos from the ascent went out into the world, and all at once I was internationally known. Without realizing it, we had ushered in a new era.

"Salathé" was, in every respect, the beginning of a fruitful and successful partnership not just for me as a climber but also for Heinz as a photographer. Now, it was no longer just isolated news items here and there that announced my most recent modest achievements in ten lines. Now they asked for whole articles: six, eight, ten pages long, and not with some little picture tucked away somewhere in the back of the magazine, but entire series of photographs. Images from "Salathé" graced the covers of no less than fourteen different publications worldwide.

It was no wonder, then, that soon afterward, a sports agent approached me about giving a lecture. I had no notion of what such a lecture would include or how much I should charge, but I simply followed my instincts. As though it was quite old hat for me, I accepted immediately and asked for 1,000 marks. To my surprise, this was promptly accepted, and before I knew it, I was giving lectures all over the place. The part-time jobs in bars and sporting-goods stores were now a thing of the past. Without putting much effort into it, I quickly arranged for no less than fifteen lectures for the coming winter. Suddenly, I no longer had to wrack my brains to figure out how to finance my next trip.

The only thing that still held me back at this point was my studies. It was early in 1997 and things were getting serious. I would have liked nothing better than to go back to Latok II the very next year, but I couldn't possibly take another semester off before graduation. There was my master's thesis to write, the qualifying exams, and, in May, the last examination for my master's degree in physics. Nonetheless, I did manage to find time to organize my next expedition to Latok II. None of the participants of the last expedition seemed to really believe we would be successful in our assault of this gigantic wall. Nonetheless, I was able to put together the perfect team for this face, the core of which consisted of my brother Thomas, Toni Gutsch from Munich, and the Californian Yosemite climber Conrad Anker. All of us had experience on big walls, and I knew that this would be the key to our success.

Islamabad, Pakistan. A "briefing" is what they call the last meeting with the Ministry of Tourism, at which they finally grant you permission to set out for the mountains. We had made careful preparations during our first five days in Pakistan, and we'd assumed that right after the briefing, that very afternoon, we would be able to set off for Skardu, the capital of Baltistan, in our chartered bus. Unfortunately, the minister was in a rather bad mood that day. Although I had already submitted the documents for every one of the expedition members to the Ministry two months before, at the briefing it turned out that Conrad's paperwork was missing. I was boiling mad but there was nothing to be done. I had to keep calm.

I noticed the ceiling fan out of the corner of my eye. Its gentle breeze had blown some of the file's loose pages to the floor. I showed the minister the letter he had sent me in reply to my application, in which he'd confirmed all the participants present. Unimpressed, he informed me that this didn't change the way things stood, and we still had to wait for the Secret Service to check over Conrad's papers. Thus, we were not allowed to leave the capital under any circumstances. And the bus was already waiting!

Mercifully, in the end the minister offered a compromise: The bus with all our equipment and most of the team could go, but I, as the leader of the expedition, would have to wait here with Conrad until the Secret Service gave him the green light. We would be given an additional trekking permit for the ride to Skardu. And to make sure we didn't go astray, we would be assigned a guide.

The next day, the minister's mood had improved considerably, and Conrad and I were actually given permission to follow the others. Out of financial considerations, we—and our guide—took the public bus. This is very cheap, extremely crowded, and quite intense. Here, you are literally cheek-to-cheek with the local Pakistanis. After twenty-four hours, the unique smells of the numerous passengers seated around you are as familiar to you as your own.

During the night, things got particularly exciting. Our utterly exhausted driver rear-ended another bus, and a brawl broke out. Fifty worked-up Pakistanis stood opposite each other, arguing and scuffling over the rather unambiguous question of fault. The drivers, it seems, were concerned less with legal liability than with personal honor. After a quarter of an hour, the bellicose crowd suddenly scattered, and our guide grabbed my shirt and pulled me back into the bus, saying, "Gun, gun!" It was like the Wild West. The two drivers faced off, each standing alone with a revolver, ready for a shoot-out. After a minute of silence, they stuck the weapons back in their pockets, started shouting at each other again, and eventually returned to their buses.

Thank God, we are on our way again, I thought, breathing a sigh of relief. The driver took one last opportunity to express his anger by tormenting the starter and the clutch, and with a blue cloud of exhaust, our slightly battered bus continued on its journey. This was rough country.

As day dawned, we were already riding in the desert high above the imposing Indus Gorge. After the oppressive humidity of Rawalpindi, it was now dry and hot. The first mountain ranges of the Himalayas capture so much moisture that in the area that lies behind them, there is hardly any precipitation over the entire year. It was difficult to imagine glaciers covering mountain peaks somewhere nearby. Inside the bus it was a sauna. Sixty men produce huge quantities of sweat, and since the windows could not be opened, the humidity was nearly 100 percent. Far below, on the banks of the Indus, the carcasses of burnt-out buses were strewn about as constant reminders of the consequence of driver exhaustion, and testified to the Pakistani attitude toward life: "Inshallah"—God willing. On a packed bus in the hands of a driver who was constantly dozing off while speeding full throttle toward Skardu, we were completely powerless.

In Skardu, we were met at the K2 Hotel by Ismail and Kassim, who had been on our first Latok expedition. Ismail was actually the cook, but he also organized everything else. With his help, the kerosene and all the provisions had already been taken care of. We would be leaving the very next day. A crowd of Baltis was gathered outside the hotel, pressing up against the fence as they usually did whenever an expedition turned up. They were here to snag jobs as porters. Ismail and I negotiated a price for him, Kassim, and the porters, and by evening, the jeeps that would take us on the next leg of the journey in the morning had already arrived.

We started before dawn. This early start was necessary because there are numerous glacial streams along the 100-kilometer stretch of gravel road through the Braldu Gorge, and by midday they swell and become impassable.

The Braldu Gorge leads right into the center of the Karakoram Range. The literal meaning of the name *Karakoram* is sobering; in Turkish, it means "black crumbling rock." In the Braldu Gorge, this description was more than apt. Our jeeps seemed like toy cars winding their way through the sandbox of the titans. The valley of the raging Braldu is cut deep. The path along it allows no glimpse of the icy giants of the Karakorams. The dry gravel slopes are occasionally interspersed with green fields watered by glacial melt streams.

Our motorized journey ended in Askole. Located at an altitude of 3,000 meters, it is the last permanent settlement before the high mountain desert of the Karakorams. Here, we found hundreds of Baltis already waiting for us—more men seeking work as porters. For the inhabitants of the most-remote regions of Baltistan, being a porter has become a fixture in their lives. Although they only make the equivalent of about 10 euros a day, and certainly do not grow rich on such meager wages, portage is their only opportunity to earn any money at all. The work is accordingly much sought after, and the crowd of job seekers very large.

Bringing order to the resulting chaos is the task of the *sardar*, the head porter. He distinguishes himself from the rest of the Baltis mainly by the fact that he can read and write a little and is able to speak broken English. Here, such few skills are enough to grant automatic leadership status. The sardar's job is to distribute the 25-kilo packs among the porters, and to keep an eye on them throughout the entire trek to the base camp.

Leaving Askole meant leaving civilization behind for good. With our eighty porters, we set off for the isolation of the high mountains. At first, we still followed the wild Braldu, which is fed by the giant Baltoro and Biafo glaciers, but then we began to climb higher and higher along the traditional Balti hunting paths, and soon saw the first six-thousanders: precipitous, ice-covered needles of granite— the hallmark of the Karakorams. We followed a small saddle pass to the side of the main path to the Baltoro Glacier, the last time our feet would touch secure ground, and then we were finally going up the 60-kilometer-long Biafo Glacier, which at first didn't look at all like a glacier.

The ice was covered by tons of scree, and it was a hard stretch for the porters. Swaying to and fro between the enormous granite boulders, they hauled their packs in all sorts of weather: through rain and snow, and under the blazing heat of the sun. To protect themselves against the nighttime cold, they brought along nothing but a blanket, which they also used to pad their backs under the weight of the packs. Each also carried a little sack for his chapattis (a handful of flour mixed with a couple handfuls water, and baked on a stone over the fire). The conditions were harsh. Everything was reduced to a minimum. And yet, in their simplicity, the Baltis were a satisfied, joyful people.

Reinhard Karl has written some sobering things about the Baltis and their way of life. But at the time, he had just returned from his failed attempt on K2, frustrated to the core; perhaps for that reason, he was particularly receptive to negative impressions. I take a different view of things. When I look into the faces of the Baltis, I don't think I'm kidding myself. They are satisfied with their life—much more satisfied than many a person in our culture—because they have a job to do that offers cash and a change of pace.

After three days and 30 kilometers on the Biafo, we reached Biantha, one of the traditional Balti campsites located around the edge of the glacier. Biantha is situated at about 4,000 meters. Here, we left the path of the Biafo Glacier and began to follow the Uzun Brakk Glacier, which leads into the heart of the Latok group. The final, daylong leg of the march to base camp lay before us, and the excitement was palpable—for the Baltis, because the next day they would be able to set down their loads and return to their villages with about a third of their annual income in their pockets. And we were excited because, with the exception of myself, everyone else on the team had only ever seen our ultimate destination in pictures, and the very next day, Latok II would stand directly before us, large as life.

Just as in 1995, we arrived at our base camp. At an altitude of 4,400 meters, the camp was located directly at the confluence of the Uzun Brakk Glacier and the nameless flow of ice that comes down from the west face of Latok II. On Nanga Parbat, at the foot of the Rakhiot Peak, there is a base camp that the German expeditions of the 1930s christened "Fairy-Tale Meadow." This is understandable, since after you leave the dry, stony desert of the Indus Valley, you arrive in a vegetation zone that resembles some of the loveliest alpine valleys.

That's what it was like for us. Just like over on Nanga Parbat, our base camp lay in a fairy-tale meadow. Hemmed in on all sides by huge glaciers, sheltered by their lateral moraines, the meadow stretched out in a rich, verdant blanket. A stream meandered through its middle, emptying out into a little shallow lake, in which we could even have a swim when the weather was nice.

After our porters had deposited all their various loads in the middle of the meadow and were paid, we suddenly found ourselves all alone among the wild, rocky towers of the Latok group. There was no wind, no avalanche, no rockfall—indeed, the uncanny calm didn't seem to fit the intimidating surroundings of the stone land-scape. The first thing I did was to train my telescope on the moraine. Did my plan come off? In August 1995, the snow and ice cover had already receded quite far, causing tremendous rockfall that thwarted any chance we had of climbing up the west face of Latok II. That was why I had scheduled this expedition six weeks earlier in the season, to catch the ice while it was in a better condition. And indeed, I could breathe easy; my strategy had worked! The west-face couloir lay under a deep blanket of snow, and it was pure white—not a single incriminating black stripe of fallen rock to be seen. I studied the rock structure of the top 1,000 meters of the west face through the tele-scope. Outlined by their shadows, the cracks and dihedrals stood out in the sun against the smooth, featureless sections of the wall. Each one of us took turns with the telescope and tried to resolve the great confusion of barely recognizable structures into an ideal line.

We had caught the fever.

Before we could set out up the mountain, however, we had to put together the gear and provisions we would need on the big wall. A thousand meters of vertical rock would need some time. We intended to spend at least ten—if not fifteen—days in this granite labyrinth. That meant reducing the necessary provisions to a bare minimum. We calculated down to the very last gram. Per day, each man would need 125 grams of fuel for cooking, 300 grams of freeze-dried food-stuff, and 200 grams of carbohydrate bars. With four men and fifteen days, it worked out to 30 kilograms of food and 7.5 kilograms of fuel. On top of that came all the climbing equipment and the bivouac gear. And all this was supposed to be hauled up the couloir to the start of technical climbing at an altitude of 6,000 meters before we could get going!

During the next few days, we set up our Advanced Base Camp at 4,900 meters, directly at the foot of the west face. It took a good week, and then we were ready to begin transporting our stuff through the couloir. On June 24, Thomas, Conrad, and Toni climbed far up the couloir for the first time and set up the Balcony Camp at 5,600 meters. But after one night in the camp, it began to snow, and in no time, the whole mountain was on the move: spindrift blew from the walls, snow slid down the couloir. It was no place for my three companions, and they immediately began their descent. Every minute counted. The fear of being swept down into the abyss by an avalanche drove them down the couloir. Fueled by adrenaline, they ran, leaping over the snowslides. An hour later they reached safer ground, before the first big avalanches thundered down the couloir.

In the days that followed, it snowed over a meter, and the nasty weather kept us gathered at Base Camp. We spent a lot of time discussing our tactics. How should we tackle the huge wall? How much material did we need? How should we split up into teams? On July 2, the weather finally improved, and the very next day we climbed back up to Base Camp. At one in the morning, we pressed on. Because of the rockfall, we wanted to use the security of the coldest hours of the day and be at Balcony Camp by sunrise. Silently, we climbed up one after another through the couloir.

Each of us felt the same oppressive tension in the face of the most dangerous part of our undertaking. I tried to keep from thinking of the rock slides of 1995, when I experienced a real onslaught here one night. This time, it was quiet, but this only diffused the situation in part; for thirty minutes, we were forced to climb under an overhanging serac before we could cross over to the right into seemingly secure terrain. Conrad's eyes looked different, and he didn't crack his usual jokes. Again and again, I saw him looking upward, and at last he came out with a phrase that at first appeared nonsensical, but I understood its meaning later: "Dancing in the ballroom of death with the fat lady of faith." From then on, we would refer to this serac affectionately as "The Fat Lady."

The exertion took one's mind off the danger lurking above us and directed it more to what was happening in one's own body. Just hang on, and keep prodding yourself, meter by meter, to bring the 30 kilos on your back a little bit further. At 8:00 AM, we reached the more or less secure Balcony Camp under a rock overhang on the right edge of the couloir. Exhausted, we sat before our tents, nothing more than tiny points in this gigantic drainpipe for avalanches. Above our heads, the big wall thrust up into the blue sky. Its dimensions were overwhelming, and only magnified by the monotonous homogeneity of the ice. But at the same time, we were completely enthralled by it. It dominated and controlled us.

The next day, while Toni and Conrad went to bring another load of provisions from Base Camp to Balcony Camp, Thomas and I climbed the ice slope, which now lay at an angle of 55 degrees, up to 6,000 meters, where the over-1,000-meter-high wall began. Once

The Huber boys—exploring the mountains together from the time they were little.

Temporary anchors opened up a whole new world of opportunities for us: the ascent of "Long Schoat" on the Fleisch-bank with Fritz Mussner.

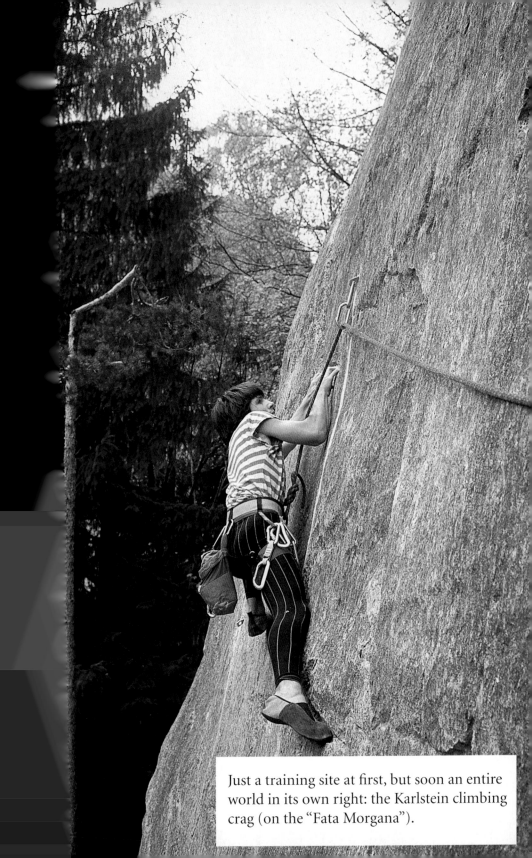

Just a training site at first, but soon an entire world in its own right: the Karlstein climbing crag (on the "Fata Morgana").

On the classic Karlstein route, "Entschlusskraft." Emulating our role model Wolfgang Güllich, we trained hard and improved quickly.

After many attempts, the realm of grade eleven was finally opened to me in 1991 with "Shogun."

At the start of the long journey up: headwall of "Salathé" on El Capitan.

Crack climbing with no end in sight—If you haven't mastered the technique, you've got no business on "El Corazón."

Topsy-turvy world: free climbing on the giant, upside-down steps of the great overhanging roof on the route "Bellavista."

again, we hacked out a platform in the ice, which would serve as a camp for the first pitches on the granite wall that now rose up directly in front of us.

In the evening, we climbed back down to Balcony Camp so we could bring up more gear the next day. Once again, we started out in the middle of the night, this time with all four of us together. Even though we knew that this was the safest time of the day, a certain tension was ever-present. Below us, the light of our headlamps disappeared into the abyss, and somewhere above us hung the serac; invisible in the darkness, our unpredictable nemesis was a constant, lurking presence. The power that drove us on was the motivation to finally get up on the wall. Up in the camp at 6,000 meters, we agreed that Thomas and Conrad would go back down and spend the next two days getting a fresh supply of provisions, while Toni and I would begin the climb.

Fifty carabiners, twenty friends, thirty chocks, fifteen pitons, six different skyhooks, hammer, etriers—I stood in the snow beneath a kilometer-high block of granite like a heavily decorated Christmas tree. At 6,100 meters, the air was noticeably thin. My brain cells had already been suffering from oxygen deprivation for hours due to the heavy work of carrying the packs. With trembling legs, I stood on the first footholds—a slab in grade 7, bad protection, long run-outs. I had to really struggle with myself and with the rock. My field of vision became increasingly narrow, restricting itself to nothing but each respective handhold. Only routine made it possible for me to make solid progress despite it all.

At last, after 15 meters with bad protection, I arrived at the lower end of the crack system that I had set my sights on. Now, I could finally relax and rest, protected by the first solid runner. Oh, God, my poor brain . . . I was nearing a state of complete inebriation. With hammer and pitons, I worked my way ponderously over the first roof. Luckily, aid climbing is less strenuous than free climbing, and this gave me the chance to slowly recover.

After the second pitch, it started to get dark. We rappelled down and set up our bivouac at the foot of the wall. Our first night at 6,000 meters. We kept waking up, gasping for air. Our breathing centers had not yet adapted to this altitude and reacted with Cheyne-Stokes respiration: two minutes of shallow breathing followed by panicked gasping for oxygen. Nonetheless, the next morning, Toni turned in a phenomenal performance, advancing over a roof that appeared unsettlingly smooth. Rurps, knifeblades, and a hook—the first A3 pitch was perfect!

During the next two days, Toni and I were relieved by Thomas and Conrad. While we brought more equipment from Balcony Camp to the foot of the wall, the two of them pushed the route up to 6,450 meters before a bad weather front on July 9 brought us all together again at Base Camp.

The weather finally cleared up again on July 12, and the very next day, Toni and I were on the wall again. Starting at the end of the fixed rope we had put down on our retreat, I climbed up along a perfectly shaped layback flake until the crack petered out in total blankness. The only possibility was to traverse to the right with skyhooks over a series of horizontal edges that were only a few millimeters wide. Unworried, I pressed on. I was just starting to look for the right skyhook for the next mini-edge when I suddenly took a dive and found myself 10 meters lower, hanging upside down in the rope. Shit! Now I had to do it all over again from the beginning!

Once again, I made it to the top end of the flake, and again I crossed to the right. This time, I hoped to have more luck with another skyhook. The hook bent under the load, but it held. And it went on in that vein. The next pitch was thorny. After a truly delicate slab, which I had to climb exclusively with the help of skyhooks, there was a moderate hairline crack 10 meters long waiting for me. In contrast, the 6-meter-high flake that followed was pure dynamite. It seemed to hover, fully detached, above our heads, held at its base by nothing more than ice. I preferred not to have to go for a test flight on such an un-flightworthy object. Using skyhooks once more, I crept past the flake. After this pitch, my nerves were shot, and I was glad to let Toni take the lead.

The next day, at sundown, just as Toni and I had finished with the second pitch of the day, we met up with Thomas and Conrad, as agreed. They had slogged away just like us the last two days, and with truly backbreaking labor had managed to haul up the entirety of their supplies for ten days of life in the vertical, all the way up to 6,500 meters. While they would continue to press on with the route in the next two days, Toni and I would have the same torturous labor before us. We were truly happy when, two days later, we finally got all the stuff up and were able to watch the sunset from the portaledges. Gradually, the wall had come to seem like a prison to us: During the day, we performed the forced labor of climbing, and after sundown, the cold of the night forced us into our little cells, the portaledges. Here, in the space of a single square meter, we would take care of all the things for which people normally have an entire house: dry your clothes, straighten up, organize your equipment for the next day, melt water, cook, eat, sleep . . .

Shortly before sundown, Conrad and Thomas glided back down to us from their day's work. Supper was already bubbling on the cooker. Cozily, we sat together, slurping soup. There was not a breeze stirring. It was completely still. The last rays of the sun kept the temperature comfortable and bathed the wall in a red glow—a last, magical flare of light and warmth before darkness and cold won the upper hand. This was one of those moments when I know why I will always return to the mountains again and again. I enjoyed the stillness and took pleasure in knowing that I was among the chosen few to be allowed to witness this unique spectacle of nature at 6,500 meters. Down in the valley below, darkness had long since fallen, while far behind us on the horizon, Nanga Parbat was still brightly lit. I thought of Hermann Buhl, who must have stood there at the summit at just this time of day, in the light of the setting sun . . .

The daily routine of getting up was far less peaceful and romantic. During the night, temperatures would fall to 20-below, and we were sitting on a west wall, where no sun would reach us until the early afternoon. While the neighboring Ogre, the main summit of the Latok group, was already shining in the morning light, we sat in the cold and tried to come out of the starting gate as quickly as possible. But when your fingers are numb, the speed of things like eating breakfast, taking care of urgent business, and getting dressed is quite considerably reduced—to say nothing of returning to the point where we had turned back the previous day and climbing on. The yearned-for afternoon hours, on the other hand, flooded the wall with sunshine, and temperatures hovered just around freezing. This made it possible to climb without gloves, and when there wasn't anything to do at the belay, it was even known to happen that one of us could be found dreamily lost in thought.

On July 17, we had finally reached an altitude of 6,800 meters. Up here, the wall turned out to be less steep and compact. It looked like the summit could be reached from here in one day, but we were tired from all the arduous labor of the past week on the wall, and spending that length of time above 6,500 meters had taken its toll. We considered our options. There wasn't a trace of cloud in the sky, and in the end, the stable weather pattern of the last few days gave us confidence. We decided to take a day off to rest.

After resting for a day in the portaledge at 6,500 meters, we set off at around midnight on July 19. It would be our day—the day on which a four-year-old dream, and so much more, would come true for me. It would simply be wonderful when all the work was over and we could put aside our tools—when we could step back and look at our accomplishment as something near and dear to our hearts, precisely because it was the fruit of our own labor.

Four little lights worked their way up through the night. Around 4:00 AM, just before sunrise, we reached the end of the vertical wall at 6,800 meters. No, man—oh no! Please, not now; not today, not here.

You've gotta be kidding. Two hundred kilometers away, on Nanga Parbat, a violent storm front had built over the entire width of the sky. It was a gigantic fireworks display. Every second, a bright-blue flash appeared somewhere along the horizon. It was a gamble against time. In as little as an hour, the whole thing could be over here, forcing us back down in a snowstorm. The last stage to the summit was a terrorizing onslaught on our nerves.

The mixed ground was more difficult than we'd expected, and I was able to make only extremely slow progress on this tricky stretch. At last, in the light of my headlamp, the rock tilted away from me. Standing on the front points of my crampons, I balanced on a slab covered by a razor-thin verglas. Two meters above me began the ice couloir that would bring us to the summit. Carefully, I struck my ax into the hollow ice. I didn't like it. I began to have some doubts about what I was doing. We weren't in the Alps here, or on some other lowly peaks. We were at nearly 7,000 meters in Karakoram, in the middle of nowhere. If I took a dive here . . . Your only lifeline is yourself, so my mind was telling me to go back down; go slowly back down, step by step—anything else would be senseless. This ice wasn't 100 percent safe. I should go down now, slowly, step by step . . .

I take the steps, two quick ones—but not back down. Rather, I go up; I watch myself tear the ice ax out and, before my body has a chance to tip backward, bring it down dynamically above me, sinking it into solid ice.

As I stood on the flatter ice of the summit couloir, I began to feel the cold. Dynamic climbing on ice at 7,000 meters! Thank God it didn't go on like this. It was getting lighter, the climbing gradually grew easier, and we made quick progress. But the most important thing was that the storm front seemed not to be moving; it remained stalled, far away on the horizon. Above us, the sky was a steely blue. Someone was definitely watching over us. Toni climbed over the last rocky step, and then there was just a short snow slope and nothing more.

Together, we climbed the last few meters to the highest point. We had done it—as a team. All four of us were at the summit together—Toni, Conrad, Thomas, and me. The summit was only a small, flat heap of snow at 7,108 meters, and yet it was so much more. For us, the summit meant the end of a yearning that had gripped us for years. Now we were free from it, if only for a short time.

The descent was an adventure in itself. We abseiled the haul bags down into the couloir, the condition of which had rapidly deteriorated in the last few days due to rising temperatures. A huge rock slide swept two of our haul bags down into the precipice. Fifty kilos of equipment—half of what we'd had with us on the wall—was lost. During the night, at 5,600 meters, a stone the size of a fist ripped through the tent and through the foot of my sleeping bag. Not even under the overhang were we safe from the rockfall. The mountain gave us to understand in no uncertain terms that we were no longer welcome.

We packed up the entire camp. In order to bring down the huge amount of material, we climbed through the couloir two more times during the night. Each one of us was loaded up to the point of complete exhaustion. And though our goal, and our safety, were almost within reach, for the first time during that night, we were truly afraid. Afraid of what could happen.

At 9:00 PM, we were finally standing on the glacier, on secure ground. Ahead of us still lay two hours of tiresome descent down to Base Camp, where we would be welcomed by Ismail and Kassim with a huge celebratory feast: luxury at 4,400 meters. Only now, when we had reached complete safety, did we finally have the feeling that we had really done it. The summit was certainly the high point of our undertaking, but it was only now that we had achieved the actual objective: to come back alive.

"We still have something to learn from one another."
Thomas Huber, the other half of the Huberbuam, *on sibling rivalry*

THE FOLLOWING IS AN INTERVIEW KARIN STEINBACH CONDUCTED WITH THOMAS HUBER

Karin Steinbach: *Your shared success on Latok II in 1997 made you both into mountaineering names to reckon with far beyond the borders of Berchtesgaden.*
Thomas Huber: Standing on the summit of Latok II—that is one of those moments with Alexander that I find particularly memorable. Whenever we've ascended a peak together, it has always been a very intense experience. But Latok II was our first great success together. It brought us public attention.

Did this success change your life?
Our success on Latok II made it possible for us to make a living on the mountaineering lecture circuit. And what's more, expedition climbing also had a lasting effect on the relationship between me and Alexander.

How so?
I discovered that expedition climbing is my strong suit. My later expeditions to Shivling and Ogre confirmed that I have great reserves of strength and can take a lot of punishment at extreme altitudes.

So your success on expeditions was a way for you to hold your own against Alexander?

If you want to look at it that way, there's a bit of truth to that. In the past, it was the case that Alexander was usually the number one, and I was number two. Alexander was more determined to make it to the top, but in our performance as a whole, when we were climbing alpine routes together, we were absolutely equally matched. A lot of times, this ranking really bruised my ego. It hurt me, to be honest with you, because I was ambitious too, you know!

Has this ranking changed in the meantime?
It changed the moment I became successful with my own expeditions. At the beginning of our professional careers, for example, I had approached a sponsor and got the response: "Thanks, but one Huber is enough for us, and if we can have the better Huber, then we'll take the better one, and not the second-best one." That kind of takes you aback. But it's all ancient history. Today, we are absolutely on equal footing.

For all your fraternal feeling, are you in direct competition with one another?
Well, really, it's like this: Although we make a perfect team, we can also be our own greatest competition. But over time, we've learnt to go our own ways more. Each of us has his own vision. I always hope that nothing happens to Alexander on his projects, I delight in his successes, and I'm always happy when we can do something together. And there'll always be projects for us to collaborate on, beyond speed climbing, just like each of us will always keep on doing his own thing.

But hasn't the rivalry between you and Alexander also led to both of you becoming as good as you are?

Naturally, we each put an extreme amount of pressure on the other. We didn't begrudge each other our success, but still, we did want to be better than the other. For Alexander, for instance, it was important that at the time of my successful ascent of the Ogre, he was able to free his "Bellavista" route on the Cima Ovest. The end result of the competition between us was a positive thing, because it made us so good that we were able to turn our passion into a profession.

And are you both over this rivalry now?
The fact that we tend to go our own separate ways more has made us both freer of it. He does his thing, and I do mine, and it's much healthier now this way, actually. And there's still a place for collaborative projects, such as the speed record on the "Nose."

Was there anything in particular that made you think differently about the path you were on?
Everything changed the moment I had a family. Then, my brother was no longer the focus for me, but my family, my children. Before, Alexander had been the most important person for me. We grew up together. There was absolutely nothing that we had not experienced together. There's just this unbreakable bond. But still, we often fought. He had always been more concrete in his thinking, and so he often got his way. Today, my brother and I are partners on the same level. It's a very emotional relationship, but he's no longer the most important person in my life. Today, I can say to him: Alexander, I'm taking this path, and if you want to, you can take it with me, but you don't have to. He is a little more independent in his life than I am and has fewer responsibilities. He goes out for a beer in the evenings,

while I put the kids to bed. Of course, you can ask yourself: which is more important, and more enjoyable?

Is climbing not such an important part of your life since then?
I don't define myself exclusively through climbing anymore, but I still need it. I'm addicted, I know that now. Addicted to physical exertion. If I don't get it, I become tired, insufferable; I really just fall apart. But if I've been bouldering or running for two hours, then I can breathe freely, I feel good, I'm wide awake. For me, exertion is the best relaxation.

Watching your film, Am Limit, *one might get the impression that your mutual breaking away from each other was actually occasioned by the shoot itself.*
I tend to see it more as something that developed over the last six, seven years. And at some point, success makes you free as well. In my case, it was success with expeditions. On Shivling, in 2000, I was thrown in the deep end. Alexander became ill, and coincidentally, I had the opportunity to realize our plan—a very difficult route—with the Swiss climber Iwan Wolf. This gave me enormous self-confidence. I realized that on long climbing expeditions, there is practically nothing that can stop me. I just get this incredible, terrific feeling inside. On the mountain, I function not so much rationally as emotionally, by gut feeling.

Do you have a greater sense of self-confidence than Alexander?
You can't really say that in general. With respect to expeditions, I've developed a great degree of confidence, perhaps

even a little more than Alexander. But if you take another climbing discipline, then the picture looks quite different; for instance, if I had to free-solo a difficult route, I'd be shitting in my pants because I simply wouldn't have this basic level of confidence.

And you aren't afraid of frostbite, especially on your fingers, which you need for climbing?
I can feel it. When I feel it coming, I turn around. If I had fears like that, it would be better to stay home. Then I would just let it be. I wasn't put on this Earth to battle my anxieties. I'd like to experience something. I'd like to reach the height of my own personal potential when I climb. Mountain climbing is just a means to an end for me. The Ogre, the Shivling, these are tools that I was handed in childhood to make a path in life. My path goes over the mountains. With other people, the path goes elsewhere. If I had grown up near the ocean, I'd probably be a surfer, or a sailor, or a scuba diver.

That sounds a little bit like Hindu philosophy.
Except we're Christian. In my first climbing journal, it says: "Many paths lead to God, the one through the mountains among them." I got that from my father. That is the original purpose of mountain climbing for me. The mountains are a means to an end, to what I want to have in life—which includes my wife, my kids, the mountains, our environment . . .

So it could happen that ten years from now you're still living in this house, the kids are ten years older, the whole family goes hiking together, and you're not climbing anymore?

Why not? At some point, I'm probably going to wake up and realize that I don't have to go climbing anymore—although I can't really imagine that right now, since climbing is going better than ever for me, but it could happen. But then I suspect there'd be something else that I'd pursue just as intensely—like photography, for instance. That's another difference between Alexander and me: He's still much more concerned with making plans. He says, I've got four or five more years in which to do this or that. For me, the question of aging is relative. The way I feel at the moment, things are super. I can imagine that it'll still be that way in ten years. I don't necessarily have to go climbing then, but it can certainly turn out that way.

You don't ever think about whether your joints will still cooperate in ten years?
Not at all! In fact, they might not cooperate anymore tomorrow. You've just got to be prepared for that. Not to court disaster, but if anything were to happen to me and I survived, I'm certain that I would find something else to do if I couldn't climb anymore. Of course, it would be a real shock at first, but I'm sure I'd find something else to be enthused about.

To go back to Alexander and his free-solo projects—that was never something for you?
Well, it could have been something for me if I didn't already have a family at the time. Then, maybe, I would have let myself be swept up in that direction too, just because we're brothers, and we have this athletic rivalry. But, like I said, I had this responsibility toward my family.

But you have this responsibility toward your family more than ever now, with three kids, and it hasn't stopped you from going base jumping?

I see basing as different from free solo, even though no one agrees with me there. I'm actually a real safety freak, when it comes down to it. I don't rush headlong into anything. I'm very meticulous in my preparations and have a healthy dose of respect, or fear, if you will, for the undertaking. I'm not someone who subscribes to the notion of "minimal investment, maximum yield." I don't do any super-dangerous jumps. I'm fully aware of the risks.

So, in your opinion, is base jumping, where you leap off a cliff into the abyss with only a parachute on your back, objectively less dangerous than solo climbing?

No, I wouldn't say that. Both are dangerous. But for me personally, I have a better sense for basing, and therefore, it's less dangerous than solo climbing for me—at least, when it's above technical grade 7. It's only when you understand the dangers that you can go to the limit, which was always our aim, after all. I would even say that speed climbing is more dangerous than either solo climbing or base jumping. Of course, I hope that in the fall we'll pull off the speed record on the "Nose," so that I can put that whole subject to rest. Speed climbing is pretty much the most dangerous thing I've ever done in my life.

Because when you're both climbing at the same time, the appearance of security is just a sham?

The rope suggests a level of protection that, objectively speaking, often isn't actually there. Along the route, there are situations where, if one of us should fall . . . though he may be tied on to the rope, the result would be just as tragic as with a free-solo fall. That doesn't really come across at all in the film—how spectacularly dangerous speed climbing really is. Even if we're only climbing in grade 8, speed climbing is absolutely uncompromising. Everything that we have ever learned about climbing in twenty-five years of experience—the most extreme technical levels of difficulty, dynamic movement, team tactics, risk-taking, experimentation—all of that is speed climbing.

And despite all that, the objective is so clear for you, and so important that . . .
We started it, and we want to finish it. If we hadn't already come so far on the last ascent, it would be different. But after three hours and ten minutes, we got to the top completely relaxed. It went so well, and we had such a positive feeling. I'm certain that it's doable for us. There's definitely the potential there that we could make it in two and a half hours.

Your fall didn't make you feel unsure of yourself?
Above all, the experience of my fall reinforced the lesson that I really do need to listen to my gut in every situation, and if I don't feel good about something, I should let it alone. That's what I do with expeditions. There, you've gone to all this trouble and expense, you've flown to India, and there's one single solitary window of good weather— but if I've got a shitty feeling in my gut about it, then I let it be. Or with base jumping, when everyone's already jumped, and I'm standing there alone, and things just aren't right for me, then I've got the maturity to say no, pack up my stuff, and go back down. On the other hand, I know just as well that when things are going well, when

the feeling's positive, then you just can't be beat—you're practically invincible, and you've got everything under control. You have to be patient and wait for this feeling. If this feeling hadn't materialized on the "Nose," I think I'd give up on the speed record. We can only make it in two and half hours if we can get this positive feeling, this flow, going again.

The way the film shows it, the conflict between you and Alexander in Patagonia was completely unplanned?
The conflict arose completely unexpectedly, and it was quite vehement. At the time, actually, it almost spelled the end of our climbing together, because we had completely differing conceptions of mountain climbing. We had gone to Patagonia to attempt the traverse of Cerro Standhardt, Punta Herron, Torre Egger, and Cerro Torre, which had never been done before. That was our objective, and I wanted to wait for the right opportunity. Alexander was prepared to take on another, shorter goal. But for me, that was out of the question, because if we did that, it's possible that at the decisive moment, when a longer window of favorable weather opened up, we might turn out to be in the wrong place, and totally exhausted on top of it. I didn't want to lose sight of the main objective. And so the team fell apart.

In the end, the traverse you planned to undertake together was thwarted by bad weather, while Alexander completed a first ascent on the south face of the Aguja-Desmochada with Stephan Siegrist. Will you attempt the traverse together again?
Yeah, sure. Definitely. And I think, in the end, Alexander will have to take something from me after all—namely, that we will have to focus on our actual goal. That it's not

about coming home with just anything in hand, but about keeping your eye on the prize. We still have something to learn from one another.

What does your team structure look like on expeditions?
We've got a few years of experience under our belts there, too, by now. A large team is always problematic. I would never go on an expedition with a large team again. A team of three, four at most, or even just two. Perhaps a cameraman, as well. Of course, the expedition needs to have a team leader as an official spokesperson to deal with the Ministry in Pakistan or Nepal. But that's just a name on paper. Within the group, decisions are always made democratically. Even when it's just the two of us, Alexander and I, as soon as we get on our way together, under normal circumstances, we're generally of one mind. These are rational decisions. One or the other of us will have more experience with this or that particular issue.

What would you say is Alexander's most notable quality?
His most notable quality is certainly determination. Then, of course, there's his intelligence. Although, sometimes that can also be a stumbling block, whenever he assumes that he knows everything. Alexander is more communicative, while I'm more reserved, but also more impulsive. It's just like with twins—the one has this, the other has that. With us, one is governed by the right half of the brain, and the other by the left. It would often make my life a lot easier if I had a little bit of Alexander, and vice versa. And then, of course, he's also got this incredible willingness to help everyone. Alexander will truly give you the shirt off his back. He's one of the most obliging people I know. A good listener, always ready to hear you out. Probably that's

an outlet for him, to compensate for the fact that, on the other hand, he's so single-minded in pursuing his own path—a balancing of accounts, so to speak, to justify how radically he's sometimes gone in his own direction.

What makes you into such a good team when you're climbing together?
I don't really know. Somehow, we just perfectly complement each other.

What are the obstacles in your way?
As I've said—his intelligence, which makes him think he's always right. Once Alexander gets going, he just won't let go. He's so convinced he's right, there's no other possible point of view. But then there's also my stubbornness, and my aggressive attitude when I find something annoying.

In a nutshell: does competition give you wings, or is it a roadblock?
Ultimately, it's a roadblock to your own development as a human being—but when you recognize that, you learn a lesson for life.

Were your parents aware of the competition between you?
Sure, they were aware of it, and in some ways, they even reinforced it, because from the start, they always fanned the flames of our ambition. They were very ambitious themselves. Marion and I—and especially Marion—are just the opposite: We're always trying to avoid competition between our sons as much as possible, to steer them in another direction. But it's already beginning to emerge that Elias and Amadeus want to trump each other just as much as Alexander and I did, and not only with climbing,

though there as well. Obviously, I wouldn't deny them the opportunity to pursue competitive sports, but I won't encourage it. I don't want to burden my sons—or my daughter—with the *Huberbuam* baggage. Let them pack their own bags.

∞

CHAPTER TWENTY

CHO OYU—THE GREAT MOUNTAIN

Reinhard Karl called it a building without any stairs, floors, or doors, which becomes a prison when you want to get to the top. The invisible prison bars are your ambition. And freedom? Freedom is something you get only after you've returned from the summit.

Being a mountain climber means you climb mountains. Extremely high mountains, as well. "What's someone like you doing on Cho Oyu?" The question would be put to me with astonishment and incomprehension. Me, the rock climber, trudging up Cho Oyu? Hauling a load, gasping for breath, bundled up like a polar explorer? What did I think I was going to do in the flat ice-scape of the Turquoise Goddess? Late in March 1998, as more and more of my acquaintances heard about my plans, I was increasingly confronted with this question, and I always gave the same banal response: "What am I going to do up there? Climb a mountain!"

The plan to climb Cho Oyu was in principle nothing more than the fulfillment of my childhood dreams—the vision of mountains that I'd had when I had climbed to the summit of my first four-thousander. Of course, in the previous decade, the eight-thousand-ers had forfeited much of their inapproachability. They had become a playground for the masses and an arena of vanity. They had lost their exciting aura of being reserved exclusively for the best and most extreme alpinists. Still, the eight-thousanders had always remained an objective for me. I had never stopped dreaming this dream, even though in the intervening years I had neglected the alpine stage in favor of sport climbing.

The object of my desire, Cho Oyu, is generally considered among experts to be an easy eight-thousander. It is, however, all too often overlooked that this judgment simply means that Cho Oyu is rela-tively easy to ascend along its least demanding "Normal Route," only in comparison to the so-called difficult eight-thousanders like K2. But at 8,201 meters, it is actually the sixth-highest peak in the world, which presents a certain level of difficulty in itself—a difficulty that has very little to do with climbing prowess. From a technical stand-point, Cho Oyu does not require much more than a demanding four-thousander in the Alps, and any climber well-versed in the western Alps possesses the technical know-how for this mountain. Neither does the altitude of over 8,000 meters require any particular qualifi-cations; almost any healthy person is in a position to acclimate and adapt to great altitudes. What defines this particular difficulty, rather, is that anyone who sets foot on such heights is playing with fire: The body is pushed to the limit of its ability to function, and becomes far more fragile than one is willing to believe.

The high art of climbing the Earth's biggest mountains, then, does not consist simply in reaching the top. What is decisive is the manner in which the top is reached—namely, with your mental faculties intact and sufficient strength in reserve. Only then would it be possible to master unforeseen problems with an alert mind, and to compensate for weaknesses sufficiently, so that you can return safely from the death zone. When I selected Cho Oyu, together with Barbara Hirschbichler from Berchtesgaden, these considerations were paramount in our decision to avoid the more-difficult eight-thousanders. Up to that time, my experience extended to 7,100 meters in the Karakorams, and Barbara had been at 6,700 meters in South America. But 8,000 meters—a good 1,000 meters more—in the Himalayas is a whole other dimension, so both of us had good reason to approach our objective with the requisite quantity of respect.

We took our preparations as seriously as we took our objective. We outfitted ourselves with the best technical climbing gear, clothing, and camping equipment; I simply could not allow myself the slightest chance of frostbite. For rock climbers, no mountain ascent in the world is worth the price of losing an appendage, like so many others have done. Of course, the preparatory conditioning was important as well. Not that I was planning a record-breaking ascent of Cho Oyu, but a solid level of fitness enables you to climb quickly at high altitudes, which shortens the amount of time you spend in the death zone and enables the body to produce sufficient heat, which in turn lessens the danger of frostbite.

Our most important preparation, as far as we were concerned, was acclimatization. A whole two weeks before the start of expedition, Barbara and I set off on a trek in the Everest region. At the highest point, we went up Gokyo Ri, an easily accessible, almost 5,500-meter-high summit, from which we could enjoy the most breathtaking mountain views. Four of the highest peaks in the world could be seen up close from here: Mount Everest, Lhotse, Makalu, and Cho Oyu. Our objective was almost within reach. Only a few kilometers and some 2,500 meters of altitude separated us from the summit. Nonetheless, we had a long road before us.

The first great obstacle arose for me even before we started, during the trekking trip. I developed a tonsillitis infection so stubborn that in the end I could not avoid taking an antibiotic. I was hardly the first to have been felled by the infamous "Khumbu cough." Still, I cursed the situation. The antibiotic kept the infection in check, but I was never really able to shake it completely throughout the entire expedition. I was apparently so weakened by the infection and the medication that a week later, on our drive from Kathmandu to Tibet, I had a relapse. I had no choice but to remain temporarily at a lower altitude while Barbara marched on toward base camp with all our expedition gear.

I began to feel some doubts. They nagged at me, dragged me down into a depressive swamp out of which I found it difficult to escape. Had staying behind already put an end to all my dreams? Would there still be enough time to reach the summit? Waiting around for my health to improve became a kind of psychological martyrdom. Time was running out, and I railed against this damn pain in my throat. In comparison to the gigantic mountain, the bacteria making my life so difficult were laughably tiny—and yet so significant. In the end, though, waiting proved to have been a wise decision, and gradually, my body got the infection under control. At last, I stumbled forth, still somewhat weak at the knees; soon, my momentum got the better of the situation, and after a three-day march, I arrived at base camp at 5,800 meters.

From that point on, everything went fairly quickly. The very next day, I climbed with Barbara up to 6,300 meters in order to put up our first advance camp there. After resting a day at base camp, we went up to Camp 1 again to spend our first night there. Sleeping at this altitude takes its toll, and we weren't exactly feeling great the next morning, so we took the day to rest there. The next day, we were feeling decidedly better, and laden with full packs, we climbed up to 7,000 meters, where we would set up our camp for the final, rather martially named, "assault" on the summit. We believed this would suffice as preparation for the ascent. We were both feeling good, and just waiting for good weather. Also waiting for their opportunity were

Horst Fankhauser, well-known as the former keeper of the Franz Senn Hut in Stubai, and Georg Simair, a mountain guide from St. Ulrich bei Lofer. We had agreed that we would set off for the summit together as soon as good weather came.

During the entire time that we had been busy with preparations, the weather had been uncertain, with strong winds at the higher altitudes. But now, just at the right time, after two days of idle waiting at base camp, the weather conditions improved. Was it a turnaround? We hoped so! In the morning, we were still undecided, but in the end, some hours later, the four of us set off and climbed up to Camp 1 together. We slept badly. This was due in part to the altitude, but also undoubtedly to the strain. There was always agitation the night before an assault that would not let you rest. The more you dwell on it, the more insistently the doubts creep in. Were we really acclimatized enough?

But in the morning, when we finally set off, the bad feelings had dissipated and confidence and momentum returned. Press on—just press on! Our backpacks once again acquired substantial weight as we climbed up over the snow ridge and a 60-degree ice bulge toward Camp 2. The afternoon up there at 7,000 meters could have been quite restful, except the rays of the sun were so strong that our tent practically turned into a sauna. What a crazy world.

To make up for the afternoon heat, the night was bitterly cold. I tossed and turned inside the sleeping bag in my down jacket, far too nervous to sleep. My first eight-thousander was within reach! I could already feel it, despite the 1,200 vertical meters that still separated us from the summit. I dreamed without sleeping, thought about what could happen, was gripped by the notion of climbing to the top that very same day. An eight-thousander was an eight-thousander. Cho Oyu was a goal that I had undertaken as a mountain climber, and I threw myself into it completely. It didn't matter to me that it was just the normal route, that it was an easy eight-thousander. I had to get up there, for my own sake, and I had to come back down again. Then I would have something that no one could ever take from me—an experience of my own making that I shaped for myself.

We couldn't sleep, so to kill time, we occupied ourselves by melting snow and drinking as much of it as possible. The interior of the tent was covered with hoarfrost because of the condensation from our breathing, and the smallest movement brushing up against the walls would set off a snowfall. It was fascinating to watch the delicate crystals dancing in the pool of light from the lamp. Here, in the calm of the tent, I still couldn't quite imagine that we would soon begin. Time stretched slowly on; the hours just didn't want to pass. But at some point it was finally 2:00 AM. The countdown began. We got ready slowly, without any rush. Barbara and I took a whole half-hour to put on all our stuff and crawl out of the tent into the cold of the Himalayan night. I felt the majestic scale of it, this terrific sense of exposure. I was an insignificant person, caught out in the seemingly endless space, lost on this great mountain.

Horst and Georg had already left a half-hour before us, and had a good head start. Their footsteps in the snow seemed laborious but not grueling. I trudged on, working my way step by step directly in their tracks. After an hour, I'd caught up with Horst and Georg and took over the track-laying work. The effort of catching up to them so quickly had been great, and I could feel how difficult it was to lay the track. I was only able to take over the laborious task for short periods at a time. Repeatedly, I had to step back behind the other two, gasping for breath, but still confident. At 7,500 meters, we took our first break. We were not quite at the halfway point yet, but we took our time to free ourselves from the tunnel vision of our labors to enjoy the grand spectacle of the sunrise, a truly moving and sublime experience.

Just as Horst and George were getting ready to continue, Barbara came up. I waited with her for another fifteen minutes, and then we left our resting place as well. We had tackled our mountain quickly at first, and had put the first 500 vertical meters behind us in two and a half hours. But now, with the increasing altitude, we became considerably slower. I wasn't worried. The weather could not have been better, it was barely six in the morning, and up ahead of us we had two strong mountaineers in Horst and Georg.

Slowly, we worked our way up, each for him- or herself, step by step, one foot after the other. The rests came more frequently. Much later—it was by now almost noon—I saw Horst and Georg, and shortly after that, I was standing with them on the summit. But this time, I could not indulge in any great feelings of rejoicing. The exertion in the cold, dry, thin air had weakened me, and my tonsillitis, which had just barely abated, was starting to flare up again. At this point, I was still not feeling too plagued by the infection. I still had energy and was completely alert. But I felt instinctively that I shouldn't spend any unnecessary time at this altitude. No time for euphoria, joy, or pride—for taking pleasure in a liberating look around; instead, I immediately began my descent with Horst while Barbara followed later with Georg.

My agitation drove me down. I put meter after meter behind me at a good clip, and after just two hours, Horst and I reached Camp 2 at 7,000 meters. Barbara and Georg turned up an hour later. Having reached the camp, I felt free of worry, and now, at last, joy set in: Despite the disadvantageous conditions, I had done it! The tension of the last few days, the last few hours, was gone. The strain gave way to a feeling of freedom. There was no more pressure weighing on me. My tonsils were infected again, but it was not important anymore. There it was—that feeling of authentic joy, which I hadn't had the chance to experience very often on this particular expedition.

Although (or perhaps precisely because) Cho Oyu was my first eight-thousander, I had felt very few moments of pleasure while enduring quite a few moments of concern. Nonetheless, this eight-thousander was still a first-class experience for me. The extreme degree of willpower necessary for the ascent gives you the feeling of having accomplished something great, even though nowadays, the normal routes up the eight-thousanders hold few surprises and offer little adventure. The real unknown here is you, yourself, on your first foray into these icy heights.

I feel that today's climbers don't have the same opportunity for adventure. The multitudes of climbers taking the same routes have robbed the mountains of their wildness, and taken the hurdle down a notch. Clever logistics and travel in large groups reduce the adventure and make it predictable. Adventure—the spice in the mountaineer's soup—is something I can only find by going somewhere no one else has gone; where I am at the mercy of the enormity and danger of the mountain; where I am lost on a gigantic wall and must find my own way out; where I can feel that survival is everything. In the end, the attraction of the eight-thousanders today no longer lies in the search for adventure. The attraction lies above all in the fact that there are no nine-thousanders. Ambition always draws people to the fastest, the best, and the highest. And that is exactly why the eight-thousanders are so spellbinding. People always have a desire to be high up. Here, in the eight-thousanders, they can be higher than anywhere else in the world.

Back home, I once again picked up the fabulous books of Reinhard Karl and traced my journey up Cho Oyu in his experience of the eight-thousanders:

To climb an eight-thousander is to play for high stakes. You have to keep trying, over and over, and never give up. Whether you will ultimately succeed is for fate, or God, or Allah to decide. Standing atop an eight-thousander is certainly no quick path to happiness. The happiness of an eight-thousander is a slow happiness, the happiness of impassioned suffering, anchored deep within you, forever, unforgettable.

Reinhard Karl's last book, *Berge auf Kodachrome*, ends with his photographs of Cho Oyu. The last picture shows the memorial pyramid for Reinhard Karl in Gokyo Valley, his name engraved on a stone slab, "Cho Oyu" below it, and the day he died: 5/19/82. Exactly sixteen years later, to the day, I stood on the summit of the mountain that would be his last. The mountain whose summit he would never reach, and which would become his grave.

∞

CHAPTER TWENTY-ONE

MATTERHORN

I knew Bernd from my time in Munich. He had studied medicine and was by now immersed in the workaday world as a surgeon at a pediatric clinic. Still, he continued to be quite active as a climber, and we often ran into each other at the ZHS, the university fitness center, where there was a small bouldering wall for training. Over a few beers in the bar at the student union, we came up with the idea of undertaking a winter ascent of the north face of the Matterhorn together.

This was a perfect objective for me: The north face of the Matterhorn is the ultimate classic, one of the greatest testimonials to the art of Bavarian climbing. The golden age of alpinism in the western Alps had been shaped predominantly by British alpinists working with French and Swiss mountain guides, and they had conquered more or less all the summits. The turn of the twentieth century ushered in the age of big alpine faces. This was the time of the Munich climbers, and although the western Alps were difficult to reach from the Bavarian metropolis, still, men such as Willo Welzenbach, Hans Ertl, the Schmid brothers, Rudl Peters, and Anderl Heckmair managed to divvy up the last great walls of the Alps among them. Bavarian alpinists managed to bag practically every one—above all, the three great north faces of the Alps: the Matterhorn, the Eiger, and the Grandes Jorasses. Of all the many successes, the first great sensation had been the first ascent of the Matterhorn north face by Franz and Toni Schmid. This north face was something true alpinists just had to accomplish!

The key to a winter ascent in the Alps is the right weather for the undertaking. We wanted to avoid at all costs having to drive to Zermatt in vain. For Bernd, especially—as a working doctor—leisure time had become more than priceless. We would have to wait for the right opportunity. In February 1999, we finally had our window of good weather: three days of a stable high-pressure system should have created the conditions we were looking for.

I met up with Bernd at his house, and we packed up the necessary equipment. We didn't take too much with us because, above all, we wanted to be fast, and we hoped to be able to make it in one day. To bivouac on the north face of the Matterhorn is, in any case, anything but pleasant. Although the wall is not super-steep, the rock is downward-sloping from top to bottom, so that there isn't a single decent place to bivy on the entire wall. It would be much better to do the whole thing in one day and forget about the sleeping bags—lighten up the load on your back! A bivy bag, two layers of underwear, a fleece sweater and jacket, a Gore-Tex jacket, a small gas cooker, and a few granola bars for provisions—fitted out with these supplies, we would survive a bivouac if need be, but our strategy was aimed at climbing through.

Bernd and I left Munich at 2:00 AM and drove through the night toward Zermatt. Out of place in the midst of the crowds of holiday skiers, we made our way through this tony wintering spot. The weather was perfect: clear blue skies and perfect calm in the atmosphere. The cableway took us up to the foot of the Matterhorn, and around noon, we finally began the climb up to the Hörnli Hut.

The snow was untouched, at times seemingly bottomless, which made laying track correspondingly difficult. On top of that, the sun shone brightly on the steep slopes, and the sweat streamed down my back with the effort. It was difficult to imagine that the next day, up on the north face, it would be freezing cold. When we reached the top of the ridge that leads directly to the hut, it became more comfortable. A gentle breeze blew away the pent-up heat and cleared our heads.

The winter room of the Hörnli Hut provided a refuge in the midst of the icy winter landscape. In the evening, we cooked a little, drank a lot, and went to bed as soon as darkness fell. At 2:00 AM, we were already up again so we could get a start on the north face while it was still dark. From the Hörnli Hut, we followed the ridge of the mountain for just a few meters and then crossed over to the right, out onto the glacier underneath the north face. Now, in the middle of the night, the air was bitterly cold, and this time I was very glad to have the warming effect of our efforts to lay down track in the deep powder. Above us lay the eerily black shadow of the north face, a bulwark that seemed even more threatening in the darkness than in the daytime.

At the bergschrund, we roped in. There was complete silence around us, like a soundproof room. The few words that we exchanged were muffled by the light powder. I was surprised by the great awe that overcame me in the face of this wall. The north face of the Matterhorn—one of the central ideas of alpinism. And in the winter! Not that I was feeling afraid, really, but there was a certain apprehension—the expectation that I was about to be confronted by something very great.

I climbed up the first pitch, secured myself with ice screws, and belayed Bernd up. Now that we were standing around a while at the belays, the cold was really making itself felt, full force. We had managed to choose probably the coldest day of the winter. The biting, icy air made our lives difficult, and the entire ascent became a continual struggle against the cold. We were even freezing when we were climbing the pitch. Even when we would warm up a little from the exertion of climbing, our toes would feel that much colder from the pressure of climbing on the front points.

Shortly before the initial ice field ended, we crossed over to the right into mixed terrain. Contrary to our expectations, we met with extremely unfavorable conditions there. Because of the condition of the snow, we had thought we would be able to get most of the way up the north face climbing on ice fields and sheets of compact snow. But, in fact, the entire north face lay under a deep layer of fresh snow—and underneath this monstrous amount of loose, light powder, there was nothing but bare rock. No ice, no compact snow: just rock. We had to laboriously clear the snow from the rock, meter by meter, in order to find the hand- and footholds. It was a peculiar picture: Above us stretched an utterly white, snow-covered wall, and below us we could clearly follow the dark path over which we had worked our way up. The dark stripe we had left behind ran up the wall like a long scar.

Unfortunately, the conditions in the diagonal couloir were not any better. During the summer, the whole middle section of the north face is completely free of ice. Usually, the first snow falls in autumn when the temperatures are still moderate, and it's wet enough to stick to the steep wall. Apparently, during the prior fall, the temperatures must have dropped very quickly, which meant that it was too cold for the first snow accumulation to stick to the wall. The time-consuming business of looking for holds under the loose powder continued, and Bernd and I struggled on laboriously with the pitches, taking turns in the lead. From a technical standpoint, we were both completely up to it, and we weren't concerned about the difficulties, but it was costing us an enormous amount of time—time that, on this short winter day, was quickly running away from us.

At the end of the diagonal couloir, it was clear that a bivouac was unavoidable. Things weren't any better in the upper portion of the wall, and climbing in the dark in this terrain under the prevailing conditions would have been playing with fire. Two pitches above the diagonal couloir, we found a small ledge that was just about big enough for both of us to sit on. Fifteen meters further up, I discovered a small patch of ice, into which I sank two ice screws. Now, at least, we had good protection. I climbed back down to Bernd, who had in the meantime completely freed our bivy seat from snow and ice. By Matterhorn standards, we could consider ourselves more than happy with our half a square meter of horizontal surface.

In the fading light, we started the cooker and spent a good half-hour melting snow, since throughout the entire day, we had drunk nothing more than the 1 liter of water we'd each had in our respective packs. We had to replace at least some of the fluid we had lost to the cold, dry air during the day. It was already dark as we got ready for the bivouac and crammed ourselves into the bivy sack. It was pretty darn tight in this millimeter-thick cocoon, but it was our only protection against the cold—and at least the close quarters let us feel each other's warmth.

The cold was merciless. I was glad that we didn't have a thermometer with us, and couldn't tell with any certainty exactly how cold it actually was. Everyone always talks about how unbelievably cold it gets up on the eight-thousanders, but you don't necessarily have to go there to experience extreme cold. A winter bivouac on one of the alpine north faces has everything you need to get just as close to your limit. Nowhere do the hours drag on so slowly as in an extremely cold bivouac night. Every glance at your watch only increases your desperation. Ten minutes stretch to an hour, an hour to an eternity. The only thing that helps you bear the cold is the certainty that time is unstoppable, and you know that as soon as you can move again in the light of the new day, warmth will spread throughout your body, and then a great feeling of well-being will come over you as your body comes to life again and puts an end to this indescribable cold.

Around 2:00 AM, I noticed for the first time that star after star was gradually starting to disappear. A deep layer of stratus clouds covered the sky. According to the weather report, the first clouds were not expected until the afternoon, followed by snow showers which were not supposed to have set in until the following night. Bernd and I didn't speak much, but we each felt the other's uneasiness. It was clear what awaited us. At this point, everything was still calm. I almost had the impression that since the cloud cover had started to come in, the brutal cold had actually lessened. But perhaps it was just the anxiety that revved up my inner engine, knowing what would happen as soon as it started snowing—when the wall would come alive, and the constant spindrift would make our progress very difficult.

An hour before dawn I turned on the cooker to heat up the tea we had prepared the previous evening. But despite the hot tea, the cold still dominated. With first light, I climbed the 15 meters up to take out the ice screws. Due to the impending storm, we had decided not to climb directly up to the summit but to take the steeper but shorter wall up to the shoulder.

The cold of the night had taken a lot out of me, but I still felt strong. Bernd, however, was badly worn out. It was clear that it was now up to me to fight my way up to the top of this wall. Pitch after pitch, I led upward. Bernd fought for every single meter, and it was astounding how well he was able to apply his technical climbing skills despite his utter exhaustion. We made slow but constant progress, so I still had the feeling that despite the lousy circumstances, we had the situation under control.

Snow began falling heavily around 10:00 AM, but by then we were already past all the difficulties, and there were only two pitches left to the top. Never in my life had I climbed under such conditions, but now that our objective, the Hörnligrat, was within reach, I could almost enjoy the situation. The cold had dissipated, the effort of climbing had suffused my body with warmth, and I had the feeling that Bernd had gotten himself somewhat under control as well. As I glimpsed the last ice slope through a gap in the clouds and saw the edge of the ridge above it, I was filled with a genuine sense of joy.

Another 40 meters, and then my hand broke through the delicate edge of the snow ridge. We were on top!

Bernd had to take his time to follow, but that didn't matter now. We had done it! Overjoyed to have put the most difficult part behind us, Bernd and I sat up on the Hörnli Ridge. All that awaited us now was the descent. Even though it was not so easy to keep your sense of direction in the thick fog, we made good progress, and at one o'clock, we were finally standing before the Solvay Hut—the refuge on the Hörnli Ridge, about two-thirds of the way along its length, at 4,000 meters of altitude. Bernd was completely spent, and we decided to call it a day. Given his state, it was surely sensible to let him rest up a bit and give him the opportunity to gather new strength overnight.

We searched the hut in vain for something to burn, and with the dwindling remains of our gas supply, there was not a lot to drink. But that wasn't important, because by the middle of the next day, at the latest, we would be back in civilization again, living it up like kings— at least for one day. As darkness fell, we bedded down for the night, covered with everything we could find, and enjoyed the warmth.

In the middle of the night, I was suddenly awakened by the sound of Bernd moaning. I asked him what was wrong, but he seemed to be sleeping deeply, so I turned over again. Before I could fall asleep, I heard Bernd muttering nonsense. He was talking in his sleep, but in a way that made me uneasy. I looked for the flashlight.

"Bernd, what's the matter?" I asked.

Bernd sat up and muttered more nonsense. His lips were a deep blue, unmistakably cyanotic. Oxygen deprivation! I sat him up to relieve some of the pressure from his lungs, and tried to get some sensible response out of him, without success. The hypoxia was too far advanced.

Now I seemed to recall vaguely that two weeks earlier Bernd had had a serious case of bronchitis. Although the symptoms had abated, the infection must have still been lurking in his lungs. That was why he had been so weakened after the bivouac—it was the early stages of pulmonary edema, which is always preceded by a phase of total exhaustion. How could I have guessed that, here in the Alps, at 4,000 meters? Obviously, the infection was the cause. Bernd's lungs had simply not yet completely regenerated—an extremely dangerous circumstance when you are trying to spite the winter under the worst possible conditions on the north face of the Matterhorn. What could I do?

I used the hut's emergency phone to call the first-response station in Visp, and explained the situation. They put me through to the dispatcher at the Air Zermatt rescue service. Here up on the mountain, the skies had cleared completely by now, but down below, a thick fog still hung over Zermatt. A rescue flight was out of the question at this time. I suggested the possibility of my bringing Bernd down on my own, but the doctor on call persuaded me that it was an utterly futile plan, which my friend would not survive. We didn't have any Adalat with us, either—a drug that drastically reduces blood pressure and can slow further fluid buildup in the lungs. There was nothing I could do but wait. Wait for the fog to clear over Zermatt. Wait for morning. Wait . . .

This time, the waiting was far more wretched. If time seems to slow to a crawl in the cold of a bivouac night, in this situation it was infinitely harder: to have to look on, condemned to uselessness, as my friend lay slowly dying. I could only hope that Bernd's heart would be strong enough to survive the strain and keep him alive long enough to be rescued despite the lack of oxygen.

I paced up and down the little hut like a caged animal, constantly looking out to see if the fog had finally lifted. As the first lights of Zermatt finally began to appear, I called Air Zermatt again, full of hope. But the heliport was on the other end of town, and so I still had to wait. The pauses in Bernd's breathing were getting longer and longer, and I was afraid that he would not survive the next few hours, now that rescue was so close at hand. I felt a profound sense of powerlessness, to be confronted by an event with a potentially catastrophic outcome, and be unable to do a thing about it.

And then, at last! The heliport informed me that the helicopter was ready to take off and would arrive in a short while. The head of rescue operations gave me instructions on how to prepare Bernd for the airlift: dress him in warm clothes to protect him from the cold, and put on his climbing harness to tie onto the long-line. Finally, there was something for me to do. I was needed. It was hard work getting the clothes and harness on Bernd's unconscious body, but I managed.

Just as I finished up and opened the door to the hut, I heard the helicopter coming. The air rescue medic hovered on the long-line right in the doorway—and tears of joy were running down my face. While the two of us together carried Bernd to the door and readied all the gear to strap him and the medic to the line, the helicopter briefly disappeared. But as soon as we were done, the long-line was hanging in front of the door again. I supported Bernd's weight with all my strength to enable him to get clipped in, and seconds later, the two were whisked away in a breathtaking curve in the direction of the Hörnli Hut.

Bernd lived—just barely, with only a few minutes to spare. One might say that it was entirely our own fault that we got into this situation. But despite the harsh conditions that we found and had to overcome on the north face, it had never occurred to us that the danger would catch up with us afterward, in the shelter of the hut. I have asked myself often enough why, having made it to the Solvay Hut, we didn't just continue our descent. Had we been lower down, it could all have been avoided.

Should have, could have, would have . . . hindsight is 20/20.

CHAPTER TWENTY-TWO

THE OGRE—THE MANEATER

The Ogre—French for "man-eating monster"—has earned its name. Piece by piece, it slowly devours us, nibbling away at our souls, just as in 1977 it had demanded everything of the team that first ascended it: Doug Scott broke both his legs just a few meters below the summit; a cold front brought a sudden storm; Chris Bonington fell several meters and suffered broken ribs and pneumonia. After a desperate, weeklong fight for their lives, the Ogre finally let them go, though not without having taken everything they had. The first ascent of the Ogre—undoubtedly one of the most dramatic examples of a successful retreat—made the mountain famous.

The Ogre, however, is no eight-thousander, so there has never been a particularly great rush to scale its peak. Still, with every new, failed attempt to climb it a second time, the mountain increasingly acquired the aura of a precious gem that an extreme mountain climber would gladly add to his collection. In 1999, Toni Gutsch, Jan Mersch, Thomas, and I set off to try and capture the repeat ascent for Bavaria. In the twenty-two years since Chris Bonington and Doug Scott had brought home the prize, no less than fifteen expeditions had foundered on the Ogre. The probability of succeeding was therefore pretty small, and that's exactly what excited us.

We didn't intend to follow the route of the first ascensionists, as it is threatened over long stretches by seracs, and this incalculable risk seemed too high for us. Not even this mountain was worth it! Instead, we had chosen the south pillar of the Ogre—an imposing, well-defined rock buttress, which, although seemingly intimidating at first glance, upon closer inspection offers a great advantage: Because it is so exposed, it is safe from rock- and icefall, and thus, safe from avalanches. The French team of Vincent Fine and Michel Fauquet had already been the first to climb the pillar fifteen years before, but high above it, at 7,000 meters, they were caught by a storm and nothing came of their summit attempt.

Jan and Jochen Haase had been the last team, in 1997, to attempt the Ogre along the South Pillar. They had reached the top of the 1,000-meter-high pillar in only six days—faster than any of their predecessors. But they, too, were surprised by a storm, and never reached the summit of the Ogre. When it came to "Operation Ogre," weather was, after personal ability, the most decisive factor. We worked out a tactical strategy, and it was as follows: Be quicker than the bad weather. Our intention was to go from base camp to the summit in only four days—climb the South Pillar in two days, ascend the big ice field to the foot of the summit tower on the third day, and on the fourth day, descend after the summit all the way back to the top of the South Pillar. From there, we could get down even in bad weather. Just four days of good weather in a row—that is all that we would need to take the summit.

Now, July was almost over, and we'd only had five days of usable weather all told and never more than two days together. If the weather pattern didn't change, we wouldn't be able to make a single attempt at the Ogre. Thirty days of sitting around in base camp had gradually made me wonder what the point of mountain climbing was; I'd never felt so unproductive in my entire life. Unavoidably, at some point, I'd have to ask myself what I've actually been getting out of the whole business here. In fact, I didn't have to ask myself that question at all, because I already knew the answer: frustration. It was impossible to overlook at this point, as it was written on everyone's faces. That's right—frustration was what you got in exchange for your hard-earned money and all the time spent training! Nothing helped, not even the little garden I'd cultivated in the apse of my tent out of sheer boredom and hatred of being unproductive. It was clear to me that as soon as I returned home, I wouldn't have a single second to spare again. With no transition, I would be sucked right back into the whirlwind of my normal hectic routine, as unwillingly as I now found myself trapped in this oasis of idleness.

The idleness was eating away at me! Climbing the world's greatest mountains is paradoxical: When you're on the mountain, you wish for the calm and security of base camp. But then, back in base camp, it doesn't take long before you start to feel restless, before you want to go up again. These are two mutually exclusive worlds, and no matter which one I happen to be in, I always want to be where I'm not. Two, three days of doing nothing is just about the greatest thing there is, but then the restlessness begins to grow, more and more with each passing day. We've been shaped by our society: If you spend long periods of time doing nothing, there must be something wrong with you. Even if there's nothing you can do about doing nothing, you still feel guilty about it; you're useless; you're good for nothing; you're a bum!

We mountain climbers often believe that we're wild and independent. But all of us, almost without exception, are just as caught in the prison of society. Though we may seem to be cut off from civilization for two months out of the year, we always come back to it.

The expedition is not an escape but just a furlough—and there, too, we naturally have to comport ourselves in accordance with society's rules. And now, base camp has become our prison, the walls of which are built by civilization. Every idle day includes a walk on the moraine at the edge of the camp, where we stand around telling some story or other from back home, gazing yearningly at the Biafo Glacier. It points in the direction of our retreat, in the direction that leads back to civilization.

What was holding me here? Who was holding me up?

Oh, yeah, there was the Ogre. It would be wrong to say that I had almost forgotten about it. It was exactly the opposite: It hung over my head like the sword of Damocles, weighing mightily on my mind, which sought refuge in repression. But the mountain was stronger. The Ogre repeatedly broke down my defenses, and though I tried to forget it, it stood before me, clear as day, and oppressive.

We'd been waiting on the Ogre for weeks. Though we still had two weeks left—enough time for a realistic chance at the summit—I no longer had any real faith in our success. I had lost the feeling that we could do it, and with every successive day of waiting, it became harder and harder for me to motivate myself for an opportunity that I no longer believed in. At the end of each day, I was happy to be able to crawl back into my tent. Once again, another day less.

It is difficult to motivate yourself when things just aren't going well. And this time, it didn't go well from the start. Even the preparations for the expedition had seemed ill-starred. A week before the start of the expedition, Thomas had hurt his knee. Our equipment came to Pakistan ten days late. What could we do in the meantime? Play cards until we were sick of it, hang around in the hotel, and run in desperation to the British Airways office one more time. Then came the telephone call from the German embassy with a travel warning: The Kashmiri conflict seemed on the verge of escalating. Where the conflict could lead, and how far India and Pakistan would go, no one at the embassy could really say. How could anyone know? But in any case, if the situation did escalate, Skardu would be an attractive target for India. It's the only place to land a large plane in Pakistani Kashmir, and it's home to a garrison. An additional brigade had already been transferred to Skardu, according to the German embassy's information, and more would follow if the conflict intensified.

Did we really want to go there? No—we *had* to go! It was the only way to get to our mountain. Skardu is the gateway to the central Karakorams. Anyone who wants to get to the heart of Pakistan's highest mountains has to pass through here. For now, Baltistan's provincial capital was as secure as ever, and there would be no problem getting there. We would be safe in the Latok group, as well. There, we would be a good 100 kilometers away from the theater of war, and the high chain of mountains in between continues to be an insurmountable obstacle for ground troops.

But what about on the way back? Naturally, no one could tell us what the situation would look like at the end of August. That was nearly three months from now, and the combat season in Kashmir had just gotten started. The snow had just started to melt in the war-torn areas, many of which were located at altitudes as high as 5,000 meters, and combat there was already more severe, more bitter, and bloodier than ever.

We felt like we were in the wrong movie. For fear of what might happen, we delayed our departure from Islamabad to Skardu for the third time in a row. Perhaps our luggage would come on Thursday? Perhaps by Thursday, the talks between Pakistan and India would start to show positive results? We hoped, but we didn't really believe it.

Thursday. We had been discussing the war at great length. Our trip to base camp and our stay there would not represent a problem at all. But what would happen if our return was blocked, if the conflict had spread to Skardu? We examined our alternatives in the event of emergency. The border to China was only 30 kilometers away from base camp. It would be possible to reach China in six days over the 5,400-meter-high Lukpe-La. It was not at all a problem from the mountaineering point of view, but what the Chinese would have to say about it remained an open question. At least I had managed to get the number of the German embassy in Peking. I also bought a map for our escape route, so we considered ourselves prepared for all eventualities. The next morning at ten o'clock we were once again standing in the brutal heat in the airfreight depot. Finally, a good sign: There were our long-awaited bags. Our supplies were complete. We could start.

Man, was that wall steep! As Jan and I came up the base camp moraine in the vanguard, Latok II showed itself in all its glory. The west wall was still in shadow, which made it seem even more other-worldly and inapproachable. Thank God that task was accomplished, and I didn't have to go up there again! I sat down on a stone, and for a brief time, I was right back up on the wall, remembering vividly exactly how it was. What a wonderful feeling to be here again! Setting up base camp, sorting equipment, preparing the gear—and with the best possible weather. It looked good. Operation Ogre was under way.

The war. For the past two weeks, we'd been hearing the muffled rumble of heavy artillery along the "line of control." It was to be expected that Pakistan and India would not find a quick resolution to the long-standing conflict that had once again flared up, and that it would have to come to massive combat operations. But we did not anticipate that we would actually hear the weapons themselves. It was quite nerve-wracking.

Ismail, who had been with us on previous Latok expeditions, listened to the news every day. He was worried about his younger brother, who was a soldier in the Pakistani army. And on June 15, a messenger brought the bad news: Ismail's brother had been killed on the Kashmiri front. That very same day, Ismail left us to return to his brother's family of ten, of which he was now the head.

For days, heavy clouds had hung over the summits of the Kara-korams. Another five days of miserable weather. We were crushed.

All this sitting around in base camp had drained us. Being up on the mountain would be a diversion, would help to bring order to our thoughts. But the weather pattern was just too unfavorable, and as long as nothing changed, we couldn't count on the four days of stable weather we needed for this expedition.

I looked up at the Ogre. There it stood, as it always has. But with each passing day it became more difficult for me to find my way to the summit. Of course, I didn't want to miss a single opportunity, and that's why I was still here in base camp at all. But in fact, I'd already washed my hands of it. Like a cat sitting for hours before a mouse hole waiting for its prey, so I sat here now, for weeks on end, in base camp, waiting patiently and stoically for my prey. If the prey doesn't appear, the cat goes on its way. If the summit of the Ogre didn't show itself soon, I'd have to go on my way too. Outcome of hunt: negative. Nothing unusual for the cat, and nothing unusual for the Ogre.

This time, it was everyone else who was getting positive results: "success" on Broad Peak, "success" on Gasherbrum II, "success" on Trango Tower—the radio regales us with announcements of successful expeditions. We look upon those who have already accomplished their objectives with a certain degree of envy. If only we had chosen an easier task, we'd have had our summit in the bag by now. And yet the celebrations take place repeatedly on the same peaks: brand-name destinations with a high probability of success. When I consider this, the envy quickly fades. I look up at the Ogre again and remember why it was that I'd chosen it as my objective to begin with: because it has an extremely high chance of failure, and therefore represents a pure and authentic challenge. A challenge that was still ahead of us, where we still had a chance—even if I was no longer capable of seeing it clearly. Another fourteen days of base camp left. Fourteen days of hoping, but also fourteen days of torturous waiting for better weather.

July 27. Yesterday, at sundown, it suddenly cleared up, and we decided to set off in the middle of the night. For the third time, we climbed up to the pillar camp at 6,000 meters. And once again, as we climbed to advance camp, through a heavily creviced area, through the couloir, and up the first several pitches of the pillar—it was all gradually starting to get on my nerves. After eight hours, Thomas and I were finally sitting in the portaledge, Jan and Toni in the ledge next to us.

It was always the same story: In the ledge, I felt right at home. I could reflect with calm and ease on what awaited us the next day: fifteen pitches of classic rock climbing. Not too difficult, but we wanted—no, we *needed*—to get through it in one day, because we were not going to take the portaledges with us, which meant we had to reach the head of the pillar in time for the bivouac. There were three heavy packs to be hauled up, so the climbing itself became secondary. The primary concern was the logistical problem of getting all the gear up to the top of the pillar as fast as possible.

But during the night, the cirrus clouds that had already begun to appear during the day thickened to a dense cloud cover, and once again, a high-altitude storm blasted the mountain, especially above 6,500 meters. At 2:00 AM, we decided not to set out yet, and to wait till morning. When the conditions didn't improve and the chances of getting good weather in the next few days seemed slim, we didn't waste our energy on a hopeless attempt, and decided to bet everything on one last opportunity.

We climbed down, for the third time, without ever beginning a real assault. Jan, however, didn't just climb down to the base camp; he threw in the towel altogether. He had already attempted the south pillar route in 1997. He'd invested far too much energy for no return, and now, two years later, he was done with the Ogre for good.

The last attempt. The weather had only gotten worse. Four nights in a row, we had gotten up at 2:00 AM. The clouds hung low over our heads. Three times in a row, Thomas, Toni, and I set off for the Ogre, and each time, snow and rain washed us down the glacier. Twice, we turned around just before advance camp, but the third time we pulled through—by the calendar, it was our absolute last day, the last opportunity we had. We climbed up the pillar, fighting strong winds and a blizzard. The ropes were completely iced over, the wind tore around the pillar's edge. If it got any worse, we wouldn't even make it up to the pillar camp to get our gear.

August 5. We considered ourselves lucky to have been able to break down the pillar camp and so at least leave the field without any material losses. The topic of the Ogre was closed. The many long, torturous days of idleness were over, and two weeks later, I was home again. I had put it all behind me: three months abroad, isolated, removed, while everything piled up here at home. Now, the dam had broken, and the pent-up forces of civilization hit me full bore. I had a hard time finding my bearings again.

This time, I had no success to prop me up, and I was cognizant of how difficult failure is. After all the endless weeks of waiting, I was happy to finally leave the field, and put an end to the tense lying-in-wait for the summit. But with every step toward home, I became more and more aware of what would await me there. What I actually needed now was rest. Success would have compensated for much, if not perhaps for everything. Euphoria would have carried me through the exhaustion. But this way, every step back to the everyday world reminded me not only that I'd had no success, but above all, that I was completely burned out psychologically.

Coming home with the summit in hand would have meant feeling energized despite all the strain. But without the summit, you come home and fall into a deep rut; you are sucked dry, completely spent—but you must keep going, must work to catch up after a three-month absence. On top of that, the hunger has not been quelled. We don't climb up mountains just because they're there. We climb up mountains because we want to stand on top of them. The failure to reach the summit weighs upon us so heavily because it is an unresolved problem. We want to reach the summit to leave our footprints for a brief time on the highest point of a mountain, to stand high on top and achieve the goal we'd set for ourselves so we can be free again.

If we don't reach the summit, then we remain prisoners of our own selves and our uncompleted task.

Experience is based on the recollection of what you've previously undergone. For me, the intensity of having to come to terms with an unresolved problem will be as deeply anchored in my memory as any of my successes—of course, predominantly as a negative phenomenon. But even this will at some point come to constitute an important experience, a significant building block of my life.

CHAPTER TWENTY-THREE

THE WAY BACK TO MYSELF

After the Ogre, pretty much everything imaginable went to hell in a handbasket. For one thing, I had come back home from the expedition utterly frustrated; I didn't really want to accept our failure. I simply refused to acknowledge that it's obviously an unavoidable part of extreme mountain climbing. Though I had already failed once on a big mountain—Latok II in 1995—at the time I hadn't seen it as a failure at all. I had just redpointed "Salathé" shortly before, and had traveled from Yosemite directly to the Karakorams. My first expedition was a brand-new experience in and of itself, and on top of that, I had been able to climb the two fantastic granite towers of the Ogre Thumb and the Spaldang. The latter was even a first ascent. At the time, these experiences had given me the feeling of not having failed at all on the west face of Latok II. I perceived our attempt as a necessary preparation—which was in itself proof that in the end, I never had any doubt that I would return as soon as possible in order to attack the west face again.

But now, after the Ogre, it was all very different. We had not only failed to climb the Ogre on this expedition, but for me, at least for the time being, it also signaled the end of the dream of climbing the Ogre at all. I wasn't ruling it out entirely, but at least for the foreseeable future, I intended to stay far away from this mountain, and the entire range. Three expeditions to the Latok range in five years were quite sufficient. For now, I first had to get some distance, get back in the swing of things at home, and learn to take mountain climbing a little less seriously again, now that it had become my livelihood.

Sport climbing had always brought me happiness in my life: to have breakfast with friends, pick up your backpack, take a short walk, and then spend the entire day at the crag, ending it afterward at the Kugelbachbauer, or some other pub. That's a way of life that I still enjoy to the utmost today, after all this time.

After many years, I finally had enough free time to visit the Frankenjura. A true climber's paradise in the forests north of Nuremberg, it is undoubtedly the best-known sport-climbing area in Germany. I was traveling with a small group and wanted nothing more than to have a good time and to recover some of my strength, which had stagnated during the expedition to the Ogre. One day, we paid a visit to the "Zwergenschloss," where a new route in lower grade 11 had recently been opened. I was curious, and wanted to take a closer look at "Powerplay." As it turned out, the moves were even better than I'd expected. Admittedly, the individual moves were already at the limit for me, but what did I expect? I could consider myself lucky to be able to manage them at all! And so, a half-hour later, I inspected "Powerplay" again. This time, I managed entire sequences, but there still remained the crux, which I managed to pull off only with luck.

I was so fired up that I could barely sit still afterward, and instead, climbed right back on the route a third time. But this time, predictably, it was more like a hard shift in the mines. I had not yet had a chance after the expedition to rebuild my endurance, and the more often I tried my hand at the crux, the quicker my strength would ebb. Once again, I found myself hanging in the air in the overhanging section, feeling like a piece of climbing trash. In order to get back up to the roof, I grabbed the rope with both hands, did a pull-up, and then let go with a jerk. In the brief moment in which my body remained paused at a dead stop after the upward motion, my belay partner could take in enough rope so that, afterward, I could make contact with the roof above me. But that's when it happened—during the brief moment in which the rope was slack, it had wrapped itself around my right hand, and right after that, my body came down and pulled the loop tight with all its weight. My hand was crushed to mush as if by a vise, and above all, my index finger was completely deformed.

Shit! Stunned, I hung in the rope 4 meters above the ground. My finger! How could this happen? *My finger* . . . I could have screamed curses till I was blue in the face, but I didn't even have enough rage for that. I was simply resigned. My index finger was mobile in every direction, and although in these first few minutes I couldn't really feel the pain yet, I guessed that this wasn't a good sign.

The very next day I was in Innsbruck, consulting with Thomas Hochholzer, the doctor I most trusted when it came to my fingers. My index and ring fingers had taken the brunt of it, but Thomas was convinced that, despite the extensive injuries, I would be able to climb seriously again at some point. I did, however, have to resign myself to a long convalescence. Despite the optimistic expert opinion, I was tormented by uncertainty. I had doubts about the significance of medical predictions, and about the body's regenerative powers. The healing process for an injury is so complex, even in something as small as a finger. The outcome of a physics experiment is generally predictable, but the outcome of healing an injured finger?

The only thing certain was that, at least for the time being, there would be no more climbing. Now, of all times, when I was so sorely in need of it to help me put the fun back in my life, and to take some pleasure in what I was doing. More than ever, I was now a prisoner in my own skin. I had played all my cards and lost everything. I had no other strategy for dealing with the situation in which I now found myself. I was completely burned out and done with this world. I couldn't climb any longer, at least not for the next six months. I even had to forego the piano and my motorcycle—things on which I would otherwise draw for strength and comfort. And although I was practically drowning in work up until that time, wouldn't you know it—now of all times, it was dead quiet. Not a soul wanted a lecture. And there were no articles to write, either. What would I write about, anyway? I was without work, without sport, without hobby. I was simply empty.

While I was feeling this inner emptiness, Thomas and I were planning our next expedition—this time, to India, to Shivling. But like so much else in my life at the time, this, too, seemed cursed by misfortune. Shortly before the expedition, I was once again laid low by tonsillitis. My damned tonsils! Ever since the severe infection I had contracted at Cho Oyu, I had never really completely recovered my health, and this added to my desolate psychological condition. Things did not take a turn for the better. I'd barely gotten to Delhi when I caught another infection and had to resort to antibiotics again. Rather worse for wear, I struggled up to base camp.

After a few days, I was able to get myself in hand. The medicine had beaten back the infection, and I was able to take an active part in the proceedings again. While Thomas had to take a break to battle a stomach ailment, I climbed up to nearly 6,000 meters with Swiss climbers Iwan Wolf and Bruno Hasler, in order to prepare the camp for the ascent of the direct North Pillar.

But there was no avoiding fate. The tonsillitis flared up again, and that finally put an end to it for me once and for all. It wasn't just my tonsils that were infected. This time, I was sick all over, down to my soul. Deep inside me something that had always sustained me had broken: my passion for the mountains. Now, all at once, the mountains seemed so far away from me that I couldn't even see them anymore, even though I was standing right in the midst of them. The two days I stayed on in the camp, waiting for the ultimate outcome, were agony. I hated myself, my body, the world around me. The Shivling, one of the most beautiful mountains in the world, turned into a hateful silhouette, and I no longer wished to set eyes on it.

I left, and spent the remaining two weeks of the expedition in Rishikesh, wandering around like a lost soul. Each day I felt more lost than the last; aimless, without a plan. I was dug in deep. After two weeks, I was finally released from my lethargy. Thomas returned— and he had done it! Together with Iwan Wolf, he had been the first to ascend the direct North Pillar of Shivling. I was glad for my brother. But it wasn't an inner joy that I experienced as a genuinely positive feeling. Rather, I understood on an intellectual level that it was something positive for Thomas, and I was pleased on his account. As for myself, I was too sick in my inner being at the moment. All I could hope for was that I would at least be able to find my way back to myself when I got back home. The two weeks of waiting in India had drained all my energy, and I could feel that I was at the absolute end of my powers—not only physically, but mentally.

There was no relief in sight. Back home, I saw nothing before me but problems and seemingly insurmountable obstacles. When it came to anything that had previously filled me with energy, I now stood in my own way. Whatever I would have wanted to undertake before, suddenly there were a hundred reasons why it couldn't be done, or why it was unattainable. I couldn't even manage to get up a simple mountain. Everything seemed endlessly difficult for me, so complicated that I couldn't even muster up the courage to make any concrete plans. I was incapable of getting anything done, and I feared that my beloved life as a mountain climber was slipping away from me.

The idea that perhaps I might never want to go up into the mountains again scared me. I was afraid that I would never take pleasure in climbing again—that I would never be able to look upon the great mountains of the world with joy. I couldn't even imagine going training with my friends anymore. I didn't even want to see any of them. I was afraid that someone would ask me what was wrong with me; all the anxieties I had to battle every day robbed me of my last bit of energy. Every time I thought I had conquered one fear through rational thinking, the next one was knocking at the door, and every new fear that presented itself seemed even more difficult to control than the last.

As the fears grew in me, things escalated to an existential crisis. If I were not going to climb anymore, then everything that I had talked about in my many lectures would lose its credibility. After all, who would be impressed by a mountain climber who has become bogged down by fears and has long since lost any sense of clear perspective on the mountains? I could no longer imagine standing up in front of an audience and talking about my experiences. Experiences that had long since disappeared in the fog of my anxieties. The intervals at which these irrational fears surfaced in my life were getting shorter and shorter. At some point, I reached the threshold: Before I could even get one anxiety under control, I would already be overtaken by the next, and as this development became more evident with each passing day, I finally began to feel an all-pervasive, ever-present anxiety. I could no longer find my way out of all the various anxieties I had, and I now had a general fear of anxiety itself.

I had ignored a great many things for a long time, refused to see the problems, and preferred instead to avoid them. It was a tempting strategy; anxieties are so easily suppressed by focusing on other things. But now it became clear to me that I could no longer continue to sit idly by and watch this mind-altering process unfold, as it had been for quite some time. Avoidance had become impossible. The problems had been mounting and intensifying long enough, and now they had piled up before me like an almost insurmountable hurdle.

My task was crystal clear: I had to face up to all the things that had unbalanced my psyche over the years. And I knew that in order to do that, I needed to get psychological counseling. That was the only way for me to really conquer my problems and not simply turn away from them as I had so often done in the past. I needed help to reorient my thoughts and develop a strategy for dealing with such situations in the future.

I met with a psychiatrist, and item one on his agenda: medication. He recommended one drug that would take away my feelings of anxiety in the short term, and another, a so-called serotonin reuptake inhibitor, as a long-term treatment to put my supposedly dysfunctional synaptic processes back in order again. The psychiatrist and I discussed the consequences this would have for me as a mountain climber. I was skeptical that medication was the way to go for me, and came to the conclusion that I had enough trust in myself to be able to take care of this problem some other way. I just had to commit to it! I was absolutely determined; I erased everything from my life and concentrated only on this one task. I was prepared to push everything else aside and, as a result, I was no longer accessible to anyone. No work, no commitments, nothing to come at me anymore—something that had seemed impossible to me previously. Now, I was suddenly energized enough to make these important, necessary decisions.

I set out in search of an appropriate therapy, only to find that, outside of Munich, there was a serious shortage of mental-health-care options. There was a three-month-long waiting list for an appointment—three months that, in my present situation, simply seemed too long. I asked around, and finally had some luck. A friend of mine who had studied psychology referred me to the psychologist who had supervised his internship. Although this psychologist worked in a clinic as a youth counselor, and was not in private practice, he was willing to meet with me. He didn't offer me his services officially as a doctor, so I was therefore not his patient—at least, not directly. But because of the urgency of my friend's request, he was prepared to give me psychological advice.

The result of this was a long and difficult path, one which perhaps demanded more initiative and strength than would have been required by relying solely on medication. But it was a path that, in the long run, gave me a deep understanding of the way I think and feel. Repeatedly, I had to will myself not to let the crumbled old edifices of my mind lie around in rubble, but to dig everything out and build it up anew. I had to dig down really deep to bring up precisely those things that in the past had always been most distressing. My psychologist opened my eyes to mental processes that were actually very clear, but which I had always ignored. He made it clear to me that I could learn how to handle situations differently than I'd handled them in the past.

All the things that I used to insist on because of my high expectations for myself, I could now throw out the window. I was ready to admit things to myself that I would never have admitted before. And if in the past I had done some things because it was expected of me, I now became radical enough to refuse these expectations. If you sink low enough, at some point you'll be ready to react this severely. The first obligation in your life is to your own well-being. Only when your own well-being is secure can you start thinking about fulfilling the expectations and desires of others. I realized how many situations there had been in the past where I had felt a cold sweat on my brow. I started to understand that in these moments, I needed to think of myself first, and not about what others would think of me.

There had always been a constant, hateful criticism of what I was doing directed at me by some climbers, and, over the years, I had taken it to heart far more than I would have ever admitted. Here, indeed, my decision to pursue an uncertain future as a mountain climber was taking its toll. Now, finally, I was called upon to face up to this fact and to deal with the problems it caused. Was it really so terrible if someone criticized me? Did it affect me so much because I felt the person was right? Before, if I'd thought anyone was criticizing me unjustly, I would feel a great rage deep within me. According to my psychologist, "Getting angry means paying for the sins of others!" This maxim offered me a chance to react very differently to these types of situations. Now, when I call it to mind, I am no longer so easily provoked, and above all, I don't take everything so much to heart.

In the end, simple insights led the way out of anxiety. The governing principle had been made clear to me from the very start. I had repeatedly expressed the wish to find out as much as I could about myself (with professional assistance) so that I would never again wind up in this situation. I was soon disabused of this notion, and learned that it could always happen to me again. No one can be guaranteed to walk through life completely free of anxiety. But once you've been able to find your way out of your fears, then you will have the self-confidence to know that you can do it again in the future. Don't think about tomorrow; embrace the now!

I went on my way, and I believe that I am stronger today than I was before the crisis. I had an incredibly intense experience, a glimpse into the depths of my soul that would have remained hidden from me without the crisis. This insight has enriched my life and made me more aware of the dark underside of life—those things that people like to suppress in public. Indeed, I am often astounded when I can intuit from just a few words and gestures that a person is in psychological distress. I always try to help, whenever it is in my power.

CHAPTER TWENTY-FOUR

YOSEMITE—SOURCE OF STRENGTH

After my crisis, I set out to permanently reconfigure my life. I would not allow myself to be subject to any external force. Or, to put it better: In the future, I was determined not to do anything that did not speak to my heart.

Aside from my home, Yosemite is one of the few places that are a source of strength for me. After the first redpoint of "Salathé" in 1995, I returned to the Valley three years later, this time together with my brother Thomas. At the time, the only free-climbing routes on the big walls of El Capitan were still just "Salathé" and the "Nose," which had been freed by Lynn Hill. That meant the imposing South Pillar and the southwest wall had been "freed," but not the southeast wall, or, as the Americans called it, the "Right Side."

A close-meshed network of routes already covered the mostly overhanging Right Side; almost all of them were extremely difficult aid climbs. The first route up this wall—the "North America Wall," opened in 1964—was for a long time considered the hardest big-wall climb in the world. It was a milestone of its time. Along this famous route, Thomas and I were able to set a new milestone of our own and bring some fresh air into the climbing scene at El Capitan. We exchanged pitons and hammers for chalk bags. Where previous climbers had nailed pins into the fine hairline cracks on the compact and forbidding wall, we now climbed on the micro edges and tiny footholds. "El Niño" was born, and free climbing had conquered the most forbidding wall of El Capitan.

This was much more than just a tremendous athletic accomplishment for Thomas and me; it was also the realization of our vision, which we had carried within us for the longest time. "El Niño" is for us an unforgettable memory that illuminates our lives like a star shining brightly in the night sky—a star that I always gladly look toward whenever I want to see a thing of beauty. A star that I can always count on, by which I can always orient myself.

And that's exactly why my first big trip after my crisis took me not to the Himalayas or Karakoram—these mountains need strength—but rather home again to my little paradise: to Yosemite.

Contrary to plan, I arrived alone in the Valley in the fall of 2000. A month before, Thomas had been running downhill, had taken a wrong step, and the result was just about the ultimate catastrophe for someone who's about to go to Yosemite in a few weeks to do some free climbing. He did a forward somersault right into the rocks, with his hands out. Searing pain, and his left elbow was dislocated. Over; it was all over. All the training, all the suffering, for nothing—free climbing was a wash.

This would certainly be true for most climbers—but not for Thomas, the speed healer. Three weeks' immobilization? Nonsense! He was moving the joint after two days. No climbing for six weeks? Not a chance! Three weeks later, he was already climbing at grade 10 again. Skip the trip to America? No way! Instead, he postponed the flight by two weeks and did some physical therapy. Free climbing on El Cap? No problem.

I came to the Valley alone, with Thomas to follow two weeks later. Of course, time was tight, so we'd agreed that I would use the intervening days to work on our project by myself.

I set off on my own. My goal was a long, narrow dihedral that cuts through the wall of El Capitan for 400 meters just above the "Heart"—a prominent, heart-shaped depression in the southwest wall. But soon, I had to admit that the project would be too hard. I had only managed to come a short way back to the shape I'd been in before my accident. The serious injury I'd suffered to my finger the previous year, all my countless tonsil infections, and the psychological crisis I had experienced just that past winter had all taken their toll on my overall condition. Thomas wouldn't look any better after his own recent accident. The good thing about my exploration of the southwest wall, however, was that I had discovered another possibility that would be better suited to our current level of health and ability.

In 1995, I had not only freed "Salathé," but at the same time, I had analyzed all the rock features to the right and left of the route with the hungry eye of a free climber. One of the products of my alert eye was "Free Rider," which Thomas and I were able to first-ascend in only 15 hours and 25 minutes in 1996, after we had first-ascended "El Niño." But this was not the only by-product. Hidden away in the furthest corner of my brain, I had yet another possibility: to traverse out over a barely recognizable weakness in the wall 20 meters above the El Cap Spire. Weaving constantly up and down, it led off far to the right, exactly where I wanted to end up—in the "Heart" route.

I set off alone down this path and entered virgin territory. It wasn't even difficult. The four brand-new pitches barely scratched grade 9. Afterward, for the most part, I followed the "Heart." Another whole fourteen pitches, two of them absolutely first-rate: steep, exposed, and top-quality rock. Everything I could possibly ask on El

Capitan, and the upper 9th grade was absolutely doable for us in our present condition.

Five days after I had opened our new free-climbing project by myself, Thomas came to join me in Yosemite, just at the right time. He managed astonishingly well, given how fresh his injury still was, and soon, after just a week of training in the route, we had come far enough to start thinking about a continuous redpoint ascent. The main difficulty of our project was its length; in total, there were no less than forty-one pitches, which made it the longest route on El Capitan. But the difficulties of the "Golden Gate," our newest creation, were still within proportion, and, in fact, not as extreme as those of "Salathé." This was pretty crazy when you consider that the "Nose" and "Salathé" were once seen as the only possible free-climbing routes.

Nonetheless, the redpoint was not exactly what you'd call a cakewalk. Thomas and I had a tough fight on our hands. But the fact that the route demanded everything we had was probably exactly what had given us such a wonderful feeling of satisfaction. It had not been easy, but once again, we had done it—despite our less-than-ideal conditions. We had walked through our valleys, and now we were at the very top again, on the mountain—at the summit. And we knew how to appreciate this happiness. For it is only when you come from deep in the valley that you can see the true measure of the mountain, and can enjoy the moment when you leave the shadow of the valley behind you to stand at the very top, in the last light of the waning day.

CHAPTER TWENTY-FIVE

BEYOND THE VERTICAL —"BELLAVISTA"

After injuring my finger in 1999, for the first time in my life I found myself in a situation where I did not know how to go on. This stupid accident had not only squashed my right index finger; it had also put a significant part of my life—climbing—in jeopardy. I felt empty, and lived in a state of athletic withdrawal.

I found a little relief in January 2000, when I was finally able to begin some light training after three months of rehab. At this point, I still did not have enough insight into myself to understand that my attitude toward life had not been thrown off balance by the injury alone. Therefore, I sought to address the problem in my usual way. In order to get myself out of my funk, I needed to be active again as quickly as possible—to go out and experience something, and thus drive out the feeling of emptiness.

When I was finally able to regain confidence in my damaged finger again, there was no longer anything to hold me back, so I set out for the Tre Cime. Aside from the thirst for adventure, I had yet another motivation. In 1994, I had climbed "Schweizerführe" on the north face of the Cima Ovest, together with the Spaniard Lisi Roig Alegre. It is a classic route that requires mastery of the lower 9th grade in order to climb it free. An impressive undertaking. The two of us had enjoyed a fantastic day in the Dolomites—a real gift. And full of consequence.

During the climb, the huge roof to the right of the "Schweiz-erführe" had caught my eye. This upside-down world had gotten a hold of me and wouldn't let me go. I suspected that the great roof on the Cima Ovest could possibly contain the craziest free-climbing route in the world, but it would be a full six years before I was able to return. There had been many plans and objectives and dreams swirling around in my head, all demanding to be realized. Something else always got in the way whenever the idea of the Cima Ovest came to my mind. But now, after this difficult period of drought, the great roof of the Cima Ovest was exactly the ticket.

In accordance with my mood, I prescribed myself the motto "The harder, the better," and chose to attempt the first ascent by myself in the winter. I also set myself the goal of avoiding putting up another direct line through the wall. This line should be natural. Only normal pitons would be placed for progress up the pitches, while bolts would be used just at the belays. I got exactly what I wanted: I was scared, and it took all the skill I had to keep myself from plunging unchecked into the snow-covered talus below. The route was right up my alley: loose, demanding, and rugged.

The first ascent of "Bellavista" was something special for me for two reasons: First, I had never climbed such extremely difficult rock in winter; and second, I had never spent so much time—a whole five days—on a mountain alone. My thirst for adventure was quenched again, for the time being. And after the five days I'd spent on the first ascent, it was clear to me that the route was possible to free-climb: every meter along the line of "Bellavista" could be climbed without relying on aid pitons. It would be extremely difficult, but doable. The free ascent of this huge roof became both an *idée fixe* and a challenge: to climb in the 11th grade on the loose dolomite of a shadowed north face . . .

I knew that I was not yet ready for a free ascent. The break necessitated by my injury had left a huge gap in my arm muscles, and a three-month training period would not be enough to build up the necessary strength for this roof. I had to put off the project until a later date. Ultimately, the summer of 2000 had confirmed that my climbing career wasn't over; however, the really hard stuff would have to wait. My finger could not yet withstand extreme strain, and I would need to give it some time to regain the level of strength I'd had before the accident. I wouldn't be able to train really hard until the winter, but then, I planned to wrest every last bit of usefulness out of all the gyms and climbing centers. I had suffered from withdrawal long enough, and now I was chomping at the bit to make up for it.

My enthusiasm also gave me a clearer view of my objective. I put everything into it, and I knew exactly what to do. Sport climbing is the foundation that allows you to climb at an extremely high degree of difficulty—in alpine terrain as well. Early in the year, I began slowly but surely to ratchet up my performance in the climbing crag. After five years of abstinence, I made my way back into the realm of the 11th grade, where the holds are tiny, the overhangs really steep, and climbing moves truly athletic.

Early July 2001. It was time. I figured I was fit enough by now, so why wait? I made my way back to the Tre Cime, together with Hias Leitner from Graz. In order to take the first step toward a free ascent, I first had to climb the route with him the "traditional" way, so to speak, in order to place the protection I would need for free climbing, especially in the roof pitches. This was necessary first of all because during my first ascent in the winter, I had left behind only a single solitary fixed pin in the great roof; and second, because at this grade of steepness, you simply can't place protection from a climbing position.

And so, we set off and climbed briskly through the first five free-climbing pitches of "Bellavista." At the belay directly under the great roof, Hias loaded up with just about everything you'd need—hammer, knifeblades, lost arrows, angles, nuts, skyhooks, etriers—and entered overhanging terrain. In essence, aid climbing has very little to do with climbing in the original sense. Most of the time, you're hanging in the harness, then you're standing in the etrier again, stretching to place the next piece of pro, creeping upward like an inchworm. But despite the slow progress, aid climbing on difficult terrain is far from boring! Difficult aid climbing is characterized by the correspondingly poor quality of its protection. Thus, spending hours making your way up an aid pitch is a real psychological challenge.

After two days, we had completed the eight pitches to the start of the "Swiss-Italian Route," and returned to the entry point, suspended from the ropes we had left behind on the roof. During this ascent, I took my time examining every single meter of the great roof closely for hand- and footholds. I wanted to find out if there was a continuous chain of holds that would allow me to get through without aid. After these two days, I was absolutely certain that "Bellavista" would go free. But what was still unclear was how hard it would be, and whether I myself was in the position to free-climb the entire thing. There was also the question of how I should protect the 60 meters of the roof.

What was clear, in any case, was that I would not, under any circumstances, try and take the edge off "Bellavista" by bolting it. This was a very conscious decision, since the existing route would have been altered by retrobolting. It was also such a wonderful challenge. Sport climbing, in particular, is increasingly dominated by quantitative measure and technical grade. I wanted to put the emphasis elsewhere and demonstrate that it can be done differently. I'm the last person to deny myself the pleasure of high technical difficulty or the fun of the sport. But for many mountain climbers, climbing is more than athletics. They forego the 100 percent certainty of the bolts usually found at high grades of difficulty. What count for them are mental fortitude, ability, and a certain risk-taking mentality— qualities that every climber needs to have on the big alpine routes.

Two days later I was on the wall again and began to tackle freeing the big roof. I analyzed every single meter, examined the rock, and tried to find the optimal solution for every spot: a solution that would be safe on the one hand, but also the most economical. The point was to climb with the least possible expenditure of strength, since after I had climbed the entire route, I would still have to have enough power left to execute the last difficult move at the very end.

Three weeks later, I dared to attempt climbing through all the roof pitches for the first time, with Guido Unterwurzacher as my partner. The sixth pitch runs for some 10 meters toward the left along a stratification line underneath a roof that protrudes 6 meters out from the wall, and then you climb through the weakest point in this line of roofs. At first glance, it seems incredible that free climbing is even possible here at all! But over and over, my fingertips find space in the crack of the slot beneath the roof, and at the end of the traverse there's even a place to rest before the first crux. I gave my burning forearms a quick shake, sorted out the small edge with the fingertips of my right hand, tore through decisively to the two-finger pocket, and then right to the next one just before my body could spiral down . . . And then I was there at the belay, with the large holds in my hands. I had cracked the first pitch on the roof!

Guido followed, jumaring up the rope, and was now also initiated into the pleasures of the suddenly increased exposure. Every handhold was checked over twice, everything was considered three times over. The mental strain made itself evident. I tried the next pitch a few times, but did not get the desired results that day. I was too nervous, not relaxed enough to find a reasonable solution to the most difficult portion of "Bellavista," a 6-meter-long traverse to the left. But even this pitch couldn't withstand my permanent assault forever. A week later, I finally managed to complete what was probably the most difficult pitch, and thus, the conditions were finally set for a redpoint attempt.

Now it came down to redpointing every single pitch, from the ground up, in one day. But I had yet another hurdle to overcome. The belay between the first and second pitches is in overhanging terrain. It does not provide a no-hand-rest. For me, as a free climber, this meant I was obliged to string these two difficult pitches together into one. An uninterrupted 50 meters through overhanging terrain would be a real challenge for the endurance of my forearms.

Another ten days had gone by, and once again, I was standing below, at the start of "Bellavista." I was turning up at the Tre Cime pretty often now, for the simple reason that I had failed on my previous four attempts. This time, Gernot Flemisch was with me—a friend from the Traunstein climbing scene. As always, I felt the strain. Though I stood at the start of the climb, my thoughts had long since flown elsewhere: 200 meters further up, to the great roof. How would it go today? Would I fail again, or would I finally do it? First, I had to climb these initial 200 meters as economically as possible, so I would still have enough strength left over later for the last difficult meters in the great roof.

After three hours, we came to the belay under the roof—a moment in which all the images of my previous failed attempts played themselves out before my inner eye. In all of them, I could climb the lower portion of the wall without any problems. Each time, I arrived with the feeling that now I would have a good shot at it. Yet all of these previous attempts had ended at the crux, the 6-meter-long traverse to the left. Over and over, there came the moment when a move would not be performed perfectly, so that I couldn't get an optimal grip on the next hold, and thus the subsequent move became impossible. It was like a gravity well. Every time, there was the same fateful chain reaction, and every time I found myself sailing through the air. The moment I set foot on the belay underneath the great roof, these images would settle firmly in my mind and play themselves over and over. If I continued to be preoccupied by these memories, I would never make it.

After a half-hour of rest at the belay, I finally got on my way. The left traverse was not a problem, and today, I easily made it over the roof to reach the resting point with the large holds at the intermediate belay. It looked good! Pretty soon, my arms had loosened up, my breathing had slowed, my heart rate was calming down. All good signs. I pushed on, my thoughts on the right track. There was no up or down; I'd filtered out the exposure. Everything was under control. I completed the difficult sequences decisively, one after another.

I reached the piton 8 meters above and to the left of the resting point, where the traverse to the left began. I clipped into the pin and climbed on immediately toward the next resting point, another meter to the left. Again, I took the time to bring down my heart rate and uncramp my arms. The crux: the left traverse. Not a single good hold; nothing but open structures. Here, you needed to pull through powerfully, climb dynamically, leave gravity without a chance. Sport climbing in lower grade 11, just like on a crag, only with the small difference that your protection isn't a bolt.

Move by move, I executed the rehearsed sequence, like a gymnast at a competition performing a routine he has been working on for weeks. Move by move, I advanced, until I reached the first good hold. Reached for it, one more move, and then I'd come to the big pocket at the end of the traverse. The worst was behind me! My forearms were burning, my spirit was ready to give out; it was still a long way to the belay—a whole 10 meters in which I couldn't make a single mistake. Ten more meters where I had to give it my all.

Move by move, I battled my way to the top, just making it from one rest to the next. Fear was breathing down my neck. So close to the finish; nothing must happen now! The last move. I didn't trust the left foothold. I wanted to hesitate, but I couldn't. Both of my fore-arms got totally pumped right away. I had to risk it. Go on. There it was—the belay, the end of the pitch. Deliverance. The way to the top was open.

On July 18, 2001, my adventure was at an end. The huge roof, the route "Bellavista," had been freed.

CHAPTER TWENTY-SIX

THE OUTLOOK FOR MOUNTAIN SPORTS IN THE TWENTY-FIRST CENTURY

Mountain climbing is a sport with a future, but also one with a history. The ascent of Mont Blanc in 1786 is often considered the birth of mountaineering. The highest peak in the Alps had been conquered, and one might say that mountain climbing had been robbed of its prospects at the very moment of its birth. But mountain climbers could always find new challenges in the unbelievable variety of the mountain world. It was easier in earlier times, when it was still quiet in the mountains. People had less money, and hardly any leisure, and they didn't know very much about the alien world of the mountains. That's why the few people that did have the opportunity to go up in the mountains also had much more freedom. They could pursue their individual interests almost completely undisturbed.

They could undertake a route without ever coming across another soul. To this day, even now that the giants of the Himalayas have all long since been ascended, there are still countless possibilities for the top climbers to test their limits—including in the Alps.

Over the years, mountain climbing has developed into a popular recreation sport, and in our mobile, leisure-oriented society, it is increasingly beginning to resemble a mass movement. If in the past you could generally expect the mountains to offer solitude, nowadays you often encounter veritable crowds. Commercial tourism has made the wild Alps accessible, altering them to suit its own needs. Many who tour the mountains today no longer experience the mountain itself; instead, they consume a prepackaged "mountain experience."

When you consider how diverse mountain climbing can be, it's understandable why so many people are drawn to the mountains. It covers simply everything, from a bit of R & R on the weekends to high-stakes adventure. All the different varieties of alpinism that can be found between these two extremes correspond to the various preferences of the different kinds of people who climb mountains—those who like to have their fun and stay safe, and those who love danger and adventure. What's important is to recognize that both extremes exist, as well as the entire gamut in between. It should therefore be in everyone's interest to maintain this diversity.

Even the relatively "small" Alps are still big enough to offer all kinds of climbing opportunities, although they have become noticeably more crowded, meaning that we must have increasingly more consideration for one another. The commercial demand for the "mountain experience" is undeniably there. It would be senseless to try to deny access to the increasing stream of tourists; we humans are a part of nature too. But to destroy the variety in our sport through thoughtless development in the name of recreation would be an assault on the history and future of mountaineering.

The Alps have been under development for centuries. This development has constantly expanded, and will continue its forward march, affecting us mountain climbers for good or ill. In Zermatt, they've built all the infrastructure necessary for mass tourism: railway, hotels, cable car, the huge parking lots in Täsch. Zermatt will never again be the village it once was. Or Aiguille du Midi, with its cable car, summit restaurant, ski run down the Mer de Glace—this mountain will never regain its original tranquility as long as the cable car is there. Naturally, these numerous development measures have also altered mountain climbing itself. But sensible regulation of tourist development has still left enough room to preserve the original character of mountain climbing. Although the tourist industry has altered the image of the mountains, it has always been possible for climbers to avoid those areas. Luckily, even today, there is not enough demand to make it economically worthwhile to completely transform all of the Alps into one continuous recreational playground.

But ultimately, it is not the large-scale development of the tourist industry that will rob alpine mountaineering of its prospects. The changes that are most significant for the sport have always been precipitated by the climbers themselves. In the last hundred years, mountain climbing has been far less affected by the big building projects in the major areas of the Alps than by the micro-development along its capillaries: the huts, mountain paths, stairs, and sport-climbing routes. The process of decking out the wild rockscape with pins and bolts continues unabated, with no end in sight. After the alpine climbing clubs agreed to halt further construction of huts and paths so as not to rob the Alps of any more wilderness, it is now the rock climbers who continue the process with their own hands, even though they are the most athletically minded species among the mountaineers. It should be remembered that from its inception, alpine climbing has always had an athletic as well as an adventuring component. Anyone familiar with the history of mountaineering knows that these two factors have always gone hand in hand. Yet this is the very thing that often cannot be taken for granted anymore today.

The overwhelming majority of alpine first ascents made in the last decade are so-called plaisir routes. In the current style, first-ascent routes are bolted at regular 3-meter intervals in order to minimize risk. This style of climbing has found widespread acceptance. Adding these plaisir routes to the countless routes from earlier eras of mountain climbing provides today's climber with an unimaginable variety of possible approaches to the art of climbing. That is precisely what makes our sport so interesting and exciting! The "Dülfer" on the Fleischbank, the North Face of the Eiger, the "Rebitschrisse," the "Schweizerführe," the "Mittelpfeiler," "Moderne Zeiten," the "Weg durch den Fisch"—these are all great, classic landmark routes characteristic of their respective eras.

On the other hand, since the 1980s, the bolt has increasingly gained significance not for aid climbing, but as a key means of protection for free climbing. The Kirschlispitzen in the Rätikon, the Wendenstöcke—these represent demanding bolted alpine routes. And all over the entire span of the Alps, the mountains are strewn with an unbelievable number of plaisir routes. There's something for everyone—whatever you're looking for. At least, it's still the case today, and that's a good thing.

But things go too far when not only first ascents, but also preexisting old routes from various eras are all developed in the plaisir style. Under the misappropriated banner of "renovation," these routes are retrobolted without any consideration for the achievement of the first ascensionist or the natural diversity of alpine climbing. The routes are "renovated" uniformly, so that afterward it is no longer possible to tell whether it had once been an Auckenthaler, a Rebitsch, or a Messner. This lack of respect for the achievement of the first ascensionist, the epoch in which the route was opened, and for alpine history in general has led to a serious schism in the climbing world.

Today, in alpine climbing areas that are popular with sport climbers due to the high quality of the rock, both new and old routes are equipped with bolts—a development that is increasingly picking up speed. And as long as there are no economic barriers or conflicts with environmental regulation, the process will continue. In economic terms, this micro-level development by means of bolting is an enterprise that even a private individual can manage. As for environmental regulation, unlike the crag-climbing districts, the alpine climbing areas are overwhelmingly uncultivated, so conflicts arising from overuse of fixed climbing equipment have remained minor. But one thing is patently obvious: The more, and the quicker, climbers develop bolted routes, the easier it is to sweep away objections. If ten years ago bolts were still to be found only occasionally, usually in spots that could not be protected by other means, today there are massifs in the Alps where more than 1,000 bolts are placed each season. This kind of development is no longer self-regulating because the ethical barrier has already been broken.

Mountain climbing in the Alps has its own history and its own ethics. There have always been discussions about right and wrong behavior in the mountains. The liveliness of these debates demonstrates that ethics are not optional when it comes to mountain climbing. There are no written laws—it's not important enough for that; but there are conventions of behavior that are rooted, among other things, in common sense, mutual respect, and tradition.

Without the guidance of a positive model, rock climbers face a dilemma: They no longer maintain any boundaries, renounce any means, or respect any traditions, and they increasingly misuse the possibilities offered by technology. It is a dilemma because we as climbers must continually redefine the boundaries and set our own limits in accordance with our ethics. Without respect for ethics, interest in true alpine climbing will continue to decline. Already today, there are only a few alpinists who are willing to take on the challenge of the wild mountain world on their own responsibility. This is quite a contrast with sport climbing. Whether at the climbing crags or in the Alps, sport climbing will continue to grow in popularity; there's no need to worry about new blood here.

As for the circle of alpinists, one can only hope that the climbing areas of the Alps will not all be made to conform to a unifying standard of fixed protection, so that the variety we find in alpinism today can still be enjoyed tomorrow. Only then will mountaineering in the twenty-first century have a future not only in the Himalayas, but in the Alps as well.

CHAPTER TWENTY-SEVEN

ON THE RESPONSIBILITY
OF THE ALPINE CLUBS

As an association of mountain climbers, the Alpine Club has decisive influence over the prospects of mountaineering in the twenty-first century. Thus, the future of alpine climbing depends far less on the behavior of the individual than on the behavior of the clubs. Just for that reason, many alpinists today view both the legacy and the future of the alpine tradition as endangered. The danger, in some people's opinion, comes from the fact that alpine clubs are undergoing a crisis. Many club members believe that their club now stands at the crossroads between a mountaineering association and a service provider. There's too much marketing of services and membership recruitment on the one hand, and on the other, not enough mountain climbing and too little engagement with the bolting issue or in the struggle to maintain open access to climbing areas.

Anyone familiar with the history of alpinism will know that none of these themes are new. Such fundamental questions have plagued alpine clubs from the very beginning, but above all since the turn of the twentieth century. Back then, many of the alpine associations experienced such a rapid rise in membership that the increase in quantity had marked consequences in terms of quality. At the time, small chapters with high alpinist standards lamented the monstrous influx of new members as a problematic growth that shook the alpine club down to the core of its values. And there were many discussions; for instance, the famous debate on the use of pitons, or the rhetorically brilliant crusades of lone unguided mountaineers against the downfall of alpine tradition, as in the writings of Hermann von Barth or Eugen Guido Lammer. These issues were polarizing, and everyone fought for the well-being of mountaineering according to his own ideals. Compromises were continually sought and reached—only to wind up disputed again sooner or later in the next argument. Will the arguing never end? Are such controversial topics dynamite that will someday blow our common interest group, the Alpine Club, to smithereens? Or do they provide the fuel that keeps the constantly growing community of mountain climbers going?

Why does our association spend its time debating themes that obviously bring it nothing but trouble? It is because since its inception, mountain climbing has always had a fundamental ethical dimension. Since the birth of mountaineering, people have been talking about the right and wrong way for climbers to behave; about the ideal structure of their associations; and about the point and meaning of mountain climbing. These questions are posed on the basis of a moral-philosophical foundation—the ethics of mountain climbing. And the liveliness of the ongoing debate shows that the ethical dimension of mountain climbing is not an aspect one can do without. But, then, what exactly *are* the ethics of mountain climbing?

The notion of ethics exists on a commonly held level of thinking that generally concerns itself with thorny issues, such as: What should one think about a society in which an eleven-year-old child is prosecuted for sexual offenses, while other children shoot each other with guns belonging to their parents, and this has no effect on gun-possession laws? Mountain climbing is not a matter of official state concern, and many would say that it shouldn't be taken any more seriously than it is. And they're right! That's why there will never be laws made especially for mountain climbers.

But outside the codex of the judicial system, there are also standards of behavior that are rooted, among other things, in common sense, mutual respect, and tradition. The climbing community also experiences these standards of behavior—its ethics—as a necessary, self-imposed structure of conduct. For the community of climbers, ethical standards are experienced as the architectural frame of the alpinist abode, within which one may move about in a reasonable fashion. If we examine the history of alpinism in this context, then, we discover that this dwelling has been repeatedly renovated, and the furniture frequently rearranged. There have been times when certain climbers have felt themselves to be strangers in this house, and often enough, everyone knew better in retrospect.

Ethics are a substantial component of climbing, without which mountain sports would collapse like a house of cards—like a house without architectural support and stability. And that is why this theme must remain under discussion. For a living association, this discussion doesn't just happen once; it must be an ongoing conversation. That's because ethics is not a timeless concept; any contemporary climber who has read climbing accounts from the time between 1920 and 1950 would hardly find that era's ethical conception of mountaineering acceptable. Ethics is a delicate flower subject to the vagaries of social attitudes, as well as to the normative force of de facto reality.

An example of the influence of changing social attitudes: Less than forty years ago, the super direttissimas, with their hundreds of bolts, were considered to be a highly undesirable trend. At the time, they were described as the murder of the impossible, and had a correspondingly bad reputation. Today, in contrast, highly bolted routes have reestablished themselves as dominant once again.

An example of the normative force of fact: the bolting debate. While the participants in this debate are laboriously attempting to cobble out a compromise, climbers are drilling bolts into alpine walls all over the place. Here, facts are being called into existence, and these newly created facts will permanently alter the course of alpinist history.

Both of these examples raise the question of how future generations—say, twenty years from now—will judge the conduct of the climbers and the alpine clubs of today. How do we now judge the era of the direttissima? On the other hand, how, in retrospect, do we now view Paul Preuß, or the redpoint movement, or the traditionally oriented climbing scene in Elbsandstein?

In alpinism, as in the alpine clubs, there is continuity and change. Anyone familiar with the American Alpine Club or the British Mountaineering Club knows that ethics are valued much more highly there than in our own case if we can even speak of valuing ethics at all in our present situation. I offer an example here, as well: A couple of years ago, Swiss mountain guides placed some fixed belay stations on the Zmutt Ridge of the Matterhorn, causing an outcry of indignation among alpinists in England. The context for their outrage was that in 1879, Albert Frederick Mummery, one of the most important British alpinists of the nineteenth century, had been the first to ascend this ridge. Safety concerns were cited as the justification for the "redevelopment" of previously nonexistent pitons, and questions arose regarding the actual possession of the Matterhorn.

Two different worldviews collided in the discussion. The Swiss argued that the Matterhorn belonged to them and was the workplace of Swiss mountain guides. Accordingly, they had the right to drill bolts to ensure their safety. The English argued from a historical standpoint: The Zmutt Ridge in its original condition was, in the line of its first ascent, an alpinist masterwork of historical significance. Further, they argued from an ethical standpoint: No one on Earth could actually possess the Matterhorn. We human beings could only possess the history of mountain climbing, and in the case of the Matterhorn, the British could claim a significant share of it.

What is the attitude of our own clubs to such alpinist masterworks? Above all, what actions do they take to preserve this cultural and historical heritage? Or isn't it a cultural and historical heritage at all? In that case, why do climbing clubs maintain museums of alpine history, such as the German Alpine Club's museum on the Praterinsel in Munich? Of course, the alpine clubs also understand that their most important museum is the Alps themselves. Here is where the climbers left their mark during each respective climbing epoch with their first ascents and their distinctive climbing styles.

A climber such as Reinhold Messner, for instance, influenced modern climbing like few others. He described the unlimited use of artificial climbing aids as the "murder of the impossible," whether in rock climbing or in high-altitude mountain climbing; with great foresight, he advocated an alpinism of self-restraint. Today, in contrast, the creative achievement and courage of first ascents and the adventurous uncertainty of rock climbing have in many cases given way to the certain knowledge that if you only have a sufficient number of bolts and artificial holds, anything is possible. That's why new routes opened up in alpine rock today are hardly worthy of note, in strong contrast to the achievements of the Slovenian climber Tomaž Humar, for instance, who climbed the south face of the Dhaulagiri solo; or the ascent of the now-famous "Action Directe" by the legendary Wolfgang Güllich. These achievements are built on an athletic foundation, and they will go down in history. The loss of charismatic climber Wolfgang Güllich weighs heavily on us today. With his sense of sportsmanship, deeply rooted in ethics and tradition, he should serve as a role model for the climbing world.

Without a positive role model, mountain climbing today finds itself in a quandary along a broad front. The protagonists have no respect for tradition and set themselves no limitations. What is the common line on chipped holds in French sport-climbing routes? When will the currently unfettered placement of fixed bolts in alpine terrain cease? Where is the consensus regarding foregoing bottled oxygen on high-altitude ascents? When will climbers on their way up to the summit of Everest finally quit going past their dying colleagues without stopping to help?

Who is at fault for this quandary? It would be wrong to place the fault with the younger generation. Rather, alpine clubs would be well advised to realize that they are actively promoting this state of affairs by their failure to take a position, and above all, by their failure to act. Alpine clubs must take action; then they would be able to achieve some results, as demonstrated, for instance, by the success the German Alpine Club has had with respect to the closing down of certain climbing areas in Germany. Here, a plan was conceived and implemented in many places. In this way, the German Alpine Club actively worked to protect its future. But has it done enough? The fact that many alpine clubs do not take a position on so many important subjects means that they must be considered culpable in promoting the developments discussed above.

I therefore urge alpine clubs to take better care of their own houses in the future—to actively protect their culture and the history and tradition of mountain climbing. The Alps and the world's mountains belong to no one, and therefore, they belong to all of us alike. They are a collectively owned piece of sporting equipment, but the ethical treatment of this equipment is marked by extreme individualism. No one feels like they need to justify their behavior to anyone else. Everyone does whatever he or she wants.

The idea that you should leave the mountain just like you found it is considered outmoded. Anyone who has seen the exhibit "Schöne neue Alpen" ("Brave New Alps") or leafed through Jürgen Winkler's volume of photographs, *Das andere Bild der Berge (A Different View of the Mountains)* can ascertain the utter failure of that notion. Alpine associations have pulled out of the discussion about underlying values in many areas of mountain climbing, and have delegated this discussion to the climbers themselves. The dispute about the redevelopment of routes in which climbers find themselves mired today was precipitated by the failure of alpine clubs to take an interest in what was actually happening. The fact is that today, a schism has occurred within the climbing scene in every region where redevelopment has taken place. Is that what we want?

I know that alpine associations are bombarded by many problems from without: mass transit, tourist industry development, environmental regulation . . . The discussion about the ethics of mountain climbing has decisively suffered under this onslaught of external issues. Instead of alpine clubs using the full weight and respect of their authority to offer a clear policy in their various publications and media campaigns, we have a bunch of contentious local factions. This is where I most deeply feel the failure of alpine clubs to provide guidance for our future engagement with the medium of rock!

In principle, the bolt is currently the only means of protection considered seriously. The regular piton has been practically discredited, and it may legitimately be feared that insurance companies might begin to interpret climbing with regular pitons as negligent behavior. Today, no one wants to hear anything about the skill and ability of earlier mountaineers, the ability of our father's generation to place a piton from the most difficult position. Often, we traditionalists tend to be presented as half-mad, under the motto "For they know not what they do." This is to say nothing of whether today's mountain climbers would even be capable of placing traditional protection themselves.

The same thing goes for all manner of camming devices. Apparently, it has now become completely irrelevant whether a route has been sent redpoint, entirely without any bolts, or whether the climber used bolts placed directly next to the cracks of classic routes. As a consequence, the question of whether such behavior is right or wrong has become moot, which comes down to the loss of ethics. Mountain climbing cannot exist without ethical principles. And who should take on responsibility for this, if not the alpine clubs—when the individual is not in a position to prevent our historical heritage from being gambled away on a massive scale.

Alpine clubs actually took on this responsibility once, in September of 2002, setting down their ethical principles in the Tyrol Declaration on Best Practice in Mountain Sports. What I find disturbing now, however, is the failure of alpine clubs to implement the principles formulated in the Declaration. In fact, it ought to be their duty to do so, since that is the only way that the Declaration, as an ethical framework, could provide the house of alpinism with a stable support system again, and offer an urgently needed foundation for future confrontations with political and environmental issues. If we wish to protect the future of alpinism, we must have clarity today about how this future is to be defined, and what we mean by it.

Alpinism does not mean just thoughtlessly going up a mountain, with everyone doing whatever he or she pleases. Although alpinism has no written laws, precisely for that reason, it has ethical principles, and this ethical foundation is a complicated conglomerate of majority and minority interests, of tradition and modernity. I strongly urge alpine clubs to once again turn their attention to what has given them their name: to the Alps, and to climbing. And I expect results—a clear signal from the climbing associations that they want to be among us again, among the mountain climbers.

CHAPTER TWENTY-EIGHT

DYNAMICS, PRECISION, AND ADVENTURE —"EL CORAZÓN"

With the redpoint ascent of "Bellavista," I was more or less back at the height of my climbing abilities again, for the first time in about five years. That was already evident early in the year with the first ascent of "Adrenaline" and "Orca," two old projects in Karlstein and at the Schleier Waterfall. It was the first time since 1996 that I was climbing routes in grade 8c+ again. For me, this was proof that despite my getting older, I still had plenty left in me where climbing was concerned, and that now, more than ever, I was in the best possible position to aim for further goals.

The year 2001 turned out to be a great one; there was every reason to celebrate, not just for me, but for my brother, too. In a masterful show of tactical and mountaineering skill, Thomas and Swiss climbers Iwan Wolf and Urs Stöcker managed to wrest the second ascent from the Ogre. After more than twenty expeditions had failed, after the two of us were driven off two years earlier, Thomas demonstrated all the qualities he embodies as a mountain climber. He knew to wait for just the right moment, and even let a competing American expedition go ahead of him. And while the Americans foundered on the Ogre's massive peak, Thomas and his Swiss friends stayed out of their way by completing the first ascent of Ogre III, where they were able to get thoroughly acclimatized in advance of their actual destination. Thomas's team took their chance. They were in the right place at the right time, and in the end, they stood at the summit of what is probably the most formidable mountain in the world.

It's hard to know why there are always these phases—years in which absolutely nothing succeeds, although you're in the best possible shape and giving it your all, and then years in which everything just goes well. What's important is that in such phases, you don't let things lie, but rather seize every opportunity and grab everything that's there for the taking.

Naturally, I would have loved to have stood up on the summit with Thomas as he made his great Ogre dream come true, but I had decided on a different direction. I had realized that I couldn't possibly be everywhere at once; that I couldn't allow myself to be caught in the pull of other people's expectations; and that, above all, I had to follow my own heart, where goals like "Bellavista" were at the top of the list. But there were others, too. In the previous year, when Thomas and I completed the "Golden Gate," it was actually a different project than the one on which we had originally set our sights: the long, narrow dihedral above the "Heart" that rips through the wall of El Capitan for 400 meters. What was still too difficult a year ago was now just right. After the hard winter training season, after "Adrenaline," "Orca," and "Bellavista," I was better prepared for this mission than ever before.

I set off with Max Reichel from Bad Reichenhall and was filled with enthusiasm by what I discovered. The marvelous thing about

El Capitan is that it repeatedly shows itself in a new light, and I am never bored climbing its walls. If I had thought the last time that I was familiar with everything, I now discovered a new aspect that was previously unknown to me. A big wall is an adventure playground, where climbing plots out the path to the unknown. It is not only the technical difficulties of climbing that play a role here. Tension and fear are constant companions on mentally demanding routes, and the sparser the protection, the more adventurous is your progress. In these potentially dangerous routes, experience and self-confidence are the keys to success. To court danger, to push your limits, and still be able to calculate the risk is the game—a high-stakes game in which your muscle power is just as decisive as your adrenaline level.

Adrenaline! In the gray light of morning, I could just about make out what triggered it above me: the "Beak Flake," the first major hurdle of the route "El Corazón." A week earlier, I was able to make the first ascent of the route with Max—a rock face as smooth as a blank wall, shot through with the mere hint of a line. The fine shadow of a flake traced its course down for 80 long meters, ending 10 meters above a wide ledge in an overhanging wave of unfractured granite. It's the most difficult portion of "El Corazón." The barely 2-millimeter-wide steel blade of the Bird Beak was the only protection here. The special hook for extremely fine cracks was wedged in the rock only 15 millimeters deep, 8 meters above the ledge. The probability that the metal would not withstand the impact force was significant. I had to assume that a fall here would be fatal. The risk of this crux was only acceptable if you could master the subsequent 2 meters—if you could virtually exclude the possibility of failure.

One week after the first ascent, I had gone up again with Max for a continuous redpoint, and now found myself at the point where I had to make up my mind to go on. I was tied to the rope, running through the carabiner, which was attached by a short sling to the Bird Beak. Below, an attentive Max was belaying, and yet I was actually climbing "unprotected"—free solo, in my mind. I was afraid, but at the same time, I knew that I could do it. I was in control of the fear. It didn't grow into nervousness.

I decided to go for it. Two sidepulls, the footholds were almost at the same height—and then the jump. Both hands let go of the rock, the upper torso flying upward in a wave-like motion a hair's-breadth from the wall. Despite the great velocity, my eyes were fixed on the goal, coordinating the movement. My fingers dug deep into the start of the "Beak Flake." My gaze left my fingers and followed the fine shadow of the flake, which ripped through the granite of El Capitan in an unbroken line for the next 80 meters.

It was a short stretch in this huge wall—but for me, everything that I associate with climbing was concentrated within it: athleticism, dynamics, precision, and adventure. Accordingly, though "El Corazón" is only one of my many first ascents, it distilled the essence of everything: Yosemite, a paradise for me as a climber; El Capitan, which I consider the most beautiful wall in the world; the fantastic rock; the naturally occurring line; the mental challenge; and the resulting promise of adventure that "El Corazón" holds out for anyone who attempts it.

CHAPTER TWENTY-NINE

CERRO TORRE
AND FITZ ROY

Patagonia is an absolutely beautiful country, marked by its great expanses, the ceaselessly howling winds, and its very own unique brand of loneliness. At least, it had been lonely for a long time, until the exchange rate of the Argentine peso was de-coupled from the dollar, and all of a sudden everything was a third or a quarter of its original price. And so, around the turn of this century, this land, too, was discovered by tourism. But aside from the crowds at the tourist spots, Patagonia is a very sparsely populated land. The settlements often lie 100 or 200 kilometers apart. In between, lost in the expanse, are the *estancias*—ranches that make extensive use of the land by grazing thousands of sheep.

These *estancias* are often so wide-ranging that outposts—so-called *puestos*—are necessary in order to effectively manage the agricultural use of the land. In my travels in Patagonia, I had the good fortune to get to know not only the world of the mountains, but also the land and its people. The *paisanos* have a lonesome job on their *puestos*. From early spring until late in the fall, they are left to their own devices in their remote huts. Together with a few dogs and a couple of horses, they live in complete isolation from civilization. No telephone, no radio, no supply lines—absolutely nothing. Just some other *paisanos* who might come by once or twice a week to drink maté together. There's not much talk among them. These are reserved people. And though these infrequent gatherings mean a lot to them on the one hand, on the other, they are not particularly loquacious due to their extremely solitary lifestyle.

The winds of Patagonia are legendary. The region around the mountain of Fitz Roy lies far enough to the south on the continent to fall within the realm of the westerly wind belt that encircles Antarctica like a ring. The winds whip the land with an unrelenting constancy, and the vegetation bears its marks. The growth of the trees leaves absolutely no doubt about the direction from which the wind blows. It is, however, neither the wide expanses nor the winds that draw tourists down to the far south year after year—it is, above all, the mountains. Though these mountains are barely higher than 3,000 meters, it is not altitude alone that counts. In Patagonia, it is above all the spectacular image of the granite towers. What they may be lacking in terms of absolute height, they make up for in their impressive dimensions. The summits shoot up into the sky up to 2,000 meters above the surrounding glaciers. Fitz Roy, Cerro Torre, Torres del Paine—breathtaking natural structures in the eyes of the tourists; hallowed names that resound in the ears of alpinists.

Even the glacial world here is unique. The famous Hielo Continental Sur, the ice cap that stretches for hundreds of kilometers over the southern portion of the continent—the hidden side of Patagonia—can only be seen in a few places on Argentinean territory. These few places are all the more well-known, such as where the massive Glaciar Perito Moreno pushes out into flatland and calves into the Lago Argentino.

Anyone who travels to this country to see the mountains needs to come with lots of time to spare. The summits are stuck under cloud cover for over 300 days a year, and are pummeled by seemingly endless bad weather. When the rare periods of fine weather do occur, they are usually very brief—a particularly difficult circumstance for mountain climbers. If you're really lucky, you might get an entire day of brilliant blue skies and calm winds. It is futile to hope for more. Supposedly, stable periods of five nice days in a row have been known to happen every once in a while, but seldom when you're actually there yourself.

Thus, in Patagonia, the essential key to success is speed. Only a team that functions like a well-oiled machine and is absolutely up to the challenge can get the better of these mountains in alpine style. Unfortunately, even to this day, the ambitious first ascents here are mostly accomplished with the help of fixed ropes. There is hardly a major line in Patagonia that has not been opened in that style. Frequently, the brief windows of calm weather, months apart, are used to wrangle one more pitch along the hoped-for route, and to install a few more meters of fixed rope. And for all that, these mountains seem to be practically made for alpine-style climbing. The climbing itself is much like in the Alps, and the absolute altitude and the temperatures are moderate. Only the conditions and the terrain are that much more extreme. A paradise for alpinists!

On December 30, 2000—before the opening of the exchange rate, and therefore before the influx of tourists—Toni Gutsch and I arrived in El Chaltén, which was at the time still a small and peaceful place at the foot of the Fitz Roy. We had reached Argentina only by way of some detours, since the Argentine airlines had for a brief time disappeared from the map during the economic depression, meaning that El Calafate on the shore of Lago Argentino was no longer reachable by plane. Our trip was therefore lengthy and complicated, but ultimately that much more interesting.

Toni and I landed in Punta Arenas on the Strait of Magellan and took advantage of the comparatively cheap Chilean prices to buy four weeks' worth of provisions. The bus took us northward, across the flat, seemingly endless land. In Puerto Natales, we had to wait a day for the next bus connection to Argentina, and after we finally got on our way again, we spent six hours waiting at the border. Not that there was such a lot of traffic here—our bus was in fact the only vehicle waiting to cross over. But presumably for that very reason, the border guards responsible for checking the passengers had decided to make a whole day of it.

Another day on the bus, and shortly before midnight, we found ourselves in El Chaltén. We plopped ourselves down in the first hostel we came across, where I was glad to find that I could still order up two beers, and even gladder that they came in liter bottles. Toni would not be persuaded to celebrate the day with me. Finally, I actually had to play a real trump card: "Now you can't tell me that you won't drink a toast to my health on my birthday!" We had now been on the road in the far south for four days, and we were finally in the land of our dream mountains.

The very next morning, we set off to put the 12-kilometer-long trek to the base camp of Cerro Torre behind us. It is doubtless among the most impressive and beautiful mountains of the world, and probably also the most highly contested summit in the history of mountain climbing. The original cause of the controversy was Italian mountaineer Cesare Maestri's claim to its first ascent. In 1958, Maestri had traveled to Cerro Torre with an expedition led by Bruno Detassis. After a preliminary exploration, the expedition leader had declared the mountain to be unscalable on the east side, and Maestri began to hatch his own plans.

A year later, Maestri undertook the next attempt at the "unscalable" mountain. Together with Toni Egger, from eastern Tyrol, and Cesarino Fava, an Italian living in Argentina, Maestri organized a fateful expedition. He did indeed come home a hero, but a tragic one; according to his own testimony, he and Toni Egger had reached the summit via the east and north side on January 30, but during the descent, Egger had lost his life in an ice avalanche. Maestri came home from the trip without any pictures. The camera had been buried with Egger. Doubts about Maestri's story were not sparked by the missing evidence. Rather, it was the contradictory, often implausible, and very imprecise descriptions that made Maestri's claims seem less and less trustworthy to the alpine world, with every new publication and public appearance.

For a long time, all attempts to repeat the route foundered, and with every failed attempt it became clearer how difficult it was to realize this goal. Indeed, almost forty-seven years went by before the north face was taken by Italian climber Ermanno Salvaterra, together with Alessandro Beltrami and Rolando Garibotti. During the ascent, in November 2005, not a single one of the seventy bolts that Maestri reported leaving on the mountain were found—and none were found during any of the previous failed assaults, either. The wall was untouched. Despite so much clear, overwhelming evidence to the contrary, Maestri continues to fight for the recognition of his first ascent. But at least among alpinists, he is no longer taken seriously.

In 1970, Maestri popped up once again to try to prove to the world that he was capable of capturing Cerro Torre. Apparently, he didn't have much faith in his own mountaineering prowess, as he took with him an enormous amount of fixed rope and a compressor. This now-infamous compressor was intended to help him place the bolt ladders on which he would rely to overcome the difficulties of the projected route up the southeast arête. In the course of two different trips to Patagonia, he and his Italian companions, Ezio Alimonta and Carlo Claus, worked their way doggedly up to the top of the vertical wall. What is astounding, however, is that he ignored the ice mushroom on the summit. By way of explanation, he stated that as an extraneous buildup of ice, it did not constitute part of the mountain, and therefore did not interest him. Maestri turned around at the start of the summit's ice cap and did not even give his partners an opportunity to try for the top. The fact is that even with the help of a compressor, the ice mushroom evaded capture, and so for the second time, Maestri failed to attain his desired goal—the incontestable first ascent of Cerro Torre.

That distinction fell four years later to Italian Casimiro Ferrari, who successfully first ascended Cerro Torre on its west face with a large team from the ranks of the Ragni di Lecco group.

Today, Maestri's "Compressor Route" is by far the easiest—and for that reason, the most popular—route on Cerro Torre, by which over 95 percent of climbers reach the summit. Toni and I had chosen it as well. I wanted to find out if, eventually, a free ascent of the route would be possible. As usual, the expedition began with the obligatory waiting for good weather, but after three days, Toni and I were released from purgatory. It wasn't a perfect window of good weather—still a little windy and mostly overcast—but the mountain presented itself as climbable. We made very good progress, but I had to abandon my hopes of a free ascent very soon. The only other way around the 90-meter bolt traverse is a chimney on the right that turns into a waterfall in fine weather. Faced with the rather uninviting alternative, Toni and I went up the bolt ladder installed by Maestri like everyone else. From the wall's midpoint, the "Compressor Route" is a completely equipped via ferrata occasionally interrupted by not particularly steep stretches of ice. Accordingly, we made brisk progress and reached the summit terrace by sundown.

Transfixed, we watched as the last traces of the sun disappeared over the mountains and the reds gradually but inevitably dissolved into the cold blue of the dusk. Toni and I had agreed in advance that if conditions allowed, we would fulfill an unusual dream: to bivouac on the summit of the Torre. In the certain knowledge that a very cold night awaited us, we sat in our bivy sack, way up high, in a little cave in the interior of the ice mushroom. Since time immemorial, mankind has attempted to develop strategies to battle the cold and to evade its grasp. It may be difficult to understand why someone would willingly expose himself to the cold with almost no protection, but there is hardly another circumstance in which the outdoors can be felt so intensely: the mountain, the cold, and little, insignificant man against them. It's true that what we mountain climbers do is a provocation to reason. We obviously have a compulsion to rush headlong from one adventure to the next. I am indeed in the grip of an addiction that does not let me rest—which is okay, because I have absolutely no desire to rest, anyway! Over and over, I go in search of new horizons. I have to constantly reinvent myself and begin anew. Without this continual challenge, I would be utterly drained of energy and vitality, because this relentless activity is my daily bread. It keeps me in motion, and without it, I would wither like a plant without water or light.

The night turned seriously cold. I was able to lose myself in other thoughts for only brief moments before the cold pulled me back to Patagonia, to the summit of the Cerro Torre. The cold crept slowly into my bones—slowly, but just as inevitably as the light disappears at dusk. I was overcome by waves of uncontrollable shivering that lasted for minutes at a time, shaking my entire body. Then, calm would return, and sometimes, it even seemed like it had gotten warmer. But that was just an illusion that temporarily deceived you. The cold dominated everything, and your only hope was the certain knowledge that at some point, morning would come and the sun would rise in the east.

The moment when it finally appeared on the horizon was truly magical. Only a few minutes before the cold had had us completely in its grip, making us suffer. But now, with the first rays of the sun, which did not yet have any physical impact, our vitality returned. We took up our ice axes and climbed up the last few meters to the highest point of Cerro Torre, on the ice mushroom—one of the most bizarre points on this planet.

Morning brought an absolutely fantastic light. As hard as the night had been, the spectacle of the sun as it began to flood Patagonia with its light was, from this perspective, incomparable, indescribable, and worth any price. We spent only a few minutes up there, enjoying the extraordinary atmosphere, and soon after, we began our long descent.

By afternoon, Toni and I had already returned to base camp, utterly happy with our unusual bivouac. As is par for the course in Patagonia, the weather had already begun to turn nasty during our nearly endless rappel, and shortly before we reached base camp, the mountain disappeared entirely in a massive bank of clouds. We had reached the summit; a tent and a warm sleeping bag waited a few minutes away—what did we care about the weather? We had our mountain and we were ready to return to civilization.

Everything was packed, and we were actually planning on marching back to El Chaltén the next morning. But we were faced with an unusual problem: There was a clear blue sky and the air pressure was even higher than when we had started off for Cerro Torre. A brief survey of what might be doable in the time we had left brought us to the Fitz Roy—at 3,406 meters, the highest summit in the entire region, and like the Cerro Torre, a real climber's mountain. We wanted to go up along the route taken by its French first ascensionists, Lionel Terray and Guido Magnone: a long approach over a glacier, then a 300-meter-high ice couloir, and last of all, the centerpiece—a 600-meter-high rock pillar that, as a free climb, required mastery of grade 7.

In fact, Toni and I were still tired from Cerro Torre, but that was exactly why we chose the Fitz Roy as our goal, a mountain well worth the struggle. It actually did have one single disadvantage: The base camp at Fitz Roy is 12 kilometers away from the base camp at Cerro Torre. In addition, there was the 10-kilometer-long march over the glacier and the whole question of the altitude differential. All in all, it was almost 50 kilometers over a difference of 3,000 vertical meters. But that was just how we liked it.

And so, in the late afternoon, after we had rearranged our backpacks, we set off toward Fitz Roy. During the night, we covered the entire hike over the glacier, as well as the ice couloir, and an hour before sunrise we reached the Brecha de los Italianos—the start of the actual climb. As Toni and I waited for daylight, we heard, coming from somewhere in the darkness, the sound of familiar voices—Bavarian voices. Indeed, it was two climbers from Garmisch, Peter Anzenberger and Jörg Pflugmacher. Although we had heard of them, we had never met personally on the mountain before.

And so, the four of us enjoyed this fantastic day together: sun, best-quality granite, a wonderful route. Under these perfect conditions, I even managed to free everything—something that you can never plan on doing in advance in these large mountains, but you must certainly grab the opportunity when it arises. The two Garmisch climbers went up ahead, and we took up the rear, and by midday yet another dream was made reality for Toni and me. We had reached both of the major Patagonian summits. Soon after Cerro Torre, we were also able to stand atop the Fitz Roy.

∞

CHAPTER THIRTY

FREE SOLO

In the middle of an overhanging wall, in an exposed position—
fingertips in two tiny handholds, feet in two tiny footholds, 200
meters of air below. No harness, no rope. Nothing that could prevent
a fall. Your life is very literally hanging in the balance.

This is a situation that would make anyone fundamentally
nervous simply to imagine it. The very thought of hanging over an
abyss by nothing more than your fingertips triggers anxiety. Humans
have an instinctive fear of falling that is deeply anchored in our
psyche. Since primeval times we have encountered great heights,
which have always meant danger for humans. That is why the instinctive fear of falling is of existential significance for mankind, necessary
to ensure the survival of the species. Only someone who feels afraid
of a dangerous situation will behave with appropriate caution; then,
even though the danger remains present, it does not become truly
life-threatening.

Free solo climbing—climbing without a safety net—is the most uncompromising form of climbing. Only your own climbing prowess and mental strength can ensure your survival. There is no room for mistakes. If body and spirit are not operating at 100 percent capacity, the consequences can be fatal. The instinctive human fear of falling ensures that anyone who encounters the vertical realm of climbing will be fully conscious of the danger that it holds. With free solo climbing in high grades of difficulty, and on big walls, the risk is so patently obvious that the mental strain of it becomes the determining factor. Only a very few climbers whose technical and mental abilities are at the highest possible level can venture out on this exclusive limb. Only a very few have this extreme danger so much under control that it is only negligibly life-threatening.

The long and intensive training required for free solo climbing is above all psychological. Very gradually, starting with easy and short routes, you need to find out how secure you actually are when you're climbing without protection. Am I standing securely on the footholds? Is my climbing position stable? Do I feel secure moving on the rock? These are questions that you can only answer when you're "on the safe side"—that is, far under the technical grade you're actually capable of climbing. At this level, you can collect information—feedback from your body and your psyche. Slowly, you discover to what extent you are mentally prepared to go another little step further.

Most of the time, the fear of danger produces a more or less palpable residue of apprehension that makes your movements tense and uncertain—a reaction that for most will only be understood as fear. The horizons of a climber who feels this apprehension intensely will always be limited, and this is why most climbers would never be capable of climbing free solo on really difficult and exposed terrain. It is only when the fear of danger produces nothing more than an extraordinarily high level of concentration that you can move over the rock in a relaxed and secure manner. Only then will you be able to take very small steps toward the difficult routes and the big walls without being tied to a rope.

Still, for all the ability and concentration of a climber, there will always be a certain element of danger. This remaining risk, the actual threat to life and limb, may be calculated by means of a reasonable, competent estimation of risk factors. How much remaining risk an individual is ultimately prepared to take on is a matter of personal character. But the number of accidents in the history of free solo climbing in difficult terrain suggests that only a very few of its practitioners are in fact weary of life.

To my mind, in any case, these free solo climbers are far less suicidal than many Everest climbers who seem to believe that paying $100,000 assures their safety. It's not enough that almost all the contenders for the world's highest summit are the rawest amateurs who haven't got a clue about the complex layers of danger their revered mountain has in store for them. On top of that, with every meter of altitude they gain, they lose more and more of their minds. This process can even go so far that a significant number of these would-be conquerors eventually get the idea of bivouacking then and there—at 8,500 meters, with temperatures of 50-below. Robbed of their senses, they are no longer capable of valuing their lives. They want only one thing: to sleep. And if they aren't hauled down the mountain by a Sherpa, they'll sleep forever.

Alpinism can count many high points in its history, distinguished by the fact that the alpinists in question have pushed the limits. While alpinism may have continually evolved over the years, one thing has always remained constant: Pushing the limits is risky. Going to the limit of what's possible means seeking a confrontation between man and mountain. Risk is therefore an integral part of mountain climbing. It was no different in Paul Preuß's time than it was later for Hermann Buhl, Walter Bonatti, Doug Scott, or Reinhold Messner. It is precisely this search for the limits of the possible, this risky, direct confrontation between man and mountain, that is the very motivation driving us to seek out situations that most people instinctively wish to avoid.

Paul Preuß was one of the first climbers to take on deliberately the risk of free solo climbing. For him, it was all about climbing prowess in the greatest possible exposure, about pushing the limits. And he was probably the first to assault exposed walls deliberately without protection or a rope. The free-climbing revolution of the 1970s could also be understood as looking back to the climbing philosophy of Paul Preuß, and his call for climbers to consciously forego reliance on artificial aids. But what's really impressive with respect to Preuß's theories is the action with which he backed up his words. He put up his boldest route, the "Preuß Wall," in July 1911 on the Guglia di Brenta in the Dolomites. Paul Preuß was able to free-solo this masterful first ascent—vertical rock, logical line, great exposure. In none of his other first ascents did he express his spirit, his abilities, his own self, as clearly as he did in this route, which will forever remain a memorial to him and his vision.

Paul Preuß died in 1913. He fell during his attempted first ascent of the Manndlkogel North Corner in the Dachstein Mountains, and thus became the most prominent victim of free solo climbing. Subsequently, it has all too often been remarked that Preuß was the victim of his own philosophy. But it was precisely his most extreme ventures that filled his existence with passion and vitality. One of his most striking qualities, reflected in everything he did, was his perfectionism—his search for the perfect attitude, the perfect style, the perfect ascent. His theories were elitist, his ideas simply too bold to be generally understood at the time. But despite that, on a personal level, Paul Preuß did not come across as arrogant or above it all; he was said to be friendly and approachable, and in a certain sense, completely normal. The fall that ended his life was not the result of a harebrained idea. It was simply one of the numerous accidents that unfortunately happen in the world of the mountains.

I don't see myself as a risk-taker when I'm free-soloing on steep rock either. I understand the risk. If it seems too high to me, I retreat. If the risk seems acceptable, then I get to live out my passion, like Paul Preuß. The fundamental motivation for my engagement with this uncompromising form of climbing arose out of an old dream: to climb a big wall in the Alps all alone, with no help whatsoever. No harness, no rope. Nothing. Just as in the case of extreme sport climbing, here, too, I am concerned with the conscious search for the outer limits of what I am capable of. Free solo is uncompromising, direct, and authentic; I hadn't tried to push myself to my personal limit until I felt I'd reached a certain level of climbing ability.

Now, I felt ready to make this old dream a reality.

The Direttissima on the Cima Grande: 500 meters high, with a big overhang. When you stand at the bottom and look up at this overhanging bulwark above you, it seems completely monstrous. That was exactly why it was this very wall that I'd imagined in my dreams; there was none more exposed, blank, and inapproachable than this. I wanted the furthest extreme of what was possible, and here it was. At the same time, I knew that I could only realize this dream after traveling a long road of training and preparation.

Over the years, I had been naturally driven to free-solo various classic climbing routes in grade 6. These were always intense, lovely days for me, where I was alone with myself. Here, it was not difficulty or extremity, but the free-solo encounter that made the ascent incomparable, and turned an otherwise banal classic into something special. I knew from these experiences that my main task would be, above all, mental preparation. I had to become comfortable with moving on difficult rock without protection, but not so comfortable that I would slip into a carefree routine.

I began with short routes at the climbing crag, at first with easy ones in grade 7 and 8. Later on, I tried soloing in grade 9, followed by the first route in the lower 10. With increasing difficulty, the climbing moves that I trusted myself to perform free solo became more complex. Finally, I arrived at the point of trying the first dynamic moves, and that is the point at which free-soloing becomes extreme. Only absolute self-confidence—complete trust in your own physical and mental abilities—can create the conditions necessary to perform dynamic moves at life-threatening heights.

After half a year of training at the crag and on a number of alpine walls, my preparations for the Direttissima were finished. I was convinced that I was capable of free-soloing the route "safely." Still, in the final days before the assault, I was anxious about falling. My thoughts revolved around the moment when a hold would break, and I would tip back away from the wall into a free fall. What would be going through my mind at the moment? Would I be angry at myself for the mistake, for having chosen this fate? Or would extreme acceleration override all possibility of thought? What would happen to me when I landed on the talus slope? Would I feel anything? Despite these dark thoughts, after four days of practicing the route, I was also absolutely certain that I now knew every single difficult meter of it cold—that I had mastered every single move. Then the fear would creep back in, and I found myself on the same emotional roller coaster again and again.

In the hour it took for me to approach the start of the climb, the reality of the world around me faded away to only a dim perception. The contradictory feelings that had plagued me during the night were still with me. They would hurry my step, drive me on, nip at my heels, then abate and allow me to calm down, only to well up again. At the foot of the wall, it was clear to me that I could not start in this state. I definitely should not climb in the grip of these dark thoughts! I paced to and fro at the foot of the Cima Grande once more, then sat back down. I knew that I absolutely had to try it today. It was now or never! My thoughts were completely consumed by this route and would not allow me to break off now and postpone the decision till another time. I had come to the point where I wished I had never set my sights on this project. But I no longer had any choice. I had to go up; I had to try it. I was compelled to decide this very day whether or not I would attempt to free-solo this 500-meter route.

This compulsion hit me hard. Just two days earlier, I had not yet reckoned on it. I had believed I was still entirely free to decide what day I chose for the attempt. But now, my mind was possessed, and this was a blow to my psyche. I had wanted to avoid pressure at all costs, and now it was there. I was like a hunted animal, crouching tensely under the wall, waiting for the outcome of the decision I would make in the next few minutes. Waves of contradictory feelings churned my thoughts into chaos. I was overwhelmed.

Mechanically, I pulled on my climbing shoes, tied on my chalk bag, and climbed the first few meters. I was completely numb. I felt nothing. There was no way I could go on like this. I climbed back down and immediately had a sense of relief. I had broken it off. I felt freer.

The pressure was still there, but it no longer had such a strong effect on me. Now I knew that I possessed enough control to turn back if I could not liberate my thoughts by the time I reached the "point of no return." The first 80 meters of the wall were not really difficult, and I could always downclimb if I had to. But once I decided to climb past the "point of no return," I had to live with the consequences—from that point on, I would have to climb up the next 500 meters whether I wanted to or not.

In full awareness of the consequences, and in full awareness of my freedom of choice, I decided to try it one more time. I ascended the first 80 meters. Whereas in the hours before the ascent, I'd been afraid and exceptionally nervous, now, when I was finally moving up the wall, the numbness was dispelled by the smooth routine of my "normal operating mode." My thoughts were free to concentrate on climbing. I no longer felt any fear; I was far too focused on my movement now to have any time to be afraid.

After twenty minutes, I reached the point of no return. But in fact, the decision had long been made. The crux for me lay not here, at the critical point, but rather at the start; the barrier I'd had to overcome was leaving the ground. Free-soloing demands not only self-control but a great effort of will to overcome your fears. I had mastered the latter by leaving the ground, and 150 meters above the ground, the former now seemed a far easier task.

After eight pitches, I reached the large ledge before the crux pitches. Up to this point, everything had gone perfectly, but now I felt mentally fatigued. I would not be able to sustain this level of concentration any longer without a break. I had been climbing continuously for fifty minutes. All of the senses that had been employed in getting me up had been under constant strain. I had to refuel again. I lay down flat on the ledge and stared for a long time up into the roofs—the crux section. A far overhanging bulwark of yellow dolomite; 120 meters of climbing; three pitches in grade 8. Moreover, unlike climbing with a rope, in this overhanging terrain I would not be able to use the belays to rest, which undoubtedly raised the actual difficulty of the stretch. I would have to put it all behind me in one go, without an opportunity to recover, either physically or mentally. But I knew that my technical climbing skills were far above the difficulties of the route, so this fact did not worry me. After twenty minutes, I sat back up, checked my climbing shoes, dipped my hands in the chalk bag, and climbed on.

After 80 meters, I climbed over the belay stance for the last of the three pitches. There were 50 more meters to go before the next ledge. This last steep pitch juts out in a 6-meter overhang and is extremely exposed, and right at this point, the rock is particularly loose. That was why it was so essential to climb the route several times on the rope in advance of the actual free-solo ascent. That was the only way I could make sure that I wasn't entrusting my life to a questionable, crumbly hold. Pressing on, I was beginning to feel the strain of climbing on the overhangs without a break. But I still had enough power to remain in control. I moved in a constant rhythm, slowly and deliberately paying attention to every detail. I didn't want anything to take me by surprise. I wanted to maintain perfect equilibrium at every moment—to press my fingers into the holds with doubled strength. This doubled power gave me the self-confidence I needed to free-solo climb 250 meters above the start of the route, but at the same time, it also took its toll on me up here.

The last difficult meters, 300 meters above the start. Gradually, the end was coming within reach—and yet the crux, the most-exposed point of the whole Direttissima, still awaited me. Everything below me broke away in the steep overhang, and I hung there all alone in this very hostile world. The holds on the subsequent meters were good, but far apart. They required decisive execution of highly athletic moves. That was the task before me: decisive pulling through with no hesitation, no time to consider, and with complete focus on what was essential right at that precise moment. It was an altered state that subsided only slowly, as the difficulties began to decrease again. Gradually, I started to take in the world around me once more, to see the clouds, the shreds of fog that constantly drifted up the north face; the higher I climbed, the calmer and more liberated I felt.

With the Cima Grande, I did more than just attain a summit: I accomplished something that had seemed absolutely impossible to me from the vantage point of the bottom. As I arrived at the summit, all the tension that had accompanied me during my preparations and during the actual ascent fell away instantly. For a brief time, I was like a flash of light: I existed only in the now, in the present moment. The intensity of what I had just experienced allowed no room for any thought of the past or the future, and thus, completely liberated me.

Mentally and emotionally, the Direttissima was, and remains, the personal high point of my climbing career. Which means neither that there is nothing after it, nor that there can be no future. Man goes on living as long as he has dreams.

"I always give them God's blessing when they go."
Maria Huber, mother of the Huberbuam, *talks about her
fears*

Karin Steinbach: *Mrs. Huber, how, as a mother, do you
stand it when your own son is climbing, alone and unprotected, up a 500-meter-high wall that isn't exactly known for
its solid rock?*
Maria Huber: I don't know how I could have stood it if
I actually knew about it. Fortunately, I only found out
about it afterwards, when it was on the "Backpack Radio"
show, and everyone was calling me with questions. Alex
had every reason not to tell me about it in advance. Naturally, he knew how worried I would have been if I had
known.

*But what about when Alexander or Thomas, or both togeth-
er, are on an expedition, or in Yosemite Valley—do you know
about it then?*
Yes. And sometimes I really don't know how I can get
through the days. You sit around being nervous, can't get
up to anything. You're afraid of the telephone ringing.
I had always told them, when everything goes well, you
don't even need to call. If I don't hear from them, I know
that they're okay. And if anything were to happen, I would
find out very quickly anyway. I was always happy when I
didn't hear from them at all.

*And even when they were young, they often only told you the
half of it, didn't they?*
Back then, too, they didn't always tell me all their plans,
so I wouldn't worry. But naturally, I feared for their safety.

On the other hand, I knew that my husband had taught them everything they needed to know. They had a very good teacher in him. Actually, I could always trust them.

What sort of relationship do you have to climbing?
When I was young, I had absolutely no interest in climbing. I first came to it through my husband. We spent a lot of time climbing together, above all, here in the Berchtesgaden Alps. But those weren't difficult routes. The real extreme tours—those, my husband always went on with his friends. After we had the boys, we started taking them hiking with us very early, and they always liked it best when there was something for them to clamber up. Then, when my youngest, Karina, was born, I stayed home with her for a while and my husband took the two boys to the mountains. When Karina got old enough, then all five of us went together. That was a wonderful time back then. And that's when the seeds were planted for the children, so that they would always be drawn to the mountains later.

And so that they would be passionate about climbing, above all else?
When it comes to climbing, my husband simply passed his own passion down to them. He took them on a lot of climbing trips; taught it to them from the ground up. But he also took them up to the four-thousanders, to the Valais. They always went there early in the year, ski-touring. That was a very big thing for Alexander. At first, Thomas always said, "You can't come; you're too little." Well, that really stuck in Alex's craw, and he just kept pestering my husband until he was finally allowed to go too.

Was there already competition between Thomas and Alexander back then?

Yes, if you want to call it that. Really, it's just that their father fostered their ambition, and naturally that also fanned the flames of competition between them. But more than anything, they are a very successful climbing team together. They complement each other perfectly. They've often said, "We're always at our best together." But they also fought a lot. There's been some unpleasantness between them. I have the impression now that they've found a good solution, that each can go his own way and let the other do his own thing. Right now, they're getting along really well.

Was there competition in other areas too, not just with climbing?

Well, with Alexander, for instance, I can remember one episode. He was a very sweet child, very attached to me, a real mama's boy. When Karina was born and my husband came to the hospital with the two boys, Alex said to me, when he saw her for the first time: "Geez, Mama, enough with the babies already!" He must have immediately felt the rivalry with his sister. And with Thomas, the thing was that he didn't like his sister's name. We had actually christened her Karin, but he came up with Karina, and we got so used to it that at some point she just became Karina.

What would you say is Alexander's most notable quality?

His determination. Once he decides to undertake something, he pursues it doggedly, without stopping to look left or right. He achieves his goals. And he's unbelievably intelligent. He never had to do much for school; everything came easy for him. Thomas had more difficulties. When Alexander plans something, he calculates everything in advance. He says that comes from studying physics. His way of thinking and his worldview were shaped by his studies. He weighs everything carefully, tries to understand all the connections, and then decides.

Where does your children's determination come from, this incredible ability to follow through? It's not just true of Alexander; Thomas and Karina have it too.

This persistence, this tenacity, probably comes from the fact that even as young children they were always kept very busy. We never let them sit around with nothing to do. On the one hand there was always work to do on the farm; on the other, they had their sports, and their music—everyone at our house played an instrument. They all started in kindergarten with the recorder. Alexander played piano and flute. Thomas played the accordion and guitar. He plays in a band, where he's the singer now, and they're even making a CD. My husband plays violin. He's been the leader of a men's choir for a long time. Karina also studied violin, starting in first grade. And the four of them often played music together at home, and at parties and weddings. All three of the children have great ambition—as parents, we modeled that for them. You could say that Thomas and Alexander are such good climbers because their father pushed them so hard. He was their role model, and he had very high expectations of them. What really makes my husband happy now is the fact that both of them have managed to make their hobby, their passion, into a profession. He himself couldn't do that when he was young, even though he would have loved to. He lived for mountain climbing too, you know.

Isn't living your life just for mountain climbing a little one-sided?

Sometimes, sure. But Alexander would like to have a family with children, too. He really loves his two nephews and little niece, and they adore their uncle Alexander. He just hasn't found the right woman yet. If he feels hemmed in, then it doesn't work. He's a lot like my husband that way; you couldn't hold him down either. Ever since he retired, he's been climbing more than ever, though not such difficult routes as before. If someone feels the pull of the mountains, you can't hold him back. It's pointless.

Will Alexander ever hang up his climbing shoes?

No, I can't imagine he would ever do that. When he's older, certainly he will undertake less-risky projects, I think. But climbing will always have great significance for him. He has such a strong connection to the mountains, he would never give it up. My husband is still comfortable at the 6th or 7th grade; right now, he's in Italy, climbing with a friend of his as we speak. I'm still pretty active myself. On Thursdays, my children all know I haven't got any time for them, or the grandkids. That's my biking day. I'm always out riding with friends. Ever since I had a slipped disk, I've been doing exercises for my back. I go to the gym. I enjoy the sauna. I play tennis pretty regularly. And of course, I still go to the mountains too, but just to hike. I don't like to climb anymore. I don't need to beat myself up like that.

Are you proud of your "Huberbuam"?

Yes, of course, I'm proud of them. But I'm proud of them because they're my children, not because they're famous. I'm just as proud of Karina. Often, people aren't even aware that she exists because all they ever see are Thomas and Alex. Sometimes they say, "What, you have a daughter, too?" Then I say, yes, I've had one for thirty-three years. She's also gone her own way. She studied physical fitness, got her master's degree, works in physical therapy. She was a very good climber, but then I think she started to feel like she was under too much pressure to be as good as her brothers. Thomas, more than anyone, pushed her a lot, wanted to get her to the top. But she didn't want that pressure. She switched over to mountain biking. She's very good at it, pursues it quite intensively. And she's a passionate backcountry skier; almost every year she and her father go off on long trips together, ski-touring in the high mountains. In 2000, she even climbed Mount McKinley. She's married, and recently became a mother. Now I have another grandchild, besides the three from Thomas. She lives in Traunstein, like Alexander, and the two of them often do things together.

Did you like the film about Thomas and Alexander?
No, actually, I didn't like it very much.

Why not?
Because I don't like speed-climbing. It's too dangerous. I don't like it any more than I like Alexander's solos or Thomas's base jumping. I think these three things are simply too dangerous; they're too extreme. I would really like it if they would stop doing it. Particularly Thomas and his base jumping—with his wife and three kids at home. I just don't think that's right.

But aren't you proud to see your sons on the big screen?
Sure, and it captures them well, too. Still, I find it too extreme. They take it too far. I was particularly disturbed

by the scenes where you see them fall, though with Alex, it's only shown indirectly. I did know beforehand that it was coming, but still, I was totally nervous. I don't want to see it when they fall. I simply wish that they always come back in one piece. But I know that you can't control everything. Here in Berchtesgaden, a man recently died while working. Fell off a ladder from a height of 3 meters. Imagine! Three meters down, onto the lawn, and then dead, just like that, because he fell the wrong way. And Alexander survives a fall from 16 meters . . . He always did say that if anything happens, it will be on easy terrain, where you think you've got everything in hand.

How concretely do you think about the fact that Alexander or Thomas could lose their lives during one of their undertakings?

I am very aware that it's a possibility. I always give them God's blessing when they go. If one day one of them doesn't come back, I would have to accept it—then it was fated. But then I'll know that he lived his life exactly as he would have wanted. That he was happy with it. What good is a long life if you can't do what you want with it? They live their lives the way it suits them. I always say, they're grown up now, and I can't look out for them anymore. They've got to do that for themselves. I couldn't prevent them from going, in any case. But whether I would really be able to accept it if it happened—I don't know.

∞

CHAPTER THIRTY-ONE

GOING TO THE LIMIT

The lower 10th grade, in which I had been climbing free solo as preparation for the Direttissima, had been an extreme experience for me. On the other hand, I knew that I could push the limit even further. I would just have to concentrate my efforts accordingly and make it my goal to free-solo the hardest possible sport-climbing routes—less of a mental challenge than a big alpine wall, but all the more athletically difficult. In 2003, I focused on achieving full grade 10. A new grade, a new limit—so I believed.

On February 19, 2003, I met up with Michi Meisl at the Schleier Waterfall. On the agenda was the "Opportunist." If the circumstances were right, I would go for it. As a photographer, naturally Michi had his camera with him, and I had asked him to take a few pictures. What it was he was to take pictures of, however, I had kept to myself.

The weather was gorgeous. The waterfall sparkled in the bright light of the sun. The conditions were perfect. I was calm, with not the slightest hint of nervousness. I warmed up, bouldered a bit. Michi took some pictures. I took a short break. Then, I got ready. Michi was taken aback when I asked him if he was all set. I took no more time to focus, just jumped right in. Michi didn't have a clue that I was about to climb on the "Opportunist." Before he'd had a chance to train his telephoto lens on me, I had already gone up the first 3 meters; and before he even realized what was happening, I was at the top. Fluidly, move by move, exactly as planned, and with no trace of anxiety, the "Opportunist" had slid by under my fingers. As lovely as it had been, that was certainly not going to the limit! I had not reached the utmost of what I could do. This was clear to me immediately. And I wouldn't be me if I had let it go at that.

A year later, I set my sights on the "Kommunist," also at the Schleier Waterfall. The upper 10th grade, 22 meters long, extremely overhanging, and demanding very athletic climbing. The moves at the crux were even harder, less controllable, and more than 10 meters above the ground. Merciless. The absolute bounds of my physical abilities at that moment really did lie only a little beyond what the "Kommunist" demanded, and the reserves of strength I brought to the route were accordingly minimal. Despite intensive preparation, I was not capable of climbing "Kommunist" whenever I felt like it, and far from every time—I could only do it freshly rested, and under good conditions. And even then, my reserves were stretched quite thin. But by now I had extensive experience and knew quite precisely how I functioned while climbing without a rope. This is what allowed me to keep the reserves I required to a minimum. That was just the sort of extreme challenge I was looking for . . .

Day after day, I trained on the route, perfecting the kinesthetic sequences. Over and over, I worked away at the dynamic crux move until, after nearly a month, I finally felt ready. But my first attempt was a wash. After 3 meters, I jumped back down. I was too nervous, lost too much power because of the adrenaline, felt too insecure, and couldn't be 100 percent certain of my strength. Free-soloing doesn't allow for 99 percent; going to the limit requires that everything, absolutely everything, is exactly right.

Despite this failure, I kept trying, and five days later I made another attempt. Again, I was nervous. Again, the reserves of power were insufficient, and this time, too, I felt that I could not count on having enough strength left for pulling through super-precisely at the crux. Once again, I jumped off.

I had not yet given up hope, but it was clear to me that with each failed attempt, it would be that much more difficult to muster up the necessary self-confidence. I needed a whole week before I would trust myself to try it one more time, and I realized it would be the last attempt. If I could not completely manage to rid myself of apprehension this time around, I would simply have to admit that free-soloing a route in the higher 10th grade was too big a challenge for me to handle.

April 20, 2004. The third attempt. The first few moves would tell! And on this day, I was in the flow. No adrenaline. I put the first 3 meters behind me with precision and efficiency and climbed over the critical mark. And on it went. This time, there was no turning back. Twenty moves brought me to the crux. I got into position, underclinging to the right, edge to the right, and in this moment, all my muscles were giving 100 percent all at once. The motion was perfectly rehearsed: Pulling against gravity, my body flew up in a wave-like motion, my hand accelerated to the hold in my sights, and spot on, I pressed my fingers against the downward-sloping edge. My fingers bit into the stone with extreme force, and for a brief moment, my body froze, motionless on the rock. I was able to stabilize my position, place my foot, and pull through to the first good hold. I still had another 12 meters left to the top; 12 meters that still required the upper grade 9—no wiggle room for even the slightest slip in concentration.

Only afterward, with the last move, did the tension recede. I became calm again, like a great river spreading out onto the wide reaches of its delta plain after the raging torrent of the rapids.

∽

PATAGONIA IN WINTER

Stephan Siegrist and I met for the first time not in the mountains, but at the ISPO in Munich—the biggest sporting-goods trade show in the world. Actually, that was not such a great coincidence. Since both of us make a living from mountain climbing, trade shows and meetings with sponsors are a normal part of our professional routine. We had both known of each other for a long time through our various publications, and so we both knew where the other stood. Often enough, such a chance encounter ends with a brief exchange of news and mutual good wishes for the next project. But with us, it was different. Obviously, the chemistry was right, because before we knew it, we had already made plans for our first trip to Patagonia together. Ultimately, neither one of us knew whether this spontaneous feeling of instant affinity would be borne out and whether we really would complement each other in a positive way under extreme conditions. But it was worth a try.

Above all, we had an objective that both of us were equally passionate about: the north face of Cerro Torre in the winter. Stephan had the requisite experience with the Patagonian winter. He had completed the first winter ascent of the "Ferrari Route" on Cerro Torre's west face, and he had already attempted the north face in the winter before as well. We were joined by two more of Stephan's friends, Ralf Weber and Roger Schäli. There wasn't much time to think about it. Before I knew it, we were in Interlaken, gathering equipment for the impending trip. This would be the first time that I'd willingly say good-bye to the summer and enter into winter. At the end of August, the time had come. The three Swiss mountaineers and I were on our way into the darkness of the southern hemisphere.

Just like on my first trip with Toni, the journey to Patagonia was again long and laborious. As before, there were no flights to El Calafate due to economic problems, so we landed on the Atlantic coast in Rio Gallegos. The day was swathed in deep gray fog, and the night was long . . . It was a stark contrast to the gorgeous European summer we had just left behind. In the three days it took for us to travel from Rio Gallegos to El Chaltén, we encountered a constant string of difficulties, and I was glad that during his many trips to Patagonia Stephan had acquired a number of local friends who did not tire of clearing one problem after another out of our way.

But in the mountains, we were ultimately left to fend for ourselves. We were alone with our problems. As is well known, the biggest problem in Patagonia is the weather, and unfortunately, this time it hit us particularly hard. From his experience on previous expeditions, Stephan knew that it made no sense to set up base camp at the foot of Cerro Torre on the surface. The snowfall is too intense and the wind is too strong for the tents to remain standing for too long. So we put up our tents in a big snow cave. And there we were now, in a cave of snow at the foot of the Cerro Torre, in our tents. We lay in our sleeping bags and waited. And waited.

Inside the snow cave we naturally had no idea what was going on with the weather out on the surface. We were sheltered 2, 3 meters deep, where no wind blew, and it was calm and even somewhat cozy, in a way. And it would quickly become clear just how "cozy" it was in comparison to the conditions outside the cave. The moment anyone had to step outside, the contrast was evident: It snowed like crazy, the wind whipped about our ears, and we could barely keep our eyes open without ski goggles for the sheer amount of snowflakes in the air. Obviously, under these conditions, it was highly desirable and comfortable to crawl back into the cave. Still, with every day that we spent in the cave, the coziness lost more and more of its appeal. In time, everything grew damp, it was incredibly cramped, and the idleness hit us particularly hard. Even the best books didn't help anymore. The weather was in a permanent depression, just like our mood, without a glimmer of hope that it would improve. At some point, we did begin to have some hope when the air pressure seemed to increase by only an iota. But that was just an illusion. The fact was, the weather could not possibly have been worse.

With each passing day, the mental strain was increasing. This endless waiting! At times, I was beginning to feel like a wanderer lost in a hostile, foreign land where he doesn't know the roads—completely disoriented, in constant search of anything that could provide a point of reference and show him the way forward. The darkness, the useless waste of time, the ongoing storm, the snow—everything conspired to make things harder for us with each passing day. One week, two weeks, three weeks . . . The question of *why* became ever more pressing. Why did we keep waiting? Why didn't we just get out of there and go back home?

I felt completely out of place in this landscape, with this life I was leading—uncomfortable in my own skin. I felt like a foreign object that didn't fit into its surroundings. Like a non-native tree that only brings disorder to the forest, or like a mushroom that looks perfect but is full of deadly poison. As usual in such moments, I had great doubts about what I was doing. My actions felt like a provocation to reason, a revolt against healthy common sense. But this was the only way for me to live an authentic life, as an adventure.

This authenticity is the driving force that constantly leads me to crave and seek out danger—to expend myself in endless effort and eternal struggle. It is endless and eternal because it is not a struggle that leads to a specific goal. Beyond every aim that is achieved, a new horizon opens up, with more goals, new challenges. It is a struggle for struggle's sake, in which the goal is completely unimportant, nothing but a pretext to keep going. It remains in focus for only a brief time. When it is reached, it is left behind, inserted into a long chain of intense, memorable experiences. The goal is a fantasy that sometimes bears the name of freedom, and other times makes my life a living hell. It is a fantasy I chase in order to keep my life going. If these goals should die in me, the central cornerstone of my life would crumble too. In the end, freedom is an illusion, for in truth, the deep-seated passion that binds me to the mountains leaves me little leeway. Freedom exists only where there is nothing more to lose . . . And so we were prisoners of our own selves, our own ideas, and we held out till the last possible moment, to the bitter end.

But hope springs eternal, and we got lucky. Only a few days before we would have had to start on our return journey, Stephan, Ralf, Roger, and I were rewarded: In contrast to the hurricane-force storms of the previous weeks, the weather was now heavenly. Our original destination, the north face of the Cerro Torre, had been made far too dangerous by the weeks of bad weather. Though the long wait had driven us to the edge of madness, we were still not crazy enough to take such risks. But there were other first-rate goals standing right next to Cerro Torre—Torre Egger and Cerro Standhardt. Both summits are not as high, and not as difficult to climb as Cerro Torre itself. The route "Exocet" on Cerro Standhardt promised to be a safe climb even under these conditions.

At sundown, we enjoyed the last hours of calm at the entrance of our cave; very soon, we would set off, so we could put the entire approach to the start of the route behind us during the night. In the morning, we reached the saddle just when the full moon went down over the shimmering silver ice cap, and a few minutes later, at the foot of the actual climb, the first rays of sunlight appeared. We didn't exactly have the best conditions on the first pitches; wind-packed snow on steep rock made progress difficult. But after just 150 meters, "Exocet" wound around to the leeward, east side of the mountain, over which we arrived, climbing mostly without protection, at the central part of the route: a 300-meter-high vertical ice chimney.

One after the other, we took turns leading in this incredibly narrow tube of ice. We were climbing in the middle of the Patagonian winter. It was a good 50 degrees below zero, so the ice was cold and brittle. Still, we made good progress, and at last were just 40 meters below the exit to the summit ridge, no more than 100 vertical meters below the summit, when the typical meteorological signs appeared: wind and clouds around the summit. At first it seemed harmless, just a mere threatening gesture. But with each minute, the power of the wind grew until it had reached infernal dimensions. The storm did not keep us waiting, and hit us full force. The summit had been so close at hand, and now it was so far!

We went back and forth a bunch of times. It seemed a lost cause to try to find the way to the summit under these conditions. In the storm, we couldn't even see 10 meters in front of us. Snow came from above and below, and we were tossed here and there on the ridge like marionettes. We had to scream to make ourselves heard in this hell. We weren't sure whether going on was still a tenable option at this point, even though there were just a few meters left until the goal. We hadn't waited all that time not to give it everything we had now! We battled on, desperate to keep fighting as long as there was still strength left in our bodies.

And it paid off! The long wait, the laborious struggle—it all came to an end. There was still a difficult descent before us, but first, we were able to stand at the top, on the summit of Cerro Standhardt. We felt how the moment gave us power, how life pulsed in our veins and drove us on.

CHAPTER THIRTY-THREE

GRAND CAPUCIN

For a long time, I had been dreaming of a project in Europe's playground: the Mont Blanc massif. This range offers an incredible variety of climbing goals, and every big wall there bears the name of a famous first ascensionist. My father was absolutely in love with this mountain range. He's done just about everything he could there: the north faces of the Droites and the Courtes, the Nant Blanc face of the Aiguille Verte, the Walker Pillar, the Brenva Spur . . . But he didn't just come home with the memories of his special experience on the big faces. It was the life of the place that was special—the international atmosphere of Chamonix that he could breathe in deeper here than anywhere else. To not just read about famous names, but actually be in close proximity to them. Just to hear him tell of the sorts of climbers one might accidentally run into up in those mountains: Walter Bonatti, Pierre Mazeaud, Gaston Rébuffat. And they weren't the least bit conceited. For my father, it has always been a dream to be able to follow in their footsteps on the routes they left behind.

I, too, had often thought about trying out the granite-climbing skills I had learned in Yosemite on the difficult walls of the Mont Blanc massif. The Petit Dru, for instance, is (or rather, was) the most fantastic granite wall in the Alps. The French Direttissima, with its central stretch, the Pilier Rouge, was a five-star destination for me as a free climber. Over the years, I had collected images and information about it, and I was just getting around to tackling the project in earnest when the gigantic landslide of 1997 pulverized my granite dreams. Thus, the idea of free-climbing the Petit Dru died an untimely death.

Despite this setback, I came to Courmayeur at the foot of Mont Blanc years later, in 2005, together with my father. Our goal was the "Bonatti" on the east face of the Grand Capucin, which was one of the few dreams my father had not had a chance to fulfill in the Mont Blanc massif during his most active period.

I was glad to come along. For one thing, I wanted to support him in his quest to make this dream come true at the relatively advanced age of sixty-six. But also, I particularly wanted to take the opportunity to pursue another one of my ideas. I had set my sights on a goal on that very same Grand Capucin, and this time, fate had really played a hand in it. Was it really just a fortuitous coincidence? In the spring of 2003, in the middle of the Valley, I had met the French climber Arnaud Petit, one of the best rock climbers of the 1990s: grade 10 onsight, grade 11 redpoint, World Cup champion in competition climbing, and a mountain guide. Yosemite Valley is, after all, a meeting place of international climbers unlike any other.

I told Arnaud about the "Zodiac" free-climbing project that Thomas and I were working on at the time. We philosophized about free climbing on big walls, and Arnaud told me about his "Voie Petit"—a 400-meter-long first ascent on the Grand Capucin that he opened in 1997, together with Stéphanie Bodet. The east face of the Grand Capucin may not be as large and compact as the walls of El Capitan, but Arnaud enthusiastically described the steep granite, with its dihedrals and cracks, and the roofs that were so typical for the Grand Capucin.

I was more or less informed about his route already, of course—the activities of one of the best practitioners of our guild wouldn't go undocumented. However, I didn't know about a small but very significant detail. As so frequently happens in the alpine press, the media forgot to mention the most important thing: At the time, Arnaud had not yet managed to free-climb the "Voie Petit" the entire way. This feat had yet to be accomplished by anyone, and Arnaud himself urged me to try it. After all, I certainly had the necessary experience with granite to succeed on the route.

I am often asked where I get my ideas for future projects and whether I am guided in the process by public expectations. Nowadays, it's not enough for a climber to be technically perfect; you also need to have a lively imagination, so you can project this technical ability onto interesting goals. There aren't too many alpinists who are particularly known for their creativity—mountain climbers with a vision unlike the others. Such climbers have not necessarily been the strongest or best among their contemporaries in physical terms, but they have been the ones who achieved the pioneering climbs and first ascents.

Take Hermann Buhl, for instance; he was the best mountain climber of the postwar era, a unique man of character and charisma. There are very few climbers like him today. He not only had immense ability and endless determination, but also a creative spirit. He was a veritable fountain of ideas. More than any other climber of his generation, he was a visionary in his thinking and his execution. He had terrific foresight for what was possible in climbing.

The north face of the Piz Badile was first ascended by no less than Ricardo Cassin, and is one of the big faces of the Alps. In 1952, Buhl traveled an entire day by bicycle from Innsbruck to get there, and then climbed up the wall in under six hours. Then he went back to Innsbruck by bike. In the evening, he labored his way up the Maloja Pass, and finally, it was downhill again. Relaxed, he coasted through the night on his bike, in the direction of his Tyrolean home—and suddenly found himself flying through the air. His landing was cold and wet. He had run into a stone at the edge of the road and fallen into the Inn River. The bike was ruined. Buhl managed to travel the rest of the way on foot, with the mail truck, and by train, arriving in Innsbruck just in time for the start of the workday—"where I had to bow to civilization once again."

The exceptional ability and tenaciousness that Buhl demonstrated in the ascent of this famous alpine wall constituted the cornerstone of his most brilliant achievement: the first ascent of the 8,125-meter-high Nanga Parbat, which he completed on July 3, 1953, by himself. This made Hermann Buhl a star far beyond mountaineering circles. He was probably the very first mountain climber ever to lecture before enthusiastic audiences on the international stage. He toured in Austria, Germany, Switzerland, France, and Yugoslavia. He met with particularly great acclaim in Italy, where the Italians were overjoyed to have a top mountaineer speaking about his adventures in their own language. Volkswagen even placed a Beetle at his disposal for his lecture trips, so that today, we might describe Buhl as the first person to understand climbing as a profession.

Hermann Buhl lost his life in 1957, just a short time after the first ascent of Broad Peak. He broke through a cornice in an impenetrable fog on the Chogolisa. The exceptional mountaineer was dead, but his spiritual legacy lives on. I have always felt a special connection to Buhl, if only because he was "one of us." Though he had grown up in Innsbruck, and matured into a famous mountain climber in the Tyrolean mountains, in 1951 he married a woman from Ramsau, a village in Berchtesgaden. The Bavarian mountains where I live became a second home for Hermann Buhl. Of course, when I was just starting to go on my first ski-touring trips with my father and Thomas, I didn't yet dream that mountain climbing could be a profession and not just a calling. But the life of Hermann Buhl charted a possible path in that direction.

The idea of the professional mountain climber was for me far more explicitly embodied in the south Tyrolean climber Reinhold Messner. Not only did he practice his vocation even more as a profession, and still continues to live on the proceeds of his mountaineering achievements to this day, but in contrast to Hermann Buhl, he was around for me to experience in person. In 1986, I attended one of his lectures. He had just climbed the Lhotse, and was thus the first person to have stood on all fourteen of the eight-thousanders—a visionary who practically dominated and revolutionized Himalayan mountaineering. Lecture halls filled to capacity, enthusiastic audiences, large print runs, countless articles in the papers, a sought-after guest on all sorts of television shows—the life of the professional mountain climber often plays itself out far from the mountains.

In 1995, when my first redpoint ascent of "Salathé" in California's Yosemite Valley suddenly earned me international attention, I realized for the first time where my path could lead. Buhl, Bonatti, and Messner were the pioneers who had shown me how it was done. I could at least give it a try. I went on my first lecture tour, and it financed my studies and my climbing trips. I began to think it might actually be possible to make a living this way. Mountaineering was above all my passion—and it remains so—but back then, I started to wonder whether narrating my experiences would also allow me to live from my passion in the long term.

This was not just a pipe dream. Although as a pro I do earn my living in part from contracts with sponsors, the largest portion of my income still comes from my lecture fees. Although this means I am dependent on the goodwill of the audience, on the other hand, I ensure a certain measure of independence from the whims of my sponsors.

People often speak of the freedom that we climbers experience on the mountain. The reality often looks somewhat different. We live on our successes by speaking about them. Without success, we would not find a publisher, no one would come to our lectures, and no one would report about us. And that is why, whenever we are in pursuit of some goal in the mountains, we remain our own prisoners. As long as it's going well, I rarely feel this pressure, and it's rather under the surface. On the other hand, such pressure also has a positive aspect: It keeps my ideas fresh and gives me the impetus to keep thinking ahead.

Actually, I'm always thinking about what projects I should invest my energies into, and so it often happens that the planning stage stretches out over one or two years. In the process I am certainly guided by my estimation of how the public will react to my projects. I pursue my own original interests above all, but when I have more than one project buzzing about in my head, then I give precedence to the one that seems to me most interesting from the public's point of view. Climbing on the Grand Capucin fulfilled that requirement in every respect.

It was astounding to see how this famous granite obelisk can appear lost in the great Mont Blanc massif when you come to the Glacier du Géant from the direction of the Torino Hut: It looks like a small, red pillar that disappears beneath the Arête du Diable of Mont Blanc du Tacul. It is not until you slowly begin to get closer to it that its dimensions grow. With every step, the tower grows larger and its prominent roofs more rugged.

My father had already been at the foot of this wall before, some forty years ago, in bad weather. Throughout his life, he'd frequently had to struggle with the problem of having to make do with just two or three weeks' vacation in the mountains, and so he had about as little time at his disposal as money. Now, as he stood under the wall for the second time, the weather was perfect.

I can still remember twenty-five years ago, my mother used to say that it wouldn't be much longer before my father would be taken to the mountains by his sons, instead of the other way around. My father always replied that he didn't need anyone to schlep him up the mountain, not even his boys. He still takes that attitude today. Of course, he's glad when we are climbing together, but he wants to work his mountain himself, and certainly not be "dragged along" behind me.

The reverence with which my father approached the "Bonatti" had something almost romantic about it. Of course, the thought of climbing one of Bonatti's milestones played a role, but there was also the fact that he would be fulfilling a long-cherished dream that had come to seem so far removed over all those years. The "Bonatti" is often underestimated. Due to its complicated line, it is actually longer than one would expect, and with the increasing altitude, my father struggled more and more against the waning of his strength. But it surely would have been the last thing he would have ever admitted— not that I should get the idea of pulling him up the mountain like some guide!

The "Bonatti" is a truly magnificent rock-climbing route. Exposed, steep, impressive, and of the best quality granite that all of Mont Blanc has to offer. At 4:00 PM, we reached the small, pointed summit of the Grand Capucin, and this filled me with a joy no less than if I had just done something tremendous myself. I hope very much that I may still experience our shared passion for climbing with the same intensity that my father enjoys when I am as old as he is now. Anyone who can still live his dreams so intensely at that age can consider himself quite fortunate.

As an extra benefit of this encounter with the "Bonatti," I had also found out what I wanted to know about the Grand Capucin: There was no better granite. The "Voie Petit" was an inspiring line, a real free climber's dream, and in the summer of 2005, I had set aside plenty of time in order to tackle it seriously. I knew from talking to Arnaud that he had mostly worked with nuts and friends in the easier pitches, while the more-difficult ones were fitted with pitons and bolts. The key to free-climbing the route would primarily be found in the fifth pitch: After a 90-degree dihedral over 30 meters long, there was a roof protruding 4 meters out. Although Arnaud had been able to free-climb the individual moves in isolation, the redpoint of that pitch and a complete free ascent of the entire route still remained to be accomplished.

At first, a little cautious exploration. A day after the ascent of "Bonatti," I crossed from the Torino Hut to the Grand Capucin over the Glacier du Géant once more, this time with Franz Hinterbrandner, from Berchtesgaden. My aim on this day was relatively modest. The fifth pitch was the hardest. I wanted to climb up to that point, and no farther. The 4-meter protrusion of the roof would be the place to decide whether the project was realistic for me. These few athletic moves would clearly demonstrate whether or not it would work.

The second pitch already had me working up quite a sweat. A little taken aback, I stumbled into this demanding stretch. Two bolts; otherwise, self-placed protection with nuts, longer run-outs—big distances on a challenging climb. Two falls on steep terrain helped me to discharge some of the built-up tension. By the third attempt, I was still standing rather more next to the etriers than in them, but with a little trembling, I did finally manage to get over this airy run-out. After that, the crux: the fifth pitch. The endlessly long corner and the roof—well-protected but impressive. Powerful moves, athletic climbing—you couldn't find better in Yosemite. And above all, it was doable! Shortly after, however, the weather stopped cooperating. We were in Chamonix, and weather is a decisive factor in every undertaking here. The Grand Capucin is not exactly a giant, but it is still in the high mountains, which means that sunshine can often turn to snow in a matter of minutes.

On my next attempt a week later, I took the first big step in the direction of my goal. After several tries, I managed the first redpoint of the pitches I'd been working on. I wanted to try climbing through the whole route the next day, but the weather wasn't cooperating anymore. I had already managed to get through the lower pitches again before it started to turn, so I naturally didn't want to give up. However much I didn't want to accept it at that moment, though, there were already a few snowflakes in the air. I wanted to go on, but Franz refused to follow. We were still arguing about it—me above, Franz at the belay below me—and I was trying my best to persuade him to keep climbing when it really started coming down quite heavily. There I stood at the belay in my sport-climbing pants and tight-fitting shoes. Well done! We had to get down from there in a hurry.

A week off, and then another attempt. Once again, I managed the lower pitches, and this time, the weather remained beautiful, so I went on. As before, I was still unfamiliar with the upper portion of the route. There were three more pitches in grade 9 and one in grade 10 waiting for me. I was feeling optimistic and thought that it could work out. But it didn't go the way I'd hoped; the pitches on the upper pillar called for extremely demanding technical climbing. They were anything but an easy nut to crack. My hopes were quickly dashed, and on top of that, the temperature on the east face plummeted in the afternoon shade.

The next day's attempt wasn't fruitful either. I was at the end of my strength and considered myself lucky to be able to make it just through the pitches of the upper pillar. I still felt I was ready to attempt the entire route—only the weather wasn't. It was supposed be bad for the next two days, and moreover, Franz had to go back to work. By midnight Friday, we were home again. After having gotten up at four in the morning two days in a row, I enjoyed sleeping in and didn't get up until noon on Saturday. I felt like just lazing about and taking it easy. But around three o'clock came the new weather report. There was a slight change from the previous one. Now, it predicted not two days of bad weather, but just one—namely, today. Sunday would be bright and sunny, and on Monday conditions were supposed to worsen again for an extended period.

There was no time to waste. I had to try it now. I called up Max Reichel and Wasti Schöndorfer. A blitz operation was in the works: start time, Saturday at midnight. They weren't particularly enthused about the marathon that awaited them, but my stubbornness prevailed. I spent the evening packing and then went off to a wine-tasting that some friends and I had planned long before. They couldn't believe that I intended to complete my project the very next day. And it did sound pretty wild: At ten in the evening, we're sitting around together, enjoying a fine bottle of wine, and twelve hours later I'm supposed to be climbing on the Grand Capucin.

At 11:00 PM, we were off. We took turns driving. At least there was no traffic in the middle of the night. Brenner, Trento, Verona, Bergamo, Milan, Aosta, and at half past seven on the morning of July 17, we were on the first cable car to the Torino Hut, the gateway to the glacial world of Mont Blanc. There was no time to rest. We had our skis, so we made it to the Grand Capucin in under two hours. The whole mountain was glowing in the blazing sunlight. It was a glorious day! At ten, we started climbing, and by twelve, we were in the crux pitch. On my first attempt, I was still too worked up and fell on the last hard move—after 40 meters. I was wiped out, needed a long break, and even fell asleep at the belay.

At some point, Wasti woke me up again, and an hour later I started the second attempt. As unbelievable as it may sound, it would be the last one that day. In this pitch especially, too many attempts were out of the question because the crux came after 40 meters, and every new attempt cost too much energy. But this time, it went better; markedly calmer and more controlled, I brought the dihedral behind me, hung in the roof, jammed in my fingers four times in a row, pulled through, and was on top. That was it—but I'd already made it this far before on one of my previous attempts! The game was far from over here, and things were now getting a little tight, especially when it came to the time. By now it was almost three o'clock, and we still had nine pitches to go till the summit. There could be no more failures, and the east wall was starting to sink into shade. The sun disappeared. Clouds shrouded the Grand Capucin and it became ice cold. No more fun and games; I had to knuckle down now.

By 7:00 PM, we had made it to the top. I'd almost lost it a couple of times; cold fingers, waning strength, and time pressure did not make things easy for me. But I really did knuckle down hard. The predicted bad weather was rolling in, and there was just enough time and remaining daylight to get back to the Torino Hut without any problems. I had done it, and was overjoyed because I knew how much luck you needed to succeed on a major route on Mont Blanc—not exactly a mountain where I feel at home. It cost me a lot of energy, but the great effort was like a trigger that heightened the intensity of the memories.

When you finally hold success in your hand, your torment comes to an end. Success is liberating. It expands the space you can take for yourself, for your satisfaction, for your happiness. It makes you open to life. The tension that had been my constant companion for many days prior to the attempt, and during the actual climb, fell away from me right away. The calm after the storm is an intense moment, but at the same time, it is a very fleeting one. It is important to seize this moment and hold it in your memory—it is the reward for the fear, the tension, and the effort. I always enjoy it to the fullest and look forward to whatever life has in store for me next.

∾

CHAPTER THIRTY-FOUR

SPEED—THE THRILL
OF VELOCITY IN THE
VERTICAL

Thomas and I had been working on projects in Yosemite Valley for over ten years. Ten years in which this Valley, with its unique climbing community, had almost become a second home to us. Repeatedly, it was the giant wall of El Capitan that moved us to return. This was the case when Thomas and I traveled to California again in 2003. Even though we had decided that we were done with the big free-climbing routes on El Capitan, fate had other plans.

The previous year, I had published the book *Yosemite* with Heinz Zak. While his first-class photographs provided the visual content, I gave a well-grounded summary of the hundred-year history of climbing in Yosemite. In order to produce this account, I needed to go to California to conduct some detailed research in the spring of

2002. Unlike all of my previous visits, this time climbing was not the first item on the agenda. But, understandably, it was impossible for me to spend four weeks working in the vicinity of this climbing mecca without laying a hand on its unique granite. I was lucky; on my last day in the Valley I was standing roped in at the start of the "Zodiac" with Ammon McNeely, one of the best big-wall climbers of all. "Zodiac" is one of the most famous classic routes on El Capitan, and the epitome of aid climbing.

As is often Ammon's way, this would be no ordinary ascent of the route. At the time, he held the fastest ascent times for a total of twenty different routes on this wall, and was probably the most outstanding big-wall climber in the Valley. No one is faster in technical climbing, certainly not on hard aid-climbing routes. According to Ammon, in order to achieve such quick ascent times, you have to take on a high degree of risk, reckon with falls, and above all—"Don't mess around!" You can't take your time thinking things over. You just have to move through. It's not for the faint of heart. This kind of climbing demands a risk-taking partner who can stay on the ball when things get critical: "You need partners who stay in the game even when shit hits the fan!" I assured him that I intended to do just that.

After a little over six hours, we arrived at the top of the "Zodiac," and I was all fired up. It wasn't just because of the speed. Despite the rapid ascent, I had taken the time at the critical points to analyze the structure of the rock a little closer. Without really believing that the "Zodiac" could ever be a feasible free climb, I nonetheless did not waste the opportunity to convince myself that the impossible was doable. And now, after the ascent, I knew it. Ammon and I sat together on El Capitan and enthusiastically discussed the discovery. He is not particularly a specialist in free climbing, but that didn't mean he wouldn't be as happy about the find. He was simply glad that he could help me along on my way to a fantastic new free-climbing route on El Capitan.

In the spring of the following year, I was in the Valley again, this time with Thomas. Our common project: Free "Zodiac"—the free-climb ascent of this classic aid climb. We got a pretty good start. After two weeks of hard work, we had cracked all the questionable spots and found free-climbing alternatives to all the blank bolt ladders. We knew this route lay in the realm of possibility for us. Nonetheless, the infamous heat managed to put an end to our progress after three weeks' time. Our performance stagnated, and the only perceivable progress being made was on the thermometer. With each day, the mercury climbed at least another notch higher, and we slipped off the nonexistent holds with more and more frequency. Our motivation was gone. Our last hopes of getting through the 600 meters over two days evaporated in the heat of the merciless California sun. We had to give it up, and there was nothing for it but to wait for the cooler days of fall.

We still had two weeks of free time left in the Valley, and anyone who knows Thomas and me would know that we would never let this time go to waste. The previous year, during the ascent of "Zodiac" with Ammon McNeely, he had shown me how to climb a big wall quickly and efficiently. Now, Thomas and I sat once more in the field at the foot of El Capitan and realized that the two of us knew "Zodiac" better than anyone else. Our next move was patently obvious: Go up the "Zodiac" at top speed and taste the thrill of vertical velocity on El Capitan! We had nothing better to do, and it was definitely the best way we could think of to spend the otherwise wasted time meaningfully.

The record at the time was naturally held by Ammon himself. The task was to run the course in under Ammon's time of 5 hours, 57 minutes. Anyone expecting Ammon to react jealously to our endeavor would be completely mistaken. On the contrary; he supported us and our aims in every respect. For him, every good climber who comes to Yosemite enriches the scene, and he sees competition purely as motivation, as a fresh impetus to go attack some big wall yourself. He also supported us in our project with the benefit of all his experience, and by sharing all sorts of small but important details so we could squeeze every last minute out of it.

The conditions for a new speed record were perfect. Thomas and I knew every single move on the 600-meter route. We knew exactly what protection to place where. In addition, free climbing is in general significantly faster than aiding. Ammon's current record on the "Zodiac" was achieved almost exclusively by aid climbing, and that's where we had our most important advantage. If we freed everything up to grade 8, we would have to do no more than a third of the route as an aid climb. That should secure us victory.

Still, we knew very well that in order to secure the record, we would have to make use of all the special techniques of speed climbing. The "Zodiac" has sixteen pitches, which means that normally you'd have to set up sixteen belays and pull in and fix the rope sixteen times. During this time, the whole team is at a standstill. Nothing moves except the unstoppable ticking of the clock. On top of that, when one climber belays the other, it means that half the team is always standing still no matter what. All of this costs precious time. That's why we had to forego traditional belaying techniques, like anyone else attempting a speed record.

In principle, there are two methods of speed climbing that have been developed, which can be used interchangeably depending on the particular difficulties and challenges of the route. One method is to climb simultaneously. That is to say, leader and follower climb at the same time. The rope that connects them is generally clipped into one or two points. The tempo does not allow for more protection, and besides, the leader would run out of gear within just a few pitches. In itself, this is the most uncomplicated method of speeding smoothly through the vertical world as a climbing team without ever coming to a complete stop. However, particularly for the leader, simultaneous climbing carries a very high risk: If the follower falls, it will pull the leader with terrific force in the direction of the last piece of protection, where he will smash against the rock with no dynamic breaking effect whatsoever. The serious injuries that have been known to result from simultaneous climbing prohibit its use on technically challenging terrain because when it comes to speed climbing, especially with high difficulties, you can never entirely exclude the possibility of falling.

That is why the shortfixing technique is used on difficult routes. In this technique, the leader runs about halfway up the pitch, places protection, and then takes in the slack, ties a knot, and hangs it in the anchor. Thus, the follower can put weight on the rope and sprint after the leader with the help of jumars. At the same time, the leader now has the second half of the rope at his disposal to keep climbing on. Shortfixing works great, although it does have a slight disadvantage: In the case of a fall, the leader is only stopped after he plunges the entire length of the remaining rope. There is no method that is optimally secure in speed climbing, and big falls are absolutely par for the course, as are serious bruises and other injuries. In contrast to the often-exaggerated descriptions of other heroic activities, in speed climbing, spectacular falls are not just the stuff of legend—they really do happen!

Due to the great difficulties of the "Zodiac," it was clear we would proceed on most of the route with shortfixing. This tactic did, after all, have the advantage that the follower, jumaring up, would usually be a little faster, and if everything was well coordinated, would have the opportunity to belay the leader for brief periods in the more-difficult spots. So, after a lot of conferring with Ammon McNeely, we felt extremely well prepared as we stood at the bottom of the "Zodiac" in early July.

The last minutes before the start. We took deep breaths, both nervous, not really sure how things would go. Five, four, three, two, one . . . Thomas set to it, and after 30 meters in only three minutes came his command: "On belay." I let the rope fly out of the grigri, the belay device. As quickly as possible, Thomas took in the slack and fixed it to the anchor. He called, "Rope fixed," the signal for me to hang the jumars on the rope and sprint up after him as fast as I could go. Two minutes later I was up, belaying Thomas for a moment to protect him at a very critical point. Shortly afterward came his "Belay" command once more. Grigri open, jumars on, and up we went again.

A good deal farther up, Thomas was climbing over a traverse, and for time reasons, decided to forego placing any intermediary protection. A minute later, I came to the same spot and made short work of it: I removed the pro and sailed out a good 10 meters to the left into the free, overhanging wall. This method didn't exactly conform to the general school of thought on climbing safety, but it was the quickest mode of following, and that day, speed was the only thing that mattered. Speed means climbing without compromise. Speed means exhilaration. At some point, potentially dangerous sections no longer register as such.

After two hours, we had reached the end of the eighth pitch—the midpoint of the wall. For the second half of the "Zodiac" I took over the lead, as planned. We had worked out what protection gear we would need in advance, so that with economical, precisely calculated placement, it would last exactly to this point. As the second, I had collected everything Thomas left behind over the entire stretch of the lower half of the wall, and at the point where we switched off, I was now fully equipped to take on the second half of the route. Alternating constantly between free and aid climbing, I ran up the great dihedral in "Gray Circle." Two and a half hours had passed in the meantime, and we had ten pitches behind us as we neared a "trad" climbing party. The normal ascension time for the Zodiac is still three or four days, and so it made sense to warn the climbers above us. "Hey, you guys up there, we are on speed!" And back came the reply, in a heavy Swiss accent: "*Was hasch gseit? Sind ihr uf Droge?*" ("What'd you say?

You're on drugs?") This Swiss party already knew who we were and wanted to joke with us.

"How long've ya been at it?" they shouted down to us.

"A good two hours!" we answered. "And you?"

"Us? Two days!"

Unfortunately, we didn't have time for a longer chat. As fast as we had come upon them we passed them again. The proportion of free climbing was becoming greater the higher we got, and that meant we were increasing our speed accordingly. We were on our way to a record. I climbed the last few meters, fixed the rope at the top, and two minutes later pulled Thomas up with a powerful tug over the edge: 4 hours, 7 minutes. We could hardly believe it.

Back in Yosemite Valley, we celebrated the new speed record over beer with some friends. Although we were pleased, we weren't convinced that this record actually represented the best we could do. We had made too many errors. The individual maneuvers were not perfectly coordinated, and in general, the second time is usually better anyway. And so we decided to try it again.

Two days later, we were standing at the start of the "Zodiac" again. As Thomas tied on to the rope, he made the comment: "I can't wait to see who'll win the race today!" He pointed upward. And indeed, 40 meters below the top of the "Zodiac" were the two old friends we'd passed two days before. "Okay, we'll give it a shot. Let's go! Five, four, three, two, one!" We ran through the entire route in 3 hours and 8 minutes, and just a few meters below the top we were in fact able to overtake the Swiss. They shook their heads at us in enthusiastic disbelief, especially when they overheard what Thomas and I were talking about—for as soon as we'd reached the top, we were already discussing what possible improvements we could make that would allow us to be even faster next time.

On our third attempt, we actually managed it in 2 hours, 31 minutes, and 20 seconds. We were satisfied. We had made optimal use of our remaining time in Yosemite, and had discovered a whole new dimension of climbing. Up until this point, we had not realized what great challenges speed climbing could hold for us.

That fall, we finally achieved the hoped-for redpoint of the "Zodiac," and indeed, Thomas and I should have been satisfied. But the idea of speed had gripped us and wouldn't let go. Above all, we knew that on our last attempt the previous spring, we had not yet been perfect. That is why we made a decision that was difficult for outsiders to comprehend: We planned another trip to Yosemite for the spring of 2004 so we could improve upon our own record on the "Zodiac." We wanted to keep shaving time off until we had the feeling that we had not given a single minute away on the entire 600-meter stretch. In an ongoing race that took place every three days, Thomas and I gradually reduced each successive time until we had it down to a sliver over two hours. Eventually we found ourselves at the point where we simply refused to be satisfied with just any old time. We absolutely had to do El Capitan in under two hours! We sunk our teeth into this vision, fully motivated; we had no intention of giving up until we had done it.

June 17, 2004. This time, Thomas was able to give over the lead to me a full four minutes earlier than all the other times. This attempt was hot! That was also a reason for me to really give it everything I had this time. With all the other exchange times it was pretty clear to me that the first half hadn't been fast enough to make it in under two hours, no matter how fast I climbed. But on this attempt, it was different. Thomas had created the preconditions, and now it was up to me to finish what he'd started. This had given me the necessary kick, and just as Thomas had done, I pushed it to my absolute limit, full speed ahead.

At some point, far up the wall, I knew that this time, we would do it! Even while Thomas was still jumaring up the last pitch, the great mob of spectators down in the El Cap Meadows began to cheer. Around fifty climbers had gathered under El Capitan, and they were urging Thomas on as he climbed up the last meters. Exactly 1 hour, 51 minutes, and 34 seconds after leaving the ground, he reached the top of the "Zodiac," accompanied by the impressive roar of the "El Cap Rock Monkeys." This time, we both had the feeling that it was fast enough.

"Alex is a bubbling volcano that never erupts."
Pepe Danquart, director of Am Limit, *on the film shoot with the* Huberbuam.

Karin Stenbach: *Why did you choose to make the third part of your sports film trilogy about the* Huberbaum—*and about a speed-climbing ascent, on top of that?*
Pepe Danquart: Quite simply because the two of them had come to me with the film idea and asked me to make it. We had already met a few years before that, when we were guests on a talk show for NDR [North German Broadcasting] together. Thomas and Alex had just published their first book, *The Wall,* and I had just won the German Film Prize for best director for *Heimspiel,* the first film in the trilogy.

And you were so enthusiastic about the idea that you were convinced at once?
No. It wasn't the idea of speed climbing that intrigued me. But in the very first seconds I had seen what was up with those two. When I was alone with Alex, he talked and talked. But as soon as Thomas joined us, he would clam up. That was a pattern of behavior they would both fall into: When the two were together, Thomas did the talking. With Alex, I felt that he was holding himself back, but there was more there. On the way to the airport, he told me a lot of very personal stuff. That's what I was interested in—their relationship as brothers.

The rivalry between them?
Since I have a twin brother who is also a director, I know all about rivalry: the jealousy, the mutual pushing each other on. With twins, it's even more extreme than with "regular" brothers. Although Alex and Thomas did start doing things together quite early—and publicly, too, as the *Huberbuam*—so that you can almost say that they lead a twin-like existence. They didn't really start searching for their own identities until they were in their thirties. For me, the sibling theme in *Am Limit* stands in the foreground. It's even more important than the theme of pushing the limits.

So it's a film about yourself?
Identification is the precondition for a good film. You can't "make" films like that; you have to live them. You have to be ready to take risks—it's not enough to have the technical know-how for filmmaking. I had to make certain assumptions in order to understand the two of them. They're not so easy to understand. They don't let you get too close. Alex especially is someone who's very strongly ruled by his head; he's defined by his intellect. I told them, if we make this film together, you have to trust me. And you have to trust me unconditionally. I promise you that I'll trust you in return. Trust is the basis you need to forget that the camera is rolling. That's how intimate moments arise that have almost a therapeutic value.

You need a lot of empathy for that.
I think that emotional intelligence is one of my talents—to come at someone in a conversation in such a way that they really come out with something they normally would never say. Alex is an extreme case: a sealed volcano that's

emotionally full—it bubbles, but never erupts. When everyone says Thomas is emotional and Alex is rational, of course that's not at all true. It's just that one reacts much more from instinct and the other clearly with his intellect. But both of them are emotionally very present. When it comes to dominance and non-dominance, Alex has the advantage of being the younger brother who has always chipped away at the elder. Even when he withdraws, Alex is often the one in the driver's seat; with his extreme intelligence, he can analyze the situation and steer things the way he wants.

And you have no interest at all in mountain climbing?
Fundamentally, the sport trilogy did not arise out of any passion for the particular sport. Before *Heimspiel* I had never been to a hockey game, any more than I had ever seen a bicycle race or the Tour de France before I made *Höllentour*. I had no affinity for that. But it was different with mountain climbing. I grew up in Singen, near Constance on the Bodensee. I started skiing when I was four. Running, too, competitively. I got a coaching certificate and coached school and youth teams in my district. Later, I would go ski-touring with my Swiss friends from Zurich. The Engadin and the Silvretta were my second home. We did some challenging stuff, like the Haute Route. And I still feel the same way about it: If I haven't been to the mountains, or had skis under my feet at least once a year, something's missing.

Was climbing ever something you wanted to pursue?
When I was a student, I met a guy from Munich with whom I would go to the climbing crag, but that was within moderate bounds. During the film shoot, though,

I had occasion to climb in the 6th, even the lower 7th grade—naturally as second. I always liked being outdoors. I liked the rock, and more than anything else, I really liked the mentality of the climbers. Climbing has a lot to do with life. For me, it is a great metaphor for life. Overcoming fear, experiencing surges of endorphins, the readiness to suffer, the feelings of euphoria when you stand up at the top—but above all, overcoming fear. Those are things that I also experienced with ski-touring, and it was a basis for understanding the two brothers. I never pushed my limits in mountain climbing; but as a filmmaker, that's where I've spent my whole life, putting myself in situations in which I've reached beyond the outer limits. I've taken on film projects that were actually not feasible, and presented extreme challenges. I cut my teeth on such problems, and grew as a filmmaker. This is comparable to what extreme athletes do in their sport disciplines, especially Alex and Thomas. Of course, the fears they deal with are more life-threatening.

In retrospect, it must be said that Thomas and Alexander's goal of breaking the speed record and your goal of making a film about it in fact were mutually exclusive aims.
But that's also what makes this film special. Normally, with climbing, the high point of athletic achievement is attained first, and then afterward it's re-created and staged for the cameras. But I wanted to have authenticity, and so that was out of the question for me. My filmic concerns were opposed to Thomas and Alexander's athletic goals: They needed to take time off to rest in order to be able to perform at such a high level of climbing. In contrast, I wanted to keep to my filming schedule. Their great achievement was that they were able to handle this pressure. The

demands of the shoot led both of them to act against their own instincts—in Alex's case, by offering to help the cameraman, and in Thomas's case, by going through with the last attempt although he didn't feel fit for it from the very start. If it were not for the film, they would have acted quite differently. Thomas would never have gone up. I'm completely convinced that when they go back there in the fall this year, they're going to crack this thing.

The fact that there's no success at the end of the film makes it even more exciting, more profound, doesn't it?
The film is structured as a classic Shakespearean narrative. I've eliminated all of the background: father, mother, childhood, friends. The film has two heroes, two gods, Hercules and Achilles. A life lived not for one's own sake, but for posterity. Superhuman powers. And all of a sudden, they come crashing down and are people. We see what they achieve—something that hardly anyone else in the world is capable of—and then comes the fall. They are like you and me. They cry, they become human. And down below, embedded in the dramaturgy of the film, there are the secondary characters who support them, like Chongo Chuck, for example, who opens the film.

Dean Potter has a supporting role in the film too?
Exactly. Dean Potter is one of the biggest climbing stars in America. He's a man who understands a lot about life. There is a great deal of authenticity in what he does, and what he speaks about. He's extremely likable from the start—he wins you over right away, you trust him implicitly. In the film, he says: "If everyone could live out his own dreams, this world would be a better place." And that's right. That is everyone's personal way of going to the limit.

But back to the heroes and their defeat.

In the end, that is the greatest source of personal growth, the greatest benefit. If we stick with climbing as a metaphor for life, the end of the film means that when you find yourself flat on the ground in life, like Alexander and Thomas did after they fell, you have to manage on your own. Only you yourself can get out of it again. Highs and lows are a part of life. If you're down, you'll be up again. They both acquire human dimensions: the tears that Thomas allows himself to show after Alex falls; the pain that Alex carried in him because Thomas is no longer speaking to him in Patagonia.

But the plan was that they would break the record, wasn't it?

Certainly; I didn't steer things the way they turned out. Everyone wanted them to succeed. But for me, that was not the problem. I wanted to make a film about two brothers.

You weren't disappointed?

No. And I want to emphasize this: The entire time, I was very worried—not just about the two of them, but about the entire team. Sometimes, I would have ten, twelve people hanging on the wall. Or in Patagonia, six weeks in a one-person tent. That really took a lot out of me, because of the psychological conditions. I always felt like the weakest link in the team. Physically, I was spent. Everyone on the team had worked their asses off. In the figurative sense, I put lives on the line for a film, for a piece of art. I didn't have to make this film; this wasn't a project to further my career. I wanted to make it because the subject of the brothers had spoken to me. And because I liked them both very much. For me, their failure was a stroke of good luck, so to speak; following around two brothers who only ever succeed would be boring—like watching a soccer game when you already know who won.

But the story told in the film didn't just develop during the filming, did it?
No. There was a documentary script, a treatment. Everything you see in the film is in there, except the falls. The narrative format—that it's a story about two brothers. The fact that the narrative style doesn't leave any room for family background, that's something I first decided as we started shooting—and then I kept to it consistently.

Thomas's wife and children are at least mentioned, though.
They were mentioned because the responsibility he feels toward his family is an important aspect of Thomas's character. But I didn't want to show them on the screen. Thomas is a happy family man—and it's a happiness Alex is still looking for. That's a mountain that he still needs to climb.

Alexander seems very controlled. The feeling of having everything under control is a precondition for his projects. But how do you work with someone like that?
When you're confronted with someone like that, you have to make sure you challenge them at their level. The confrontation I engaged in with Alex involved going after his vulnerable spots, but eye to eye, with great sincerity. I made it clear to both of them that I'm not some guy from the media, but a partner. That I put all my heart and soul into this film project. To get back to your question of how you get Alex on your side: dedication is something that he

has a lot of respect for. He saw that this was two years out of my life. A commitment that I made for their sakes.

Patagonia was surely a sticking point?
Patagonia takes a huge psychological toll on you—simply because of the constant storms. The bad weather, the pressure to finally have it work. Alex has a great fear of irrational processes: sudden changes in the weather, crevasses, icefall in the couloirs—anything where he has to expose himself to danger that he can't control himself. In those circumstances, he is almost more afraid than a "normal" person because of his great rational intelligence. And add to the mix the feud between the brothers that quite evidently came to a head in Patagonia. Alex suffers greatly in such situations. He practically breaks down. But there were not only arguments between him and Thomas, but also between Alex and myself. We're talking about alpha dogs here, about very strong egos. I was the third alpha dog in the mix, and I wanted to have my way too. But in the course of the shoot, a tight bond formed between Alex and me. In difficult situations, he always understood me. On an intellectual level, he understood me in every phase of the project.

More than Thomas did?
Actually, I'd rather not compare them. I myself hate it that everyone always sees me in competition with my brother. I think the two of them feel the same way. But sometimes I find it difficult to speak about Alex in complete isolation from his brother. It's almost impossible. This twinned existence is a mode of being they sought out themselves when they were young, and external pressures have welded them together even more. The search for their own identi-

ties began relatively late, and at the same time, they did not want to lose the bond between them. I find it remarkable what they both expressed after everything was behind them. We had gone on a really difficult climb together, which was a lot of fun, but also very strenuous. Alexander said that after the film, his relationship with Thomas went to a whole new level. And Thomas said that for him, there was a life before the film, and a life after the film.

But with such intense moments as in Patagonia, there must also be a sense of discretion with respect to your subjects. They must feel some assurance that not everything they say will be packed into the film?

They put that trust in me, and I'm very grateful to them for it. They only saw the film for the first time after it was finished, not during the editing. And they were both happy with it. I revealed only as much as was necessary to understand the film, but not too much. It is always difficult to show weaknesses, but frequently, seen from the outside, that is what makes the person likable. I have heard feedback from many people that the greatest moments in the film are the ones where Alexander and Thomas are seen from a different perspective, as human beings. Absolute sincerity adds a truly stunning dimension.

It isn't possible to plan such moments in advance, any more than you could have predicted the two accidents. Was the cameraman in fact so level-headed that he was just able to switch on the camera when Alex was being carried down after he fell?

Yes, that's what happened—I would never have re-created a moment like that afterwards. It was a free day on the set. The sound crew was off recording the wildlife. The lead cameraman Wolfgang Thaler and I were taking some silent footage of the landscape. Suddenly, there was the camera assistant who had gone with Alex and one of the cameramen over to the wall opposite the "Nose" to look for a vantage point for the camera. He came running down into the valley in a panic and said that Alex had fallen. Then, Wolfgang and I spent an hour and a half retracing their path like trackers, running uphill like top cross-country athletes, over the scree slope up to the foot of the wall, and there we came upon Alex and the other climbers who were carrying him. I was completely out of breath. The first thing I did was to ask him, "Alex, does it hurt?" He said no. "Do you need help?" No. I saw that there were enough people there—okay, then, we're shooting. Sure, life takes precedence before film, but I'm also enough of a professional to see that it doesn't help anyone if I stand around lamenting. If they don't need my help, then I can film. I'm not a social worker. We're here as filmmakers, we're here to do a job. But, naturally, I didn't have any sound—that's why it's so quiet in the beginning. Afterward, I had to convince everyone to deliver some sound for me. But I didn't want to dub over the beginning of it. Rather, I wanted to leave the silence the way it was. It comes in suddenly and signals something serious is going on.

No one reproached you for it?
Right afterward, there were some intense discussions with the camera people about whether it was appropriate to film such a moment. But these discussions were productive, and as a result of them, when Thomas suddenly fell at the end of the film, they rolled the cameras of their own accord.

These are moments that are seldom seen in a mountain film.

I think you need a lot of experience for things like this. After thirty-five years and more than forty films, maybe I have the professionalism to pull something like that off. It doesn't have anything to do with being heartless. Obviously, there's a line between life and film—but when I see that there's nothing else I can do, then I'm a professional. If you don't know how to swim, you don't jump in to save a drowning man. For many viewers, these are two terribly important moments in the film, which stay with them. To capture these moments is my job—that's my own experience of my limits, my highest achievement, so to speak.

As I was watching the film, at some point I found myself sitting there with sweaty palms, although speed is actually not at all my thing.

The fact that the film is so gripping also has to do with the way in which it was filmed. We developed some filming techniques that no one had ever used before. Our cameramen, Max Reichel, Franz Hinterbrandner, and above all Marin "Mungo" Hanslmayr, all climb at grade 9, and all three were completely committed. How do you show speed climbing? How do you represent velocity? You can make the speed of the action more evident by slowing down the film during filming. I also remember a take from Kurosawa's *Seven Samurai*. As the village is being attacked and the samurai are getting into position, Kurosawa pans the camera for a really long time at ground level, with the grass in the foreground. This produces an incredible sense of proximity, speed, drama. I wanted to do that too. Only there was the difficulty that we found ourselves not in the horizontal plane but in the vertical. The cameramen created a setup for themselves with ladders and pulleys, over which the one could run down and pull the other one up. Often, they would push themselves away from the wall on long poles in order to get into a better position for the shot. Sometimes it only took a tiny movement of the camera: When Alex was hanging onto an undercling on El Cap Tower, it sufficed for the camera just to pull back a little in order to emphasize how exposed he was 600 meters above the valley.

As you were filming, who did you have in the back of your mind as an audience—climbers, or non-climbers?
The film must be comprehensible both for the pros and for the general public who know nothing about it. But it can't be boring for the pros. The tension has to be maintained—that's a question of the filmmaker's craft. Takes like the one of Alex's fist, when he pulls himself up on it, were particularly significant for the non-climbers.

What particularly stuck in my mind are the scenes where Alex tapes up his hands to protect them—these contemplative moments come up pretty frequently.
Taping his hands is a leitmotif to which Alexander continually returns throughout the film; and it's always from his very own perspective, which defines him as a character: as brother, rationalist, hand-crack climber, as a contemplative personality, when he speaks about his primal fears. In every situation in which he does it, he performs the task with an attentive care that continually builds in intensity until it's done. But there's also the scene of brotherly devotion par excellence when Thomas bites off the tape for Alex with his teeth—a touching testament of love. In the end, as Alex is tearing off the

tape, he muses that what they're doing is an assault to human reason.

To my mind, Alex has an absolute clarity. He has a clear vision of what his ultimate solo project will be, and he will quit soloing when he has attained that goal.
Very few people have such clarity. To a certain extent, this may be enviable. But on the other hand, it also stands in his way. You can really see it with the brothers: Thomas is guided by his instincts—sometimes he flails about a bit, gets to his goals by way of irrational detours, falls really low, but also flies really high; while Alexander goes in a straight line from here to there like he's on rails, and doesn't permit anything that might precipitate a change inside him. Emotionally, too, he is an absolute control freak. He has himself under control practically all the time.

In the beginning, I was afraid that the Bavarian dialect would put the film into a provincial box.
Both the brothers identify so strongly with their Bavarian homeland, with the Bavarian landscape; the Bavarian manner of speaking is one of the characteristics of their personality. It's authentic. Everyone falls into their own dialect when they're emotional—we only curse in our own language, too. High German would have seemed very implausible. There were even some serious attempts to put in subtitles, but it was completely impossible. On the flip side, the Bavarian dialect was actually really well received, particularly in Berlin, Hamburg, and Bremen. There, the audience only understood about 80 percent, but that didn't matter—instead, it's the directness, the naturalness, the

sincerity that came across. The soul has a language, and in this case, the language is Bavarian. And anyway, nowadays, Bavarian doesn't have that stigma of the "primitive" anymore, like it used to. That's completely changed now. The great success of the film *Wer früher stirbt, ist länger tot* can be directly attributed to the great authenticity of its language—also Bavarian, coincidentally.

Was Am Limit *a successful film for you?*
In its fifth week, it had 150,000 viewers, and that was after three weeks of hot summer weather. And for a long time, it was among the top ten. By the end of the summer it will likely go above 200,000. Judging by that, it is a very successful film. But whether it is worth it for me is another question. In order to be able to make such projects, I have to find other ways to make money. Commercials, for instance. But like I said, possessed is possessed; obsessive is obsessive—we're talking here about pushing the limits! For such a personal film, you're willing to make an investment. The film's greatest success in my eyes is that Alexander and Thomas had an opportunity to explore themselves, to redefine themselves, to find themselves.

When Alexander did his solo of the Cima Grande, the photographer Heinz Zak refused to photograph him because he didn't want to watch him fall. He only took pictures of him at an actual photo shoot afterward, during which some protection was used. Would you have any scruples about filming one of Alex's solo ascents if he asked you?
I would have to think about it, certainly. I'm not sure if I would do it. Probably not.

But is it comprehensible to you why he does it?

Absolutely. I understand him. To the extent that I have gotten to know him as a human being, in his soul, I understand it. What most people out there don't get is this: When you're in a situation in which there is no more going back, which is the case with soloing after about 7, 8 meters—Alex also describes this as the one point where you know now that everything's at stake—then you get this unbelievable level of concentration. A level of concentration you simply can't produce any other way. It's like the pressure on the lump of coal that makes it into a diamond. The general misconception is that you become panicked, but what happens is the exact opposite: You're super-alert, like you're on some extreme drug. All your senses are engaged 150 percent. I know this from my own experience, though in another context. When you're like Alex and you know you've mastered grade 10, then grade 9 is no problem; it's just getting your fear under control. In this state of extreme alertness, he registers everything his senses take in; he functions like a machine. Every handhold, every foothold, is spot on. He's buzzing like a high-voltage power line. It's precisely this extreme pressure that produces the feeling of freedom—perhaps not in the act itself, but afterward. No one who hasn't put himself in a similar situation can comprehend this intense feeling of joy. I completely believe him when he says that he always wants to have this feeling again. There is a clear reason for Alexander's behavior that I'm very aware of. Life is made of two things: One is already behind us, and that is birth. The other is death. In order to feel the intensity of the life in between, he gets close to the edge of death. For me, this is something very life-affirming. It's a way of getting at the meaning of life—why was I brought into this life, as unique as I am? It's a way of making your presence felt, defining yourself as an individual, especially as a younger brother.

Making your presence felt in public? I have much more the feeling that it's only about him and nothing else. That he isn't doing it because of the public.
No, that is his very own personal thing, absolutely. There is great genuineness to it. When I say making your presence felt, I don't mean to the public, I meant just to your own self: Why do I exist? What's the meaning of it? He wants to feel himself as a being before death comes. Of course, there's also the interplay between narcissistic and material interests—after all, performing, presenting themselves to the outside world, is their profession. But for me, it's evident that a man as defined by his rationality as Alexander needs these extreme experiences in order to break through the barriers in his own head, in order to experience the intense feeling that other people might get just from going for a walk, or from looking at a wonderful scene with a lake in the foreground and the panorama of the Alps behind.

How is what Alexander does related to us "normal" people?
Alexander differs from "normal" people only in degree. There are those who live on the edge, and there are the others who don't push themselves to the limit and are still happy. Maybe they're even happier than the ones who live on the edge. For the people at the limit, happiness takes a much more extreme form. They're only happy when they push themselves to that limit and can grow with their

failures as well as their successes. Their power comes from this intense way of life.

What do people find so fascinating about the Huberbuam? *Am Limit* is, first and foremost, a film that appeals to women. The sex factor plays a big role in it. It shows the body in action, in the Theweleitian sense.[6]

I'm particularly impressed by the elegance of the climbing moves, but just as much by the mental strength, when I imagine in what sort of exposure all this takes place.
Alexander does really move like a dancer on the wall, with an incredible calm and elegance. Thomas's climbing style puts more emphasis on strength. But the thing is, it's not just their physicality, it's also the naturalness, the authenticity that they've retained. The great effort they put in, the thorough preparation, their courage, dedication, and motivation result in a level of achievement that is unattainable for most of us. And people need heroes, particularly in sports. Women also respond especially to the fact that the film presents some nuances that make the undertaking of the two brothers more comprehensible. Thomas and Alexander are figureheads of extraordinary people. By facing up to their fears and emotions, they unite high performance—sex; and nuance—soul. Women are particularly good at recognizing the parallel between climbing and life. For women, it is not the technical but the human aspect of the film that matters. *Am Limit* has taken two icons of climbing and made them human.

---

6 Klaus Theweleit is a well-known German sociologist and critic whose writings often focus on the cultural interpretation of the physical experience of the male body (transl. note).

∞

AT THE FINISH

In September 2007, Thomas and I traveled to Yosemite Valley once again. My 16-meter fall on the Middle Cathedral Rock was by now two years behind me. *Am Limit* had been released to enthusiastic audiences—even though it was now no longer a film about a new speed record on the "Nose," but rather about our failed attempts to set one. After my injured feet had healed, we had given it another try, which also gave Pepe and the film crew an opportunity to wrap up the shoot. This time it was Thomas who had the bad luck. Just above the "Great Roof" he took a great big leader fall, which is documented at close range in the film. A small ledge painfully broke his fall, and severe contusions temporarily put an end to our big dream of beating Yuji Hirayama and Hans Florine's record time of 2 hours and 48 minutes.

Now we were once again standing beneath the line drawn by light and shade on the 1,000-meter-high granite pillar of El Capitan. We were not yet ready to give up on the speed record, despite all the setbacks. It had been the hardest rock-climbing route in the world when Warren Harding first ascended it in 1958, and it took forty-one days of hard work. In the 1960s, a team led by Royal Robbins was the first to climb the "Nose" in seven days. In 1975, Jim Bridwell, John Long, and Billy Westbay managed the first single-day ascent—the birth of speed climbing, so to speak. Since then, the ascent times have been getting shorter and shorter, until Yuji and Hans put a temporary end to this development in September 2002 by pushing the record to under three hours.

On September 15, 2007, we climbed the thirty-four pitches of the "Nose" again for the first time—in ten hours. We were tired and disappointed. The record appeared to be receding into the far distance. The only thing we had left was faith in ourselves. We wouldn't give up! After a day of rest, we took the 1,000 meters on another time—and another, and another. After five ascents, we had once again committed to memory every single crux on the wall and rehearsed the tactical refinements. Mentally and physically, the necessary resources were in place. Our team strategy: We would climb in four blocks. Thomas started, led up to the end of "Sickle Ledge," then I would take over until "Boot Flake." At the "King Swing," Thomas would head the team again until "Glowering Spot." After that, I would sprint up the last pitches to the summit. Our protection strategy: shortfixing and simultaneous climbing. Per block, our gear consisted of various cams (Camalots in sizes 0 to 4 and a cam hook), three little stoppers, fourteen quickdraws, and twenty carabiners.

Then, everything went much faster than anticipated. On our sixth ascent, Thomas and I climbed through the "Nose" in 3 hours and 10 minutes, from the first official pitch at the upper end of the low-angled rock until the "finish line," a tree 20 meters above the last belay. We were surprised. At the top of El Cap, we were feeling very fit and decided to venture a serious attempt the very next time, although we first took three days off to rest up for it.

October 4, 2007. We started at seven o'clock in the morning. A quick check of the time at the "Boot": We were over ten minutes faster than the previous attempt. We were making good progress. It would be tight, but with a bit of luck, we might make it. Luck could go both ways, though . . .

Thomas lost an etrier on "Great Roof," and in the middle of "Changing Corner," we had to overtake another climbing party and thus lost valuable minutes. Before the last pitch, we checked the time; we barely had a chance at beating the record, and if we did, it would be tight. On the last few meters, we gave it all we had, and the clock topped out at 2 hours, 48 minutes, 35 seconds. We didn't yet know if it was a record. Hours later, we got the confirmation on Hans Florine's home page: Yuji and Hans's exact time was 2 hours, 48 minutes, 50 seconds. We were 15 seconds faster. Unbelievable that a race over a distance of 1,000 meters could be decided by a mere 15 seconds! But a record is a record, and we celebrated.

Still, we knew that we'd lost some time on the route, and we wanted to make it up. Four days later, on October 8, 2007, we started our second attempt—this time, without the pressure of having to break the record (we already had it, after all). This time, also, without the loss of an etrier, though Thomas had taken an extra one along just in case. Once again, we had to go through some complicated maneuvers to overtake two other teams, and we lost time because of it. But aside from that, everything went like clockwork. For "King Swing," we barely needed two minutes by this point. On the last 50 meters, the spectators at the foot of the wall urged us on excitedly, and at the end, I stopped the stopwatch at 2 hours, 45 minutes, 45 seconds. We fell into each other's arms. Three minutes and five seconds faster than Hans and Yuji!

That was enough for us. We had had our release, so to speak. We would leave it to others now to break this record—and I was also certain that Hans Florine and Yuji Hirayama would try to get their record back as soon as possible.

Barely nine months later, they'd done it: On July 2, 2008, their third attempt in two weeks, Hans and Yuji set a new record, with 2 hours, 43 minutes, and 33 seconds—despite the fact that halfway up, on "Stove Leg Crack," their rope had gotten stuck and one of them had had to go back down 5 meters in order to free it.

We were immediately inundated with news of the record from all sides, and we congratulated the two at once (from the bottom of our hearts!). That fall, they returned again for additional attempts. On October 13, 2008, they undertook what is, for the present, their last ascent. Yuji again led all the pitches. They climbed 95 percent of the route free, had to overtake four parties, and ended with a time of 2 hours, 37 minutes, 5 seconds. A fabulous record!

For Thomas and me, it is a tremendous thing to have set a record on the "Nose," especially because the mental challenge was particularly great after both of our serious accidents. It is in the nature of records that sooner or later, they are broken. It doesn't matter if you hold it for a day, a month, or a year. Who knows—perhaps one day climbing teams will even get in under the magical two-hour mark. Thomas and I are glad to have been the fastest on the "Nose" once. Most likely, after this experience, the speed-climbing chapter of our lives is now closed. It is high time to turn to new objectives!